Christopher F. Schiavone

Rationality and Revelation in Rahner

The Contemplative Dimension

PETER LANG

New York • Washington, D.C./Baltimore • San Francisco
Bern • Frankfurt am Main • Berlin • Vienna • Paris

Library of Congress Cataloging-in-Publication Data

Schiavone, Christopher F. (Christopher Francis).
    Rationality and revelation in Rahner : the contemplative dimension /
Christopher F. Schiavone.
        p.   cm. — (American university studies. Series VII, Theology and
religion; vol. 169)
    Includes bibliographical references.
    1. Rahner, Karl, 1904– . 2. Revelation—History of doctrines—20th
century. 3. Faith and reason—History of doctrines—20th century.
4. Contemplation—History of doctrines—20th century. I. Title.
II. Series.
BT126.5.S3253   1994   231'.042—dc20   93-37304
ISBN 0-8204-2342-4   CIP
ISSN 0740-0446

Die Deutsche Bibliothek-CIP-Einheitsaufnahme

Schiavone, Christopher F.:
Rationality and revelation in Rahner : the contemplative dimension /
Christopher F. Schiavone. - New York; San Francisco; Bern; Baltimore;
Frankfurt am Main; Berlin; Wien; Paris: Lang, 1994
    (American university studies: Ser. 7, Theology and religion ; Vol. 169)
    ISBN 0-8204-2342-4
NE: American university studies / 07

The paper in this book meets the guidelines for permanence and durability of
the Committee on Production Guidelines for Book Longevity of the
Council on Library Resources.

© Peter Lang Publishing, Inc., New York 1994

Rationality and Revelation
in Rahner

American University Studies

Series VII
Theology and Religion
Vol. 169

PETER LANG
New York • Washington, D.C./Baltimore • San Francisco
Bern • Frankfurt am Main • Berlin • Vienna • Paris

Anyone who has been in love or disappointed in love, who has faced death or recovered from illness, who has been hounded by questions of life's meaning or confronted by a bewildering ethical dilemma, knows that no single standard of rationality is wholly adequate—that, in the end, there is mystery, which one may choose to enter trustingly or evade at all costs. To let oneself be grasped by mystery: That is contemplation.

Contents

Introduction

A basic stance toward the relationship between reason and revelation lies at the foundation of the kinds of positions people take on important theological issues. The matter of the proper interpretation of the Jewish and Christian Scriptures is a case in point: A biblical fundamentalist, for example, might hold that no special historical or critical analysis of the Scriptures is necessary or desirable, that a simple literal reading of a given text adequately reveals its meaning. This person's presupposition with respect to reason and revelation might well be that human reason is too radically distorted by the effects of original sin to be of much use in the understanding of God's word. Faith in the revelation of God is everything, and reason is nothing. On the other hand, there might be another person who would claim not only that historical and critical analysis explains the Scriptures, but that such analysis effectively explains away anything of the transcendent or supernatural. The only significance of the creation story, for example, might be that it once provided an explanation (in the primitive mythical form common to its era) of something which is more satisfactorily explained today in the language of the natural sciences. For this person, a rational positivist, if you will, reason is everything and faith in an alleged revelation of God is but one more datum of human experience to be submitted to rational analysis.

The most formidable challenge in a dispute like this is not getting these two opponents to agree; it is getting them to talk. The principal difficulty is that the operative presuppositions with respect to reason and revelation are rarely articulated in such a debate. Not least among the hidden presuppositions which one might bring to such a discussion is one's operative conception of rationality; i.e. what it means to characterize a human being or a belief as rational. If our hypothetical opponents, for example, cannot come to terms on the question of what reason is, then they will be incapable of discussing the relationship of reason and revelation, let alone agreeing on it or on any specific theological problem to which this traditionally troubled relationship has given rise.

While the difficulty of reconciling reason and revelation may be of concern to a relatively narrow audience, the further difficulty which it brings to light, that of working out a conception of rationality, has implications in a much wider arena. The philosopher Alisdair MacIntyre, for example, has recently argued that the failure to develop a useful conception of rationality, to replace the relatively uniform one which prevailed from the thirteenth to the eighteenth centuries in the West, is the very foundation of the contemporary lack of consensus over what is and is not just in the social order. Opponents in the fractious debates over the justice of employing the death penalty or permitting abortion, for example, may both adduce what they take to be good reasons for their positions. But, if what constitutes "good reason" is itself in question, then there is little basis for the hope that consensus on such issues can be achieved.[1] Clearly, then, the lack of a useful conception of rationality is not just a cause for intramural discord among theologians or even philosophers, but has and will continue to have a profound influence on the moral and political life of ordinary persons outside the "academy" as well.[2]

Although Karl Rahner, S.J. (1904-1984) is generally remembered for his contributions in the area of Catholic systematic theology, he has also made a significant contribution in precisely the area which I have marked out for special attention, i.e. the rationality question. Rahner's unique perspective and place at a critical historical juncture enabled him to develop a philosophical anthropology whose operative conception of rationality provides a viable language and thought structure for dealing with the contemporary situation. I will argue that what distinguishes Rahner's approach is its largely implicit but absolutely indispensable contemplative emphasis. Attention to the contemplative dimension of rationality not only provides a basis for working out the reason/revelation relationship and a host of related theo-philosophical problems; it also proves to be important to the future success of ethical dialogue in a world profoundly aware of its temporality and cultural pluralism.

Contemplation is certainly not a new or novel theme, either in philosophy or in theology. Ascetical theologians of both the East and the West have always sought to reflect on the contemplative life, even if at times calling it by other names. In the philosophy inspired by ancient and medieval thinkers, as well, contemplation has always enjoyed pride of place among the various activities a person could undertake in pursuit of the good and happy life. What may be novel in the argument of this study, however, is its contention that the contemplative aspect of human existence in general, and of human rationality in particular, is pivotal in working out some of the most perplexing problems in the philosophy of religion, Roman Catholic apologetics, and ethical discourse.

Inasmuch as the purpose of this study is to bring to light the presence and significance of a contemplative dimension in rationality as Rahner conceived it, it is neither necessary nor possible for us to rehearse exhaustively the history of Western thought with respect to contemplation. However, something needs to be said of the word *contemplation* as well as of the remote origins of contemplation as a philosophical category in the thinking of Plato and Aristotle.

The verb *to contemplate* is said to have come into English with its present meaning, *to meditate* or *ponder*, as early as the late sixteenth century. It can be traced to the Latin verb *contemplari*, whose origins are more ancient. The root of this verb is the word *templum* (as in temple), a space marked out for the observation of omens or portents. In all likelihood, there is some kinship between *templum* and *tempus* the Latin word for time.[3] In Greek philosophy, *contemplation* is the way in which the word *theoria* is usually rendered. Deriving from the word *thea*, which means *spectacle* or *sight* (as in *theater*), *theoria* at the time of Plato and Aristotle was used in at least three different ways: its original popular use, *looking* or *beholding*; its ordinary philosophical use, *observation, examination, study;* and its more restricted philosophical use, *exercise of knowledge already possessed.* It should also be noted, that *theoroi* were ambassadors of the state appointed to consult divine oracles; here some kinship with the word *theos* is also discernible.[4] One of the goals of the present work is to explain with greater precision what it means to say that the human person has a distinctive "contemplative capacity" or that rationality has a "contemplative dimension" or "aspect," the omission of which could have serious ramifications. At this point, it suffices to note that that contemplation involves taking the time to ponder, not simply the limited and mundane details of human existence, but also that which transcends the limits of a particular time and place.

For Plato, an explicit treatment of *theoria* is presented in the context of reflection upon a highly practical and political concern: Who ought to be the head of state? Persons of philosophical nature are preferred, those who are "always in love with that learning which discloses to them something of the being that is always and does not wander about, driven by generation and decay."[5] A just society, it seems, cannot be established except by one who knows what justice is—not simply a just act or a just man, but the idea or form of justice itself. The only ones who have this knowledge are those who have been released from the prison of sense knowledge and opinion, the world of contingency and change, into the bright light of understanding and science, the world of the necessary and eternal. At the end of his famous allegory of the cave, Socrates says to Glaucon:

> Well, then, my dear Glaucon, I said, this image as whole must be connected with what was said before. Liken the domain revealed through sight to the prison home, and the light of the fire in it to the sun's power; and, in applying the going up and the seeing [theoria] of what's above to the soul's journey up to the intelligible place, you'll not mistake my expectation, since you desire to hear it. A god doubtless knows if it happens to be true. At all events, this is the way the phenomena look to me: in the knowable the last thing to be seen, and that with considerable effort, is the idea of the good; but once seen, it must be concluded that this is in fact the cause of all that is right and fair in everything—in the visible it gave birth to light and its sovereign; in the intelligible, itself sovereign, it provided truth and intelligence—and that the man who is going to act prudently in private or in public must see it.[6]

For Plato, contemplation of the things above is the highest activity in which a human being can be engaged this side of the grave; though how precisely these "things above" are to be construed remains a very complex interpretive issue which cannot be discussed, let alone settled, here. To be qualified to lead, one must be a praciwner of such contemplation; though, paradoxically, one who has had a glimpse of the forms will not be overly anxious to assume such a burden.[7]

Contemplation, as Plato understood it, is not the kind of activity that one enters into lightly or easily. Accustomed to the relative darkness of life lived in the cave of the senses, one may at first be repelled by the blinding brightness of the light of the Good. Contemplation requires a process of conversion and habituation whereby the eyes of one's soul eventually become accustomed to the brilliance of the higher realm.[8] Dialectic, the highest form of science, is the means by which, through argument and without the use of the senses, one attains "to each thing itself that is and doesn't give up before he grasps by intellection itself that which is good itself [and] comes to the very end of the intelligible realm."[9] Although one arguably learns more about what dialectic is for Plato from participation in his dialogues than from a compilation of all the places where he makes explicit mention of this art, his remark near the end of the seventh book of the *Republic* is significant: Dialectic is "the only process of inquiry that advances in this manner, doing away with hypotheses, up to the first principle in order to find confirmation there."[10] Highly as Plato regarded the mathematical sciences, even these take second place to dialectic, the goal of which is contemplation of the non-hypothetical—that which is necessarily, universally, eternally.

For all the differences between them, Plato and Aristotle are in striking agreement at least on the primacy of contemplation in human life. Likewise, they both situate contemplation in the context of ethical concerns: What is the good for which human persons strive? In what does a person's happiness consist? What kind of social structure is most conducive to the attainment of such happiness? In the first book of the *Nichomachean Ethics*, Aristotle establishes that the good for which all persons strive is happiness and that it must be attained through "an activity of soul according to virtue, and if the virtues are many, then according to the best and most complete virtue."[11] Having devoted the better part of the *Ethics* to the moral and intellectual virtues, Aristotle returns to the happiness theme again in Book X and argues that the highest human good, that in which perfect happiness will consists, is *theoria*, contemplation.

Among the arguments in favor of contemplation: First, it must be considered the best activity, since reason is what is best in the human person, and the objects of reason (the subject matter of metaphysics) are best of knowable objects.[12] Secondly, contemplation bears the character of self-sufficiency, in the double sense that, 1) the philosopher does not require others when he is contemplating the truth and 2) this activity alone is desirable for its own sake and not for the sake of something else (as, for example, is the case with practical activity).[13] Aristotle admits that, in one sense, the contemplative life, a life spent in the pursuit of wisdom, is "too high for man." Still, he insists that we "must, so far as we can, make ourselves immortal, and strain every nerve to live in accordance with the best in us, for even if it be small in bulk, much more does it in power and worth surpass everything."[14] At the end of the eighth chapter of Book X, he concludes:

> So while contemplation endures, happiness does so also, and those who are more contemplative are more happy also, not in virtue of some other attribute but in virtue of contemplation, for contemplation is by its nature honorable. Happiness, then, would be a kind of contemplation.[15]

As may be expected, the primacy of contemplation in Aristotle is not an uncontroversial matter among contemporary commentators. Many have cited the apparent contradiction between Aristotle's overwhelming interest in the practical and political and his two chapter hymn of praise to contemplation discussed above. Some suggest that he is simply inconsistent; others argue that he changed his mind; still others claim that his position as stated in Book X of the *Nichomachean Ethics* is strictly ironic, that what he really wants to do is overturn intellectualism once and for all.[16] No matter where one stands on this interpretive issue, however, Aristotle's words on this theme have become in fact a *locus classicus* for thinking about contemplation. It should not surprise us to find, therefore, that one of his remote philosophical progeny, Karl Rahner—a thinker fully steeped in Thomism with its curious synthesis of Platonic, Aristotelian, and Christian elements—exhibits a significant contemplative emphasis in his thought. We are not far from the minds of Plato and Aristotle when we read,

> Asceticism, in the sense of the readiness to submit to self-criticism of one's own order of love, and the readiness to judge this in terms of the necessary basic elements of the true order of love and to reorganize it better according to the growing light of deeper insight, is a profound factor of concrete philosophy in a true man. Philosophical actitivity in recent centuries has completely lost sight of the fact that a true philosopher must lead the religious life of the cloister.[17]

Although I have said that Rahner's conception of rationality is distinguished by its contemplative emphasis, I must also acknowledge from the outset that this element in Rahner's thought is largely implicit. Normally, one would assume that we could begin by combining the most important parts of the author's corpus for every direct reference he makes to contemplation. In Rahner's case, however, this means of access is closed to us. Such references are so infrequent that the exercise would be largely fruitless. Therefore, a special strategy will be require to bring the contemplative aspect to light.

The strategy entails three movements: The first part establishes the reason/revelation problem in its contemporary form and lays out some preliminary indications as to the distinctive contribution which the Karl Rahner may have to make to the discussion. Chapter I looks at the historical roots of the discussion about the proper relationship of reason and revelation and argues that the loss of consensus over rationality is the most significant feature of the contemporary debate. Chapter II considers how that loss of consensus has manifested itself and been treated in the Roman Catholic milieu during the twentieth century. Chapter III takes a preliminary look at Rahner's epistemology and philosophy of religion through an overview of his seminal works, *Spirit in the World* and *Hearers of the Word*. In both works, a certain constellation of characteristics figures prominently: An emphasis on the status of the human person as a questioner and the necessary dynamism of the human spirit; a recognition of the dependence of human knowledge on sensibility and, therefore, the attainment and expression of that knowledge in time; and the identification of freedom as a condition of possibility of knowledge and the disciplined exercise of that freedom, terminating in love, as its highest realization. This constellation of characteristics is the first indication we have of a contemplative element in Rahner's thought.

The second part of the study proposes the hermeneutic of retrieval as the most promising means for bringing out this contemplative element with greater clarity. Chapter IV establishes the validity of retrieval as a method of interpretation and identifies the three most significant influences on the development of Rahner's conceptual horizon. With a view to developing a notion of contemplation which can then be brought to a reading of Rahner's later works, Chapters V through VII examine these three influences in turn: Thomas Aquinas as understood by Pierre Rousselot and Joseph Maréchal, Ignatius of Loyola as understood through his *Exercises*, and Martin Heidegger as Rahner knew him during the thirties. Notwithstanding the significant differences among the influences considered, a certain harmony is shown to exist among them with respect to the nature and importance of contemplation. Contemplation is a free modification of intentionality, whereby a human person adjusts his intellectual and moral orientation from the myriad finite particulars, concepts and systems which normally command his attention to that inner dynamism whereby all knowledge is attained and all action is accomplished. In this attitude, a person comes to recognize the utter poverty of all that is ordinarily included under the title of knowledge and the limits of every good that he can achieve or acquire and opens himself up to infinite possibility. Because it is a distinctively human activity, it always takes place in the world of space and time, requiring the collaboration of sensibility and imagination in history. But because it also implies a preconceptual affirmation of that which is more than or beyond the world of space and time, it also requires a certain asceticism. This asceticism safeguards freedom—the freedom of the human being to know what there is to know and to be what he/she is called to be, the freedom of everything which exists to be and to be precisely in the way that it is.

The third part of the book executes the retrieval prepared for by the previous part. Whereas, in Part I, the contemplative dimension emerges only as a certain constellation of characteristics discernible in human cognitive activity as the early Rahner described it; and, in Part II, contemplation itself emerges as a theme prominent in the writings of those thinkers most important to Rahner; in Part III, contemplation is shown to be the largely implicit but indispensable key to understanding Rahner's treatment of the relationship between reason and revelation. A careful reading of material representative of Rahner's later thought, in light of the notion of contemplation developed in Part II, reveals that the complementarity of reason and revelation is grounded in a more primitive and original unity which may be experienced only through contemplative living and thinking. Chapters VIII through X respectively show that contemplation characterizes Rahner's very methodology, figures prominently in his account of what distinguishes the human person from all other beings, and constitutes the condition of possibility for revelation itself and for making the very concept of revelation intelligible.

In the Conclusion, I entertain some of the standard critiques of Rahner and work out some of the implications of his contemplative model. I argue that attentiveness to the contemplative dimension of rationality provides a way of meeting some of the typical objections to Rahner's philosophy of religion. At the same time, and more importantly, an appreciation of this dimension provides a new basis for working out the relationship between philosophy and theology, developing a contemporary approach to apologetics, and facilitating ethical dialogue in a world profoundly aware of its temporality and cultural pluralism.

Before proceeding, it seems important to confront one possible objection to the overall project: What justification can there be for looking to a theologian for solutions to philosophical problems? From the side of the "pure theologian," the value of such an endeavor is dubious, since the philosopher will always be trying to prescind from the contribution made by revelation—a contribution which may be essential to understanding the thought of the theologian in question. From the side of the "pure philosopher," the situation may appear to be even more problematic: What good purpose is served by admitting into the company of reasonable men and women a participant who will be appealing to meta-physical and meta-rational experiences to bolster his view of the world?

In fact, the argument of this study is not addressed to purists of any kind, for purisms are always based on the mistaken assumption that reality can be adequately or even exhaustively dealt with from a single standpoint. Plainest experience shows, to the contrary, that every attempt at systematic investigation and exposition—theology as well as philosophy—is a human activity and, as such, intrinsically limited. Whether the object of one's science is God or something else, one never has the vantage point of the omniscient observer, but only the perspective of a concrete individual knower, having a specific personal and social history, now living at this particular time and place. As this kind of knower, one will always find it possible and even desirable to look at things from another point of view. The philosopher may benefit from listening to the theologian, and vice versa. Even more to the point, however: To pursue philosophy as if the experience of Christianity had never taken place would violate the nature of this science as a love of wisdom; just as to pursue theology without employing philosophical method would contradict theology's nature as a reasonable account of God. The method and conclusions of this study can be understood and evaluated only in the light of these basic assumptions.

Part One

Rahner
and
the Reason/Revelation Problematic

I

The Problem

Historical Roots of the Problem

Contemporary debate over reason and revelation did not emerge *ex nihilo,* but has its roots in a history which spans at least two millenia. Indeed, the reason/revelation problem emerged almost as soon as Jewish-Christian thought was introduced into the Hellenic world, particulary through the Gentile mission of St. Paul. Evidence of the conflict can be found, for example in Paul's own letter (c. 56 C.E.) to the Christian community at Corinth—a Mediteranean seaport which served as a melting pot for numerous cultures and cults:

> The message of the cross is foolishness to those who are perishing, but to us who are being saved it is the power of God, for it is written, "I will destroy the wisdom of the wise, and the learning of the learned I will set aside." Where is the wise one? Where is the scribe? Where is the debater of this age? Has not God made the wisdom of the world foolish? For since in the wisdom of God the world did not come to know God through wisdom, it was the will of God through the foolishness of the proclamation to save those who have faith. For Jews demand signs and Greeks look for wisdom, but we proclaim Christ crucified, a stumbling block to Jews and foolishness to Gentiles, but to those who are called, Jews and Greeks alike, Christ the power of God and the wisdom of God. For the foolishness of God is wiser than human wisdom, and the weakness of God is stronger than human strength.[1]

From the very beginning, there was a serious question in Paul's mind, as to whether human wisdom—presumably the varieties of Greek philosophical thought—could be of any service in the understanding of Christian revelation.

Yet, this passage from the Letter to the Corinthians could be misleading. The author of the Acts of the Apostles, writing closer to the end of the first century, describes a speech which Paul gave at the Areopagus in Athens, wherein Paul reveals some sympathy for the pagan religiosity of the Greeks. In his address, the "Apostle to the Gentiles" makes an effort to relate the Creator God of the Jewish Christians to the cosmic powers known to his audience. Rather than to dismiss their cult out of hand, Paul here seems to employ a reasoned argument to persuade the Greeks that they have been implicitly worshipping the one transcendent God of the universe in their homage to the many gods who were thought to regulate the affairs of this world.[2] And so, even if Paul harbored reservations about Greek philosophical reason, he did not hesitate to use quasi-philosophical arguments for his own apologetic aims.

This use of reason in the service of evangelical goals is also exhibited in the first Letter of Peter. To a group of Gentile Christians evidently facing the danger of religious persecution, the author recommends the virtue of hope—not a baseless hope, however (which would be more of a wish), but a well-founded one: "Always be ready to give an explanation to anyone who asks you for a reason for your hope."[3] In sum, there is strong Scriptural evidence that ambivalence about the proper relationship of reason and revelation has existed since the foundation of the first ecclesial communities.

The tension, more or less implicit during the apostolic era, became quite explicit in the patristic era. The writings of Clement of Alexandria and Tertullian of Carthage close to the end of the second century provide a striking study in contrasts.

Clement was by no means a rationalist, but he reveals far greater enthusiasm for dialogue with Greek philosophy than does his North African counterpart. To Clement's mind, philosophy was for the Greeks what the Mosaic law had been for the Jews: a human preparation for divine revelation in Jesus.[4] Just as Jesus the Messiah fulfilled rather than abolished the Mosaic Law which preceded him, it could also be said that Jesus as the Word (*logos*) of God fulfilled rather than abolished the Greek desire and love of wisdom. For Clement, it was impossible that there be two sets of truth, completely separate and contradictory; truth for Clement was one, the person and teaching of Jesus the Christ. However, God ordained from the beginning of time that men and women come to Christ by different paths. Clement envisioned an *apologetic* use for philosophy: Rightly taught and properly understood, all human wisdom points to Christ.

However, Clement also envisioned a *systematic* role for philosophy within faith: "The juxtaposition of doctrines by comparison saves the truth, from which follows knowledge."[5] A member of the famed catechetical school of Alexandria, Clement was convinced that genuine faith had nothing to fear from philosophical argumentation; quite to the contary, the use of reasoned argument could only serve to purify and strengthen true faith. His criticism of those who reject philosophy is telling:

> But the multitude are frightened at the Hellenic philosophy, as children are at masks, being afraid lest it lead them astray. But if the faith (for I cannot call it knowledge) which they possess be such as to be dissolved by plausible speech, let it be by all means dissolved, and let them confess that they will not retain the truth. For truth is immoveable, but false opinion dissolves.[6]

It should also be noted that, if Clement saw truth itself as immoveable, he also understood the human process by which it is attained as dynamic, practical, always incomplete, and fundamentally dialectical (characteristics which I will later argue are indicative of rationality's contemplative dimension). The *dynamism* of human reason is exhibited in the way the mind advances from opinion based on the uncritical assessment of the data of the senses through understanding to knowledge.[7] That this process has a *practical* as well speculative dimension to it is evidenced in the status of "right conduct" as a *sine qua non* of the pursuit of truth and love as its ultimate *telos*.[8] The essential *incompleteness* of all this is expressed in the identification of God as "a Being difficult to grasp and apprehend, ever receding and withdrawing from him who pursues."[9] Finally, the human quest for Wisdom, philosophy properly speaking, seems to possess a certain dialectical quality:

> We define Wisdom to be a certain knowledge, being a sure and irrefragable apprehension of things divine and human. . . . in one aspect it is eternal and in another it becomes useful in time. Partly it

is one and the same, partly many and different—partly without any movement of passion, partly with passionate desire—partly perfect, partly incomplete.[10]

Little is known of the life of Tertullian, but his disapproval of the kind of constructive engagement with the Hellenic world which Clement recommended is well-documented. His *Prescription Against the Heretics* makes clear his conception of revelation and reason as not merely distinct but opposed. With polemical ardor he writes:

> What indeed has Athens to do with Jerusalem? What concord is there between the Academy and the Church? What between heretics and Christians?

> Away with all attempts to produce a mottled Christianity of Stoic, Platonic, and dialectic composition! We want no curious disputation after possessing Christ Jesus, no inquisition after enjoying the gospel! With our faith, we desire no further belief.[11]

Tertullian had several objections to the use of philosophy. To begin with, notwithstanding the ambiguity of the Pauline writings on this score, he sees the apostolic witness being decidedly opposed to all admixture of Greek wisdom with Christian revelation.[12] Moreover, he sees Aristotelian and post-Aristotelian thought in particular as useless in themselves. He refers to dialectics, for example, as "the art of building up and pulling down; an art so evasive in its proportions, so farfetched in its conjecture, so harsh in its arguments, so productive of contentions" that it really treats nothing at all.[13] In his view, philosophy—far from attaining to or preserving the truth—really serves to destroy it by unnecessary complication and self-contradiction. He refers to its practitioners as "patriarchs of heretics . . . hukstering wise acres and talkers."[14]

His most serious objection to philosophy can be found in his interpretation of the famous biblical injunction, "Seek and ye shall find." If the truth has already been taught by Jesus and transmitted through the apostolic Church, one ought to seek until—and only until—one has encountered this unchanging truth. Once this truth has been discovered, there is not "anything further to do but to keep what you have believed."[15]   Any human activity which calls itself a pursuit of wisdom apart from Jesus and the Church either has not yet come upon the truth or has departed from a truth which it once securely held. If a person feels compelled to continue the search for the truth, the only promising place to look is at the already complete truth possessed by practioners of Christianity. "Let our seeking, therefore, be in that which is our own and from those who are our own, and concerning that which is our own."[16]

By constrast with Clement's thought, where the pursuit of truth is depicted as dynamic, incomplete, and fundamentally dialectical; Tertullian's thought exhibits an emphasis on the stability and sufficiency of a truth possessed by and communicated within a community of belief.

Precisely what is at stake in the debate over the proper relationship of reason and revelation becomes particularly clear in an analysis of the situation at the University of Paris during the thirteenth century. At the time that Thomas Aquinas was teaching and writing, three major philosophical movements competed for ascendency at Paris. Two were forms of Aristotelian thought; the third was predominantly Augustinian in its inspiration.[17]

On the one hand were a group that has been described as Neo-Augustinian. With Augustine of Hippo as their spiritual father, this group, though not as extreme as Tertullian in their condemnation of philosophy, sought to delineate very clear limits for reason within theology.   They took their cue from Augustine's admonition about faith and understanding: "Understanding is the reward of faith . . . seek not to understand that thou mayest believe, but believe that thou mayest understand."[18]   Like Clement, Augustine believed that philosophy may well have been an *historical* preparation for theology, the rational thought of the Greeks a preparation for the revelation of Jesus Christ. Now, however, since Jesus has revealed the truth, and since the revealed truth has been preserved in Sacred Scripture, the way to truth runs no longer from reason to revelation but from revelation to reason. Theology is the highest type of philosophical thinking, and nothing in the natural order of things makes complete sense apart from the light of faith. In the Augustinian approach to reason and faith, the Greek ideal of rational thinking is fully transfigured: Wisdom is offered by God himself to all men and women as a means of salvation by faith and to philosophers as an unerring guide toward rational understanding. Clearly, there is some value in reading the works of the Greeks, but these are not to be viewed as an independent or adequate path to truth.

Even at their best, apart from revelation, the fruits of reason are radically blemished.[19] Gilson has identified the Neo-Augustinian approach to reason and faith as a species of *theologism*.[20]

In sharp contrast to the theologism of the Neo-Augustinians was the rationalism of the second major philosophical faction in thirteenth century Paris, the radical Artistotelians or Latin Averroists. These were members of the arts faculty who, as disciples of Averroes (the great Arabic commentator on Aristotle), shared in common a number of philosophical positions on a wide range of key issues including the eternity of the world, the free choice of the human will, the nature of the human intellect, and the relationship of reason and faith.[21] Chief among the Latin Averroists was Siger of Brabant. Following Averroes in the serious study of Aristotle, Siger found that the use of reason led him to conclusions which he was convinced could not be denied, and yet could not be reconciled with his Christian faith. His solution, not unlike that of his Arabic forefather, involved the strict separation of faith from philosophy. Human reason, unaided by faith, leads to certain conclusions which—though at variance with Church teaching—must be acknowledged as necessary results of philosophical argument. At the same time, however, Christians must believe that what revelation says in all matters is true. The contradiction between the two is, humanly speaking, irresolvable: In the university setting, one must accept as necessary the conclusions of rational arguments whose truth-value (from a theological point of view) is doubtful, while, in the life of faith, one must accept as true the teachings of revealed religion whose rational justification is negligible. Siger concluded that the work of the arts faculty, philosophy in particular, needed to be protected from theology, lest the doctrinal concerns of the latter interfered with scientific progress of the former. Committed as he was to the Church, however, he also saw the need to protect faith from the speculation of philosophy. The only way to do this was by a strict separation of the two.[22]

The position of Thomas Aquinas on faith and reason may be understood in relation to the two competing options, theologism and rationalism. For all the differences between them, there was one feature which they shared in common and which Thomas sought to overcome. They were reductionist.[23]

Thomas' basic position emerges with clarity from the first three questions of his *Commentary on the DeTrinitate* of Boethius.[24] Thomas tries to establish what is required for the human mind to attain knowledge in general and the extent to which knowledge of God is attainable by unaided human nature. He rejects illuminationism as an explanation of the knowledge human beings possess of the first principles and of the world and argues that the "intelligible light" (or agent intellect) by which we come to know the first principles and recognize the forms of sensible things is unique to each person, not one for all.[25] Inasmuch as God has created the human knower as well as all that is knowable, a divine light is operative in knowledge of the natural world; but no new illumination is required in addition to that active power which the intellect possesses by its nature.[26] When it comes to the truths of faith and future contingents, however, (which are neither accessible to the senses nor deducible from first principles), "the human mind cannot know these without being divinely illumined by a new light supplementing the natural light." Being a created power (i.e. not self-subsistent in its existence), the human mind is finite and restricted in its effect.[27]

Now a further question presents itself: Does the requirement for a new illumination pertain to the human knowledge of God specifically? Thomas' answer seems to be both "Yes" and "No." "God is known only through the form of his effect," says Thomas. But effects may be of two kinds: one equal to the power of its cause (hence a source of full knowledge), and the other less than the power of its cause (hence a source of a less comprehensive knowledge). The latter case applies to human knowledge of God. Inasmuch as we know the effects of God's power (e.g. in our knowledge of the world of finite things), we know *whether* the cause (i.e. God) exists (*quia est*). However, because God completely surpasses creation in fullness of being, we cannot know *what* God is in himself (*quid est*).[28] The "five ways" or proofs of God's existence outlined in the first part of the *Summa Theologiae* all involve an application of the principle outlined here, for while they conclude with an affirmation of God's "is-ness," they do not begin the exhaust the depth and breadth of God's "what-ness."[29]

What is particularly significant in this argument is not simply that God is said to be knowable by the human intellect, but that there are said to be gradations or degrees of knowledge, even prior to the advance made possible by the added light of faith. One person's knowledge of God may be more perfect than another's according to "the degree that the relation of the cause to the effect is more prefectly apprehended." For example, one may affirm the existence of God in his power to produce things. One may go beyond this to a recognition of God's power in "more lofty effects." (Thomas is not explicit as to what he means here, but perhaps the metaphysics of human cognition would be one example of what he has in mind.)   Finally—and paradoxically—one's knowledge of God may advance to a recognition of him "as distant from everything that appears in his effects . . . by transcendence and by negation."[30] This advance of knowledge by degrees—from the things of the world to the God who is utterly beyond this world—is facilitated when the mind's natural powers are

> strengthened by a new illumination, like the light of faith and the gifts of wisdom and understanding through which the mind is said to be raised above itself in contemplation, inasmuch as it knows that God is above everything it naturally comprehends.[31]

But, strictly speaking, no new illumination is required for a human being to arrive at a knowledge of God, at least in its most rudimentary form.

Having established in the first question of the *Commentary* that the human intellect possesses a real though limited capacity to attain knowledge of God, Thomas in the second question is able to address the concerns of both the Neo-Augustinians and the Averroists. As to whether it is permissible to make divine realities an object of investigation, Thomas appeals to the *Nichomachean Ethics* to argue that human nature, with its peculiar affinity for the immaterial and immortal is required to "strain every nerve to live in accord with what is best in us."[32] With intellect as our highest power, it is incumbent upon to use that power to inquire after the highest possible object, i.e. divine things. Hence to those prone to theologism, Thomas suggests reflection on the nature of the human person as a rational inquirer.

On the other hand, he admits that even so noble a pursuit can go wrong: By presumption (treating the incomprehensible as if it were comprehensible), by making reason precede faith (as if faith required it), or by speculating beyond one's own abilities.[33] Hence, for those prone to rationalism, Thomas provides a reminder of the very real limits to human reason. Thomas' position at the midpoint of the spectrum between rationalism and theologism is reflected nicely in his reply to the argument that God is in some sense honored by our silence, i.e. by our refraining from the scientific investigation of divine realities:

God is indeed respected by silence, but this does not mean that we may say nothing whatever about him, nor inquire into him, but that we should understand that however much we may say or inquire about him, we realize that we fall short of fully understanding him.[34]

Not only does Thomas favor rational investigation into divine realities; he also argues in defense of the use of philosophical reasoning and authorities in the science of faith. At the foundation of his argument is his well-known position on the proper relationship of nature and grace. The various gifts of grace and the light of faith do not in any sense abrogate or abolish the light of natural reason which has been given to all human beings. Hence the truths attained by natural reason and the truths revealed by divine faith are not opposed, separate, or mutually exclusive. If they were, "one or the other would have to be false, and since we have both of them from God, he would be the cause of our error, which is impossible."[35] Rather, they are complementary, derived from one and the same source (i.e. the first Truth who is God), and mutually supportive. If anything is concluded philosophically which is contary to faith, it may be assumed that human reason has failed in some way. An error of this kind may itself be corrected philosophically either by demonstrating its impossibility or, at the very least, its lack of necessity.[36]

With the double truth theory of the Averroists refuted and the anti-intellectual strain in theologism challenged, Thomas is able to describe in the third question what it is that the grace of faith adds to reason. To begin with, a certain natural faith is required for all human living. Owing to the fact that no person is self-sufficient, knowledgeable in all things, there is a sense in which one person is always relying on the word of another in order to conduct his/her daily affairs.[37] In the case of divine science faith plays a distinctive role: Here the "objects of knowledge," though supremely intelligible in themselves, are nearly unintelligible to us because of the peculiarity of our constitution (i.e. the fact that we are "spirit in the world," as Rahner will later express it). Though there are certain facts about divine reality which may be known through unaided human reason, faith is nonetheless required for us to be able to give "unerring and firm assent" to that which is unclear to us, because it is not directly available to our intellects by way of reason or sense experience.[38] Drawing on the wisdom of the Jewish Aristotelian Maimonides, he delineates five reasons that faith is required, most of which are related to the extreme difficulty of the subject matter of divine science and the need for the average human person to attain knowledge of God more efficiently than would be possible were one to rely on reason alone.[39]

How exactly does faith operate in an individual person? Both by an "interior light that leads to assent, and by way of the realities that are proposed from without and that had as their source divine revelation." The former seems to some kind supernatural aid given the individual will, which enables one to assent even to that which cannot fully comprehend. The latter is most likely the testimony of the faith community as to the ways in which God has revealed himself in history.[40] But in neither case is the operation of faith to be understood as a flight from reason. Reason as a natural capacity of the human being retains its importance and validity; the role of faith is to provide the human knower with an insight into that which reason alone cannot attain. Faith, then, does not contradict or suspend reason's activity; it rather fulfills its highest aspirations by leading it beyond itself.[41]

Lest we be left with the impression that faith is a purely speculative and wholly intellectual gift, Thomas does not leave the topic without underlining the sensible and practical aspects of the knowledge of God. Thomas describes religion as "consist[ing] in the act by which we worship God by subjecting ourselves to him." Because the one worshipped is spirit, the worshiping acting is itself spiritual. Religiosity is not, however, some abstract or disembodied act which takes place outside of time:

> Because we worshipers of God have bodies and receive our knowledge
> through bodily senses, some actions of the body are also required on
> our part for the worship of God, not only that we might serve him with
> our whole being, but also that by these bodily actions we might arouse
> ourselves and others to acts of the mind directed to God.[42]

Moreover, true worship consists not merely in acts of the mind and acts of the body; true worship includes acts of mercy, since "those acts that are rendered to our neighbors for the sake of God are rendered to God himself . . . [belonging thus] to the same act of submission in which the worship of religion consists."[43] Thus reason, even in the fulfillment of its highest aspirations, remains inescapably linked to sensibility and eminently practical.

Through his distinctive way of describing and relating reason and faith, Thomas was enabled to move beyond the reductionism latent in the theologisms and rationalisms of his own day. Whereas theologism tried to secure the truthfulness of religious claims by either rejecting philosophy in its entirety or attempting to provide rational demonstrations of theological truths, Thomas identified the confusion which lay at the heart of the matter. Plainest experience teaches that a good many things in the world are knowable apart from revelation. The lunar cycle, the logical law of identity—truths like these are equally available to and the same for all, irrespective of religious orientation. To subsume these kinds of realities under the heading of faith is to mistake one kind of knowing for another kind of knowing and thus to destroy the integrity of each.

Whereas rationalism tried to secure the claims of human reason by either dismissing faith as a kind of low-level rationality for the masses or positing an irreconcilable conflict between philosophy and theology, Thomas identified the incorrect assumption which was the source of the difficulty; namely, that the same thing could be known scientifically and believed religiously at the same time. If a truth is known through rational demonstration, faith is not needed for us to give our assent to it. If a truth is an object of faith, no rational demonstration of it is possible—even if one were a philosopher.

For Thomas Aquinas, truth is one, and faith knowledge and scientific knowledge form an organic unity springing from one divine source. Reason, unaided by faith, must search tirelessly for truth about the world—including even the truth of God's existence. But what reason fails to achieve on its own, faith gives as a gift. And what faith gives as a gift does not contradict or offend reason, but draws reason beyond itself into the realm of the incomprehensible and mysterious. This constitutes the very heart of the Thomistic synthesis with respect to reason and faith and an important point of reference for the discussion of the problem at hand.

In this analysis of the historical roots of the reason/revelation problem, what has become clear is the extent to which an operative underlying conception of rationality can be determinative of the way in which the two poles are described and related. When rationality is conceived of entirely apart from a notion of being or God—as theologism tends to do through emphasis on intellect as it is affected by sin or as rationalism tends to do by seeming to posit a state of pure nature—the chances of successful synthesis seem remote. When, however, rationality is conceived of as itself a creation of God or somehow intimately related to that highest being to which all things owe their existence—as both Clement and Thomas do—then the basis on which to relate reason and faith becomes more evident. Indeed, both Clement and Thomas conceive reason's pursuit of truth as a spiritual dynamism which is never complete (at least this side of the grave). Both describe the possibility of reason's encountering God in dialectical terms, "already . . . not yet," "partly . .

completely," and so on. Neither proposes a fully abstract criterion of rationality—an unchanging standard of truth which is somehow available to the human intellect apart from experience in the concrete world. In each, the fulfillment of reason's highest aspirations is viewed in each as having a practical as well as speculative dimension. Already we can see in the historical roots of the discussion about reason and revelation that, when adequately understood, human rationality entails a contemplative dimension. It remains to be seen shether this aspect continues to find voice in the modern and contemporary periods.

Shifting Conceptions of Rationality

Creative and promising as the Thomist synthesis may have seemed, it was far from universally accepted in his own time. Latin Averroism continued to exert formidable influence at the University of Paris. The fact that the Averroists were following Aristotle's thought to conclusions about the world and the soul which contradicted orthodox teachings of faith led many late medieval thinkers to radically narrow the scope of faith affirmations which could be demonstrated through reason alone.[44] One may assume that the various ecclesiastical condemnations issued between 1270 and 1277 against a host of philosophical postions (most of them Averroist, some of them Thomist) did little to foster an atmosphere of rational inquiry.[45] In Paris, at least, the profound ecclesiastical defensiveness caused harm to scientific life, created suspicion toward philosophers, and diminished the possibilities of maintaining a collaborative spirit between the theology and arts faculties.[46] The marriage of faith and reason appears to have been dissolved before it could even be consummated. Further confirmation of the dissolution can be found in both the intellectual and religious history of the late Middle Ages. Nominalism's rejection of the human capacity to make true necessary judgments[47] and the rise of the *moderna devotio* with its wariness about philosophy[48] are emblematic of the breakdown of reason and the popular rejection of philosophical theology.

If it is in the late Middle Ages that we find the dissolution of the Thomist synthesis, it is in the Renaissance that we find the basis for the attempts at new synthesis in the Enlightenment. The general outlines of the Renaissance conception of the human person are extensively delineated elsewhere;[49] here we note only those features of immediate relevance to the present study. The Renaissance focus on the dignity of man (as elaborated, for example, by Marcilio Ficino[50] and Pico dello Mirandola,[51]) combined with the ideal of modern mathematical science (proposed by Galileo and others[52]) to set the stage for the rise of modernity. Francis Bacon, Galileo's counterpart and contemporary in late sixteenth and early seventeenth century England said of the "new science" born in the Renaissance: "By the agency of Man a new aspect of things, a new universe comes to view."[53] Physics was no longer the simple observation of natural phenomena and the construction of various hypotheses as probable explanations for all the available data. The creation of new tools for better observation and measurement led to development of experimental science, whereby the natural world was to be observed under a variety of conditions and under strict human control. The universe explored by modern science was not simply the world as it presented itself; it was the world as it revealed itself in reference to human projects—as it responded to human experiments and provided solutions to human problems. In a sense, in modernity, the Renaissance focus on man and focus on science came together in a new science which was uniquely anthropocentric.

This new picture of the universe is, to some extent, reflected in or presumed by the thought of most of the great modern thinkers whether British, French, or German; rationalist, empiricist or transcendental: The human subject is self-consciously at the center, attempting to get the world to conform to a rigorous standard of certitude. Descartes set the tone in the middle of the seventeenth century when he wrote:

> Some years ago I was struck by the large number of falsehoods that I had accepted as true in my childhood, and by the highly doubtful nature of the whole edifice that I had subsequently based on them. I realized that it was necessary, once in the course of my life to demolish everything completely and start again right from the foundations if I

wanted to establish anything at all in the sciences that was stable and likely to last.[54]

Although few of the philosophers who came after Descartes accepted his substantive claims, most of them did accept responsibility for solving, or at least addressing, the problem of foundations which he raised.[55]   One by one, each of the great minds of the modern period offered his own account of rational certitude. Descartes built on the foundation of an allegedly indubitable *cogito*. Leibniz saw promise in the model of the indivisible and inpenetrable monad. Locke turned to the clear ideas of the mind in search of an unfailing basis for knoweldge. Hume went beyond the ideas of the mind to the sense impressions which are their basis—ending up, according to one interpretation, in scepticism about the possibility of certainty about anything but analytic truths.

As late as the close of the eighteenth century, despite the fact that numerous attempts at identifying a universal basis for rational justification had shown themselves incapable of bringing about the hoped-for consensus, Immanuel Kant remained convinced that the goal was attainable. He expected "once for all" to come to "a definite conclusion" with respect the some of the vexing problems of modern philosophy, not the least which was the conditions of possibility for knowledge.[56]   Kant's transcendental philosophy merits particular attention here, because it is so prominent in the background of Rahner's thought.

In his *Prolegomena to Any Future Metaphysics*, Kant sets out to answer the question, "Whether such a thing as metaphysics be at all possible?" His goal is to either establish metaphysics' credentials as a science or, if that is not found to be possible, to write its death notice.[57]   What is interesting to note is the extent to which he presumes Newtonian mechanics as a model of what science is, properly speaking. All of the scholastic wrangling over being, substance, angels, the soul, and so on—not to mention the seemingly irresolvable conflict between rationalism and empiricism—Kant attributes to one basic problem: the absence of a "standard weight and measure to distinguish soundness from shallow talk."[58]

Not surprisingly, then, when Kant sets himself to the task of deducing the *a priori* structure of mind (which in turn is expected to provide the conditions of possibility for scientific knowledge), he turns to pure mathematics and to physics as he knew them. From mathematics he deduces the forms of sensible intuition, space and time.[59]   From physics he deduces the categories of understanding by which the mind synthesizes the data of sensible intuition.[60] There may be several reasons why Kant looked to math and science, but chief among them must have been the features of necessity and universality which they seemed to exhibit; it seemed as if their findings were immune in principle from infection by shifting empirical factors, including historical and cultural contingencies. The rational certitude which they offered was not to be seen as function of the in se intelligibility of the world (since, to the knower, the world is only phenomenal), and still less a function of the supreme intelligibility of a creator god.[61] The rational certitude they offered was to be seen as a function of reason itself in its pure (i.e. scientific) employment, identical in every human reasoner and discoverable through the analysis of the conditions of possibility for knowledge.

And so, Kant's answer to the question about the possibility of any future metaphysics was in the affirmative, but metaphysics for Kant was redefined: No longer an attempt to attain sure knowledge about things outside our experience (e.g. the essences of things as they are in themselves), it became the science by which the principles of pure reason and the limits of their employment are known. Kant's allegorical description of reason in its scientific employment is typical of the Enlightenment conception of rationality:

> This domain is an island, enclosed by nature itself within unalterable limits. It is the land of truth—enchanting name!—surrounded by a wide and stormy ocean, the native home of illusion, where many a fog bank and many a swiftly melting iceberg give the deceptive appearance of farther shores, deluding the adventurous seafarer ever anew with empty hopes and engaging him in enterprise which he can never abandon and yet is unable to carry to completion.[62]

To be rational is to remain on the island, whose limits are space and time and whose laws are unchanging. The reasonable person is neither taken in through an uncritical acceptance of the appearances of things material nor misled by the illusory promise of the ideas (i.e. the ideas of God, Soul, World) which the mind itself has generated to give its laws their systematic quality. In short, the reasonable person is the abstract, ahistorical subject of the transcendental philosophy.

Despite Kant's best efforts, the "standard weight and measure," which was to provide the basic for adjudicating all conflicting claims in the epistemological and ethical spheres, remained elusive. His own highly abstract and ahistorical ideal quickly proved inadequate. Like Kant, Hegel recognized the great diversity of philosophical systems and the bold ambitions of reason as facts to be reckoned with. Unlike him, however, Hegel did not see in this diversity simple disagreement between mutually exclusive propositions, but rather "the progressive unfolding of truth." Hegel understood the ideas attained through reason's dialectical ambitions not merely as marking negative boundaries for scientific knowledge, but as themselves constitutive of science in the full sense. Moving beyond Kant's historical naïveté, Hegel proposed that it was precisely through history and not apart from it that truth becomes manifest. Hegel's aim was "to help bring philosophy closer to the form of Science" by bringing to light "the scientific system of such truth."[63]

The only truth worthy of the name, from Hegel's point of view, is that which has its place in the one all-inclusive system which is the life of the mind, of *Geist*. In that all-inclusive system, it is not the life of consciouness (objectivity) which dominates (as was the case, for example, in Medieval philosophy); nor does the life of self-consciousness separated from objects (viz. the *a priori* laws of reason as distinct from "things in themselves"), as Kant would have had it.[64] It is in the dialectic between these two perspectives that truth may be found, as history converges toward Absolute Spirit, where consciousness and self-consciousness, object and subject are seen in their unity and identity. For Hegel, to be rational is to think and live in accord with that system which comes to light through rigorous study of the history of the human spirit.[65]

Hegel's effort to move beyond Kant's abstract, ahistorical conception of reason immediately became itself the object of attack, as first Kierkegaard and then Nietzsche brought to light the limitations of the concept of system which was so central to Hegel's thought. As much by their literary style as by the substantial content of their writings, the two called attention to the place of the existing finite and individual subject who, they argued, had been completely overwhelmed in the elaborate system which Hegel and his followers proposed.

Against the objective notion of subjectivity put forth by German idealism, Kierkegaard puts forward his own notion of radical subjectivity. For him, subjectivity rightly understood engages the existing individual in a never-ending process of becoming. The subjective thinker is the one who reproduces this existential situation in his thoughts. Those to whom Kierkegaard disdainly refers as "Systematizers" are far from this. "They occupy themselves now and then with a little striving, but this is only the parsimonious marginal note for a text long since complete."[66] Uninterested in the labor and afraid of the risk entailed in constant striving, these objective thinkers seem to prefer the articifical certainty of their rational science to the difficulty of authentic existence. Though Hegel was right to reintroduce the notion of dialectic into the pursuit of truth, he failed to recognize the radical incompatibility between the contingency and striving implicit in dialectical movement and the necessity and order which are the hallmarks of system.[67] Kierkegaard does not deny that reality is in some sense systematic; but it could only be thus for God.[68]

Nietzsche goes further than Kierkegaard. For him, positing God as the only legitimate systematician would be as inimical to the life of the existing individual subject as the Hegelian system which Kierkegaard sought to overturn. Through the madman's famous announcement of God's death, Nietzsche observes that modern culture, decentralized and pluralized in rational as well as religious perspective, can no longer turn to a single notion of god—be it the god of medieval Christianity or the Enlightenment god of reason—for its meaning.[69] Each person must find his own meaning, create his own value, take a stand on life. Man, as known by all previous systematic thinking is to be overcome, and the overman is to be born.[70] The overman is not to be identified with any particular historical figure or way, but with the unique way each existing individual assumes responsibility for and takes hold of his own life.[71] Will this lead to chaos, as most every philosopher from Descartes on seems to have believed? Absolutely, replies Nietzsche; but it is in this chaos and not in some belief structure imposed by a dominant religious or rational elite that the fulfillment of authentic human existence is to be be found: Thus spoke Zarathustra: "I say unto you: one must still have chaos in oneself to be able to give birth to a dancing star."[72]

And so, if it may be said that modernity begins with the hope of establishing once and for all a stable and lasting foundation for the sciences and ultimately for the moral life, it must then be concluded that, on the eve of twentieth century, this hope remained largely disappointed. What MacIntyre says of the Enlightenment with respect to practical rationality applies *mutatis mutandis* to the question of rationality in general: This is the legacy of the Enlightment to those who live in the twentieth century: "the provision of a an ideal of rational justification which it has proved impossible to attain."[73]

Alternatives in the Face of Crisis

The post-modern crisis of rationality may be said to consist in this: A collapse of the metaphysical concept of reason, which perdured until the Renaissance, under the weight of an anti-metaphysical ideal of reason, which remained nonetheless meta-physical. In other words, "Enlightened" philosophers rejected what they took to be medieval appeals to an otherworldly standard (e.g. Being, First Truth) in the effort to ground human knowledge, and they sought to replace it with a standard which was scientifically rigorous and accessible to all, regardless of religious or cultural orientation. Yet, this strategy proved no more successful than the one it replaced, for the many conflicting standards to which it gave birth lacked consciousness of their roots in the concrete physical, historical, and social lives of those who bore them. The search for a new conception of rationality in the Enlightenment led paradoxically to greater chaos.

Though there are a number of possible responses to this set of circumstances, I will outline only three: First of all, one could resolutely continue to search for or claim to have found the elusive standard. Second, one could despair of the possibility of rational agreement and thus see in the present situation evidence of rampant irrationality. Or, third, one could let go of the illusory promise of agreement and see in the present situation compelling evidence of the historically-constituted dynamism of the human person as a free questioner.[74]

The first may be characterized as the position of the objectivist or the rational positivist who, through the consistent employment of a particular paradigm claims to be able to provide definitive answers to every question or else to show the meaningless of those questions for which the paradigm at stake does not account.[75] However, appealing to the insights of Martin Heidegger and Thomas Kuhn, John Caputo finds something deceptive in this approach, "the hollowness of a pure 'logic of science' which prescinds from the institutional circumstances in which scientific ideas are generated and debated."[76] MacIntyre seems to be describing as similar phenomenon when he writes of "secular fideism": One party may describe another's position as arbitary or irrational

> not so much because they themselves are genuinely moved by rational argument, as because by appealing to argument they are able to exercise a kind of power which favors their own interests and privileges, the interests and privileges of a class which has arrogated the rhetorically effective use of argument to itself for its own purposes.[77]

Often enough then, what is considered rational and irrational by the objectivist is more a function of unconscious political exigencies rather than the abstract philosophical exigencies which are publicly expressed.[78]

The second response—to despair in what is seen as evidence of irresolvable irrationality—is the position of the relativist or irrational positivist. Such a person sees the everyday world as constituted of pragmatic necessities and sees every concrete historical tradition as equally unjustifiable from a rational point of view.[79] The various concepts which philosophers have taken to be most fundamental can only be understood "as relative to a specific conceptual scheme, theoretical framework, paradigm, form of life, society, or culture."[80] One who takes this position may be led, therefore, to live life on the surface, consciously avoiding exploration of the peculiar history and tradition which may even be unconsciously guiding his/her own relativistic option. Or else such a person may go the way of religious fideism: unquestioning commitment to a particular system of meaning and value whose lack of intelligibility is not only considered unproblematic but may actually be viewed as the certificate of its divine origin. In the end, both of these approaches amount to the same thing: A theoretical rejection of the possibility of distinguishing the rational from the irrational and a practical reduction of the world to one's own individual perceptions, needs, and decisions.[81]

Recently, however, an alternative to these options has begun to emerge. Bernstein, for example, has argued that the dichotomy between objectivism and relativism is "misleading and distortive," based as it is upon the Cartesian assumption that the failure to find a fixed foundation for knowledge upon which all could agree will lead ultimately to intellectual and moral chaos.[82]

Starting with Kuhn's *The Structure of Scientific Revolutions,* he detects an internal dialectic in the philosophy of science and epistemology whereby preoccupation with isolated individual terms, propositions, and conceptual schemes has given way to an appreciation of the "historical dynamic continuity" evidenced in living and socially-constituted traditions.[83]

MacIntyre similarly calls for "a conception of rational enquiry as embodied in a tradition, a conception according to which the standards of rational justification emerge from and are part of history."[84] Though Nietzsche, for example, saw himself as having overcome the Enlightenment's truth claims, he was inadequately conscious of the extent to which he himself was the inheritor of the Enlightenment problematic and its terms. Progress out of the philosophical *cul de sac* of relativism, MacIntyre implies, can only be made if attention is shifted from the question of the possibility of finding a single rational standard to the actual practice of rational enquiry.[85]

In his proposal for a "radical hermeneutics," John Caputo has also put forward a strategy which exhibits substantial kinship with those put forward by Bernstein and MacIntyre. Metaphysics, he claims, has been a sustained attempt to describe that principle of constancy and abiding presence which can serve as an objective reason for everything that is and happens. As he puts it, "Metaphysics has been trying to sell us the same bill of goods, the same *ousia,* ever since it opened for business"[86]—and this in an effort to flee the difficulty of living without the comfort of such a bottom line. This shortcoming, in turn, has afflicted much of Enlightenment and post-Enlightenment thought, whose objection to traditional metaphysics is not to its pursuit of a bottom line, but to its particular method and conclusions. What hermeneutics attempts to do is to "stick with the original difficulty of life, and not to betray it with metaphysics."[87] Cultivating, as it does, a "an acute sense of the contingency of all social, historical, and linguistic structures," hermeneutics would seem to undermine the possibility of conceiving any meaningful notion of reason or rationality. Caputo argues, however, that the radical hermeneutic approach will actually rescue reason from the status of mere instrumentality to which it has been relegated in the contemporary world and restore that freedom for play which is one of reason's distinguishing marks.[88]

I want to argue in what follows for a notion of 'reason' which begins by acknowledging the uncircumventable futility involved in trying to nail things down. In the end, I want to say science, action, art, and religious belief make their way by a free and creative movement whose dynamics baffle the various discourses on method.[89]

One outcome of the Enlightenment has been that no single conception of rationality can make an undisputed claim to validity. While contemporary thinkers have taken refuge in objectivism or relativism from what they consider to be an unacceptable situation, another option needs to be considered—an option which does not see in the present situation evidence of rampant irrationality, but rather the inner dynamism of the human spirit. To the extent that I have described them here, the proposals made by thinkers diverse as Bernstein, MacIntyre, and Caputo all converge toward one important point: We will not make progress in the rationality debate until we abandon the search for universal agreement on a fixed standard of certitude and recognize in the present situation, marked as it is by a pluralism of ever-changing views, evidence of the historically-constituted dynamism of the human person as a free questioner. What these contemporary thinkers are proposing is not, in the end, completely alien from the conception of rationality which we saw operative in the thought of Clement of Alexandria and Thomas Aquinas. Dynamism, historicity, dialectical progression: These elements which we have tentatively identified as contemplative are beginning to emerge again as philosophically important. It is part of the genius of Karl Rahner that he was able to bring these elements to bear in a philosophical anthropology which is neither discontinuous with the Thomistic tradition in which the reason/revelation problem found its first resolution, nor oblivious to the contributions and questions of post-Modern thought which challenges us to reconcile reason and revelation in a whole new way.

II

Karl Rahner, Philosopher and Theologian

Catholic Responses to the Enlightenment and the Revival of Thomism
Catholic philosophy and theology are often identified with the thought Thomas Aquinas. This identification, however, can be misleading, because it obscures the tremendously complex intellectual and political developments which led to the revival of Thomism at the beginning of the present century and the subsequent emergence of pluralism within Neo-Thomism during the period prior to the Second Vatican Council. This history—only the barest outline of which can be presented here—provides the immediate context for understanding the early thought of Karl Rahner.[1]

In the previous chapter, it was noted that the dominance of one or another conception of rationality is often enough a function of political as well as intellectual exigencies. This was as true within the Roman Catholic milieu as it was outside it. When the nineteenth century began, the ideals of liberal democratic government and bourgeois capitalism were on the rise in Europe and North America. These presented not merely an intellectual but also a political threat to the Church, as the last vestiges of the Papacy's temporal power (e.g. its control over the Papal States) began to deteriorate. Throughout the first half of the nineteenth century, reigning popes tried in varieties of ways to reassert monarchical authority—their own and that of other royal governments—in a Europe rapidly loosing patience with monarchs. The ecclesiastical nationalism which had begun to evolve during the previous century was definitively crushed as the Bishop of Rome exercised an increasingly active role in the direction of Catholic thought.[2] "A debilitating feebleness of intellectual life set in. Authoritative decrees became the criterion of truth, or, rather, certitude guaranteed by authority displaced the quest for truth."[3]

What is important to see is that almost every intervention of the Holy See in a theological controversy during this century was influenced by Church-State relations.[4] Even an event so seemingly innocuous from a political point of view as the definition of the immaculate conception of Mary the mother Jesus had profoundly political inspiration and implications. Although it was certainly intended to be a positive statement about Mary's freedom from the effects of original sin, it was also to be seen as a negative statement about the rest of mortal flesh: Darkened by sin, the intellects of all required the special guidance that only the God-given authority of the Church could provide.[5] Even though the Holy See was unable to maintain its temporal authority (which was lost with the papal states in 1870), it was certainly equipped to maintain its spiritual authority—which included control over Catholic intellectual life—at least for a while.[6]

If it is true that the papacy exercised increasing control over Catholic intellectual life, it must also be said that a certain intellectual eclecticism among eighteenth century Catholic intellectuals was a condition of possibility for this to occur. At the beginning of the nineteenth century, the reaction of Catholic scholars to the development which had occurred during the Enlightenment was as varied as that of their non-Catholic counterparts. The Renaissance and Reformation had led to the decline of scholasticism; its revival following the Council of Trent was undermined by the rise of post-Cartesian philosophy in France and Germany as well as by the suppression of the Jesuits, who would have been among its strongest proponents.[7] Only among the Spanish Dominicans did the thought of Aquinas continue to figure prominently. And so, Catholic intellectuals of the late eighteenth century numbered among their ranks Lockeans and Cartesians, rationalists and fideists, as well as ontologists and traditionalists.[8]

What finally galvanized Catholic theology in the nineteenth century was the *bête-noire* of rationalism.[9] Whether in the form of Humean empiricism, Kantian critique, or of post-Kantian idealism, it was the commitment to pure reason which was perceived to pose the gravest problem for Catholic thought. The ideal of "religion within the limits of reason alone" not only undermined ecclesiastical authority over the religious life of individuals, but also provided a theoretical basis for the rejection of the intellectual and moral claims of positive Christian revelation. The major task for Catholic theology became defensive apologetics.[10]

Although this perceived threat provided a common focus for Catholic thought, in no way did it elicit a uniform response. McCool has identified at least three types of response:[11] 1) Traditionalism, which claimed that unaided human reason was incapable of reaching truth with respect to God. This option granted rationalism's confinement of reason to spatio-temporal boundaries, but sought to protect historical revelation by asserting a distinct authority for faith. 2) Semi-rationalism, which sought to appropriate the epistemological insight of Kantian and post-Kantian thought to Catholic apologetics. By redrawing the boundaries of reason, this option left room within the Enlightenment ideal of pure reason for a natural knowledge of God. 3) Neo-Scholasticism which, through the recovery of pre-Kantian scientific method (the ideal of Aristotelian science), hoped to establish a standard of certitude in Catholic theology to rival that of Enlightenment philosophy and to overcome its concomitant religious skepticism.[12] The first of these options never achieved any prominence; the second dominated until the middle of the nineteenth century; but the third achieved ascendency thereafter.[13]

The Neo-Scholastic assessment of modern philosophy was rather dim:

> In modern philosophy, reason was individual reason, separated from the Church's authoritative communication of Christian tradition. The separation of individual reason from the Church's authoritative communication had occurred within theology at the time of the Protestant Reformation. Descartes had extended it to Catholic philosophy. Rationalism and skepticism were the inevitable results of philosophy's separation of itself from Catholic tradition. Therefore, they could never be overcome until philosophy had been persuaded to retrace its steps, abandon the modern form which it had assumed with Descartes, and rebuild itself anew in vital continuity with the sound Christian philosophy of the scholastic period.[14]

Joseph Kleutgen, a German Jesuit and neo-Thomist was a pivotal figure in this movement.[15] His rigorous scientific approach to theology carefully steered clear of what he took to be the excesses of fideism on the one hand and semi-rationalism on the other.[16] His Thomism had a dual emphasis: the unity of epistemology, anthropology, and metaphysics required by the theory of abstraction; and the capacity of the human intellect to grasp, through the universal, the intelligibility of the sensible particular. Ironically, this dual emphasis eventually gave birth to two strains of Thomism, violently opposed to each other: the Maréchalian tradition with its emphasis on the subjective and historical and the tradition represented by Garrigou-Lagrange, Maritain, and Gilson with its emphasis on objectivity and realism.[17] We will have more to say on these shortly, but suffice it to say here that seeds of pluralism within Thomism were already, though unconsciously, present in the thought of one of the nineteenth century's most important Catholic apologists.

From the outset, Neo-Scholasticism appears to have labored under at least two limitations. As philosophy in the service of defensive apologetics it tended to look with suspicion at best and antipathy at worst at any philosophical system whose method or conclusions differed from its own. Hence it deprived itself of the benefits of any serious dialogue with Kantian or post-Kantian philosophy.[18] Secondly—and not unrelated to the first limitation—it lacked an adequate sense of history. The "intelligible but non-logical development of thought through the changing conceptual frameworks of succeeding historical and cultural world views" was a notion entirely foreign to Kleutgen and his neo-Scholastic colleagues. Their lack of historical consciousness not only validated their resolve to avoid dialogue with modern philosophy, but affected their approach to Aquinas. Rather than to look at the works of the master in his own distinctive historical context, Kleutgen relied on the post-Reformation scholasticism of Cana, deLugo, Vasquez, and Suarez.[19]

Kleutgen as well as other neo-Scholastics were intimately involved in the drafting of the apostolic constitution of the First Vatican Council, *Dei Filius*. Though the constitution does not endorse or mandate scholasticism specifically, the language and thought structure in which its teaching are expressed is decidedly scholastic.[20]

Vatican I sought to defend the reasonableness of faith against the "blind leap" approach of the Pietist tradition. Simultaneously, it sought to guard the supernatural character of faith as a divine gift against those who would view it merely as an intensification of natural reason. Faith, in the words of *Dei Filius*, is

a supernatural virtue by which we, with the aid and inspiration of the grace of God, believe that the things revealed by Him are true, not because the intrinsic truth of the revealed things has been perceived by the natural light of reason, but because of the authority of God Himself who reveals them, who can neither deceive nor be deceived.[21]

What we saw earlier in Thomas's commentary on the *De Trinitate* is repeated here, as both the interior and external dimension of faith are emphasized. Faith is said to involve both external proofs of revelation (divine facts, miracles, and prophecies)[22] and "the illumination and inspiration of the Holy Spirit who gives to all a sweetness in consenting to and believing in the truth."[23]

Vatican I also sought to describe clearly the proper relationship between faith and reason. In order both to defend the reasonableness of faith's (and therefore the Church's) claims and to protect the doctrine of the faith from inappropriate philosophical scrutiny, it outlines a two-fold order of knowledge, distinguishing that which natural reason can attain from that which can only be be grasped by divine faith.[24] While the second chapter of the document affirms that God's existence and essential attributes can be known "with certitude by the natural light of human reason,"[25] the final chapter marks out definite boundaries for reason. It emphasizes that even with light of faith, the divine mysteries cannot be grasped by the human intellect to the same extent that created things can, since these mysteries naturally "exceed the created intellect so much that, even when handed down by revelation and accepted by faith, they nevertheless remain covered by the veil of faith itself, and wrapped in a certain mist."[26] In light of all this, although the Church seeks to cultivate the arts and sciences, it reserves the right to condemn false opinions for the sake of the deposit of the faith.[27] The language in which the Church's role as guardian is described exemplifies the conception of truth presumed throughout the document:

> The doctrine of faith which God revealed has not been handed down as a philosophic invention to the human mind to be perfected, but has been entrusted as a divine deposit to the Spouse of Christ, to be faithfully guarded and infallibly interpreted.[28]

And so, though the excesses of both fideism and philosophical rationalism were both avoided, the abstract and wholly ahistorical conception of reason implicit in the thought of Kleutgen and other neo-Scholastics found itself enshrined in the Church's authoritative teaching. As a result, from 1870 until the period between the two world wars, Catholic theology and philosophy became even more highly speculative and existentially detached. The Enlightenment had produced a host of conflicting rational standards without any consciousness of their roots in the concrete physical, historical, and social lives of those who conceived them. The official Church responded, in turn, by proposing its own rational standard, the "divine deposit" entrusted to it, omitting (as had its rationalist opponents) any reflection on the complex dynamisms by which all such standards are formed and continue to develop.

Ironically, the correction of this omission was also the result of an action of the official Church: the promulgation of *Aeterni Patris*, which gave new impetus to studies in Thomism and ultimately gave birth to a new generation of Thomists uniquely aware of the importance of history.

Leo XIII, pope from 1878 until 1903 and author of *Aeterni Patris*, was a complex figure. Although he was keenly interested in addressing the new challenges presented by the rise of democracy and industrialization, he was linked strongly to the traditionalism which preceded him. He viewed the Church as separate from the secular world in which it found itself.[29] From his seminary days, Gioacchino Pecci cultivated an interest in Thomism and with his brother Giuseppe transformed the seminary at Perugia into a center for Thomistic studies. By 1875, Pecci together with other neo-Scholastics had been successful at establishing centers of Thomistic studies in Italy, Germany, and Belgium. In his first encyclical *Inscrutibili Dei,* he had already written of the importance of Thomism for the transformation of society and culture.[30] But it was in *Aeterni Patris* that the revival of Thomism was explicitly identified as goal to be embraced throughout the universal Church.

The encyclical begins with a diagnosis of the ailment of the times. Without being specific, the letter traces the roots of the "troubles that vex public and private life" to "the false conclusions concerning divine and human things, which originated in the schools of philosophy."[31] Later in the document, this generally negative attitude toward modern philosophy emerges again when he criticizes Catholic scholars for their attempts to seek a rapprochement with non-Scholastic philosophies:

> [T]hrowing aside the patrimony of ancient wisdom, [they] chose rather
> to build up a new edifice than to strengthen and complete the old by
> the aid of the new—ill-advisedly, in sooth, and not without detriment

to the sciences. For a multiform system of this kind which depends on the authority and choice of any professor, has a foundation open to change and consequently gives us a philosophy not firm and stable and robust like that of old, but tottering and feeble.[32]

Particularly troubling to Leo seems to have been the rise of liberalism, which he believed equated liberty with license and overlooked the divine origin of all authority. Only the teachings of Thomas could "overturn those principles of the new order which are well known to be dangerous to the peaceful order of things and to public safety."[33]

Therefore, identifying philosophical error as a major source of social evil, Leo determined that he should speak "on the mode of taking up the study of philosophy which shall respond most fitly to the true faith and, at the same time, be most consonant with the dignity of human knowledge."[34] After reaffirming the complementarity of faith and reason along much the same lines as *Dei Filius*,[35] he identifies philosophy's primary tasks: Philosophy is "to smooth and fortify the road to true faith,"[36] to provide motives of credibility (i.e. to demonstrate the reasonableness of belief),[37] to make theology scientific,[38] and to defend the truths of faith against "those who dare to oppose them."[39] While performing these tasks, philosophy should carefully avoid the transgression of its proper boundaries. As "handmaid to theology," and "conscious of its own infirmity," the systematic exercise of hman reason must accept those supernatural truths which are beyond its reach and refrain from measuring them according to its own standard. In no way does such unflagging obedience to the faith detract from philosophy's dignity, "but adds greatly to its nobility, keenness, and stability."[40] From Leo's vantage point, the philosophy best outfitted to do all this was that of Thomas Aquinas.

Leo appeals to his predecessor Sixtus V who praised scholastic philosophy for its "noble and admirable endowments."

That ready and close coherence of cause and effect, that order and array as of a disciplined army in bttle, those clear definitions and distinctions, that strength of argument and those keen discussions by which light is distinguished from darkness, the true from the false, expose and strip naked, as it were, the falsehoods of heretics wrapped around by a cloud of subterfuges and fallacies.[41]

Leo praises the way Thomas brought together in one place the teachings of all his predecessors and formed them into a complete and coherent system. Using the hyperbole which sometimes characterizes solemn papal pronouncements, he writes, "Reason borne on the wings of Thomas to its human height, can scarcely rise higher."[42]   And then he goes on to review all those papal teachings before his own which accord particular honor to the teaching of St. Thomas.[43]   The document ends with an exhortation "to restore the golden wisdom of St. Thomas," allowing, however, that anything in the teachings of St. Thomas which is clearly disproved by the discoveries of a subsequent time need not be affirmed in the present age.[44]

Despite its defensive tone and its questionable identification of post-Tridentine scholasticism with the thought of St. Thomas, *Aeterni Patris* reawakened a spirit of intellectual inquiry in the Western Church which (the set-backs under Pius X notwithstanding) has perdured up to the present.[45]   The rich developments within twentieth century Thomism—not to mention the myriad developments in systematics, scripture, liturgy, ecumenics, catechetics, evangelization, and so on—bear testimony to the fertility of the twentieth century as a period of Catholic intellectual activity.

Although *Aeterni Patris* mistakenly treated scholastic thought in general and Thomism in particular monolithically, it cannot be denied that the selection of Aquinas as normative also brought with it many benefits.   The systematic quality of Thomas' presentation; the insistence on the integration of epistemology, anthropology, and metaphysics; combined with Thomas' willingness to interact with the "new science" of his day made the Thomism of Thomas an excellent model for philosophy and theology in the twentieth century.[46]

But what is most interesting about *Aeterni Patris* is this: Though Leo no doubt assumed that Thomism would provide the basis for establishing an objective and immutable order in the world to counteract the chaos alleged to have been brought about by modern philosophy,[47] the fact is that the promulgation of this encyclical inaugurated a process of internal evolution in Thomistic studies which it neither anticipated nor would have endorsed.[48] This evolution and its resulting pluralism are not antithetical or completely extrinsic to Thomas's own thought but are among its intrinsic strengths. In an essay written for the hundredth anniversary of *Aeterni Patris*, Joseph Owens wrote of Thomas' metaphysics:

> [It cannot] be looked upon as a system neat and fixed, and merely handed down from one generation to another. Rather, the philosophical thinking of Aquinas has to be lived anew by each thinker who would profit from it. It will be different in each individual who absorbs its influence and inspiration. One has to get used to this live pluralism of the thought of Aquinas if it is to play an effective role.[49]

What forms have the development and pluralism of Thomism assumed in the twentieth century?[50] From the promulgation of *Aeterni Patris* in 1879 up to the start of the first world war, the Thomism of the commentators—Cajetan and John of St. Thomas—dominated The principal concern of the early Neo-Thomists was to refute the two errors which were taken to be at the foundation of modernism: the metaphysics of becoming and the subjective notion of truth. The "strict observance" Thomism of Réginald Garrigou-Lagrange, with its focus on the certitude of logical principles and the objective grasp of essences, was prominent in this period. Jacques Maritain, who had begun as a disciple of Henri Bergson, was also among those who turned to the scholastic commentators for their version of Thomas' thought. Some others, however, like Maurice Blondel and Pierre Rousselot, began during this period to question the rationalist conceptualism of the the scholastic manuals and move toward a more dynamic, experiential approach.[51]

During the period between the wars, a changed political situation in Europe accompanied by greater openness within the Church to democracy and secular culture, created the condition of possibility for the rise of first rate Catholic scholarship. Both the historical Thomism of Etienne Gilson and the transcendental approach of Joseph Maréchal developed during this era. So too did the less widely known participation-oriented Thomism of Cornelio Fabro. These approaches to Thomas varied in significant ways.

Gilson is remembered for his distinctive conception of Christian philosophy and his fierce defense of the epistemological realism of Thomas against those who emphasized Platonic strains or transcendental elements.[52] Maréchal continued the development begun by Rousselot, focusing on the dynamism of human intellect toward being and entering into dialogue with post-medieval thought—particularly Kant's transcendental philosophy.[53] Maréchal, as we shall see, exerted very significant influence on the early thought of Karl Rahner. Finally, Fabro endeavored to draw out the Platonic and Neo-Platonic aspects of Thomas thought, arguing that these were in fact more original than his widely-discussed Aristotelianism. He attempted to confront the history of Western metaphysics with Thomas' synthesis, convinced that Thomas had escaped Heidegger's damning judgment of this history.[54] Although representatives of these three major schools of Thomism frequently found themselves at odds with each other, they all shared in common an appreciation of the distinctiveness of Thomas' penetrating insight into esse, the act of being—something which the post-Tridentine scholastics and early neo-scholastics had missed.[55]

During the period stretching from the second world war to the start of the second Vatican Council tension was building within the Catholic intellectual community. The historical method of Catholic exegetes and patristics scholars clashed with the largely ahistorical approach of popular scholasticism. Inspired by Maréchal's transcendental method and concerned about the rise of theoretical and practical atheism, "la nouvelle théologie" turned toward the scriptures and to the writings of the Fathers and away from rigid scholasticism in its effort to explain how it that grace can reach the non-believer. Maréchal's conception of the human person as fundamentally oriented toward Absolute Being proved more adequate to the Scriptural and Patristic witness and better suited to the mentality prevalent in contemporary culture than did the older notion of man as if in a state of "pure nature." Moreover, transcendental Thomist emphasis on the poverty of human concepts of God—their status as merely analogous representations of the Pure Act's infinite reality—opened the theoretical door to greater theological pluralism. Despite some temporary set-backs just prior to the Council, the concern for the human subject and an acceptance of the ideas of pluralism and historical consciousness which marked "la nouvelle theologie" moved into the mainstream of Catholic intellectual life.[56] The time was ripe for the contribution of a thinker like Karl Rahner.

The Distinctive Place of Karl Rahner

Karl Rahner was born in Freiburg, Germany, on March 5, 1904, just as the twentieth century revival of Thomism was getting underway.[57] The child of a pious Catholic home, Karl entered the Society of Jesus in 1922. Even as we prepare to look to Rahner's writings primarily for their contribution to philosophy, we do well to bear in mind that their author saw himself first and foremost as a disciple of Jesus Christ, a priest of the Roman Catholic Church, and a Jesuit, a follower of St. Ignatius.

When Rahner undertook philosophical studies for the first time (one year at Feldkirch and two at Pullach), he displayed a particular interest in the thought of Kant and in Maréchal's attempt to bring "the critical philosophy" into conversation with the thought of Aquinas. After his regency , Rahner went to Valkenburg in Holland to study theology. In 1934, he was sent to Freiburg to take up the study of philosophy for the second time; it was the intention of the Society that he earn the doctorate there and then teach the history of philosophy.

At Freiburg, Rahner found himself the beneficiary and victim of the Thomistic pluralism discussed above. On the one hand, he brought with him the interest in Maréchal's attempt at rapprochement between Thomas and Kant which he had developed at Feldkirch and Pullach. His enthusiasm for coming to terms with Enlightenment thought was further stimulated by his contact with Martin Heidegger, in whose seminars he participated. On the other hand, the chair of Catholic philosophy at Freiburg was occupied by Martin Honecker, a rather traditional neo-Scholastic who disdained all attempts to harmonize the thought of the Angelic Doctor with what were considered the less-than-angelic strains of modern philosophy. That Rahner was the beneficiary of this pluralism (and even of its accompanying tensions) is evident in the shape of his thought, which is neither discontinuous with the Thomistic tradition nor oblivious to the contributions and questions of Enlightenment and post-Enlightenment culture. That he was also a victim is clear in that his dissertation (later published as *Spirit in the World*) was rejected by Honecker for an alleged lack of faithfulness to Thomas' epistemology.

Honecker's judgement turns out to have been a *felix culpa*. In 1936 Rahner went to Innsbruck to finish doctoral work in theology and to begin his teaching career. In 1937 he gave a lecture series in Salzburg on the foundations for a philosophy of religion. These lectures, based in large part on the metaphysical anthropology worked out in his rejected dissertation, attempted to lay out the conditions of possibility for revelation. These lectures were eventually published under the title *Hearers of the Word*.

Aside from a couple of individual essays,[58] most of his published work from the late thirties on was theological rather than philosophical in character, though it is by no means clear that Rahner would have approved of the rigid separation such a distinction implies. His corpus includes a number of major theological reference works in the editing of which he was prime collaborator, a number of devotional and short pastorally-oriented works, hundreds of essays in systematic theology (gathered in his *Theological Investigations*, the English version of which numbers twenty-three volumes), and various collections of interviews. One of his last major works was *Foundations of Christian Faith*, which begins with much the same metaphysical anthropology and philosophy of religion that *Spirit in the World* and *Hearers of the Word* had elaborated nearly forty years earlier.[59]

In addition to teaching and writing, Rahner lectured widely and continued to do pastoral work. He was a significant participant in the *aggiornamento* which took place in the Roman Church just prior to and during the Second Vatican Council. Like his thirteenth century mentor, Rahner did not always enjoy the blessing of his ecclesiastical superiors. Still, when the dust of the Council settled, it was evident that much which Rahner had brought to light theologically—in apologetics, christology, ecclesiology, sacraments, and so on—had become part of the mainstream.

And yet, Rahner did not see his formidable achievement as finished business, but simply as a modest and essentially incomplete contribution to the thought and life of his own culture and age. As he neared the end of his life, Rahner spoke of a systematic theology which was, nonetheless, anything but a final system:

One should never stop thinking too early. The true system of thought really is the knowledge that humanity is finally directed precisely not toward what it can control in knowledge but toward the absolute mystery as such; that mystery is not just an unfortunate reminder of what is not yet known but rather the blessed goal of knowledge which comes to itself when it is with the incomprehensible one, and not in any other way. In other words, then, the system is the system of what cannot be systematized.[60]

This is only one of many places in the Rahner corpus where a contemplative dimension to rationality, as Rahner understood it, is prominent and decisive. His ability to deal both soberly and creatively with the challenges posed by rapid change and extraordinary pluralism in theology and culture was, at least in part, a function of his operative notion of rationality: One which was supple enough to bend and grow to accommodate newly-emergent realities and yet firmly rooted enough not to degenerate into arbitrary dogmatism, meaningless chaos, or thought-less superficiality. Philosophically, this was Rahner's major contribution.

Admittedly, Rahner's primary work was theology. His self-description and the evidence of his scholarly output dictate that Rahner be thought of as a theologian. Yet, it is also indisputable that Rahner's philosophical options (elaborated in his first two major works) had a significant impact on the shape of his entire theological corpus, just as it is possible to glean from his theological work insights of profound philosophical significance. There is a certain circularity in Rahner's thinking: Philosophy begins where it always must, with the human person as questioner; and philosophy's reflection on what it means to be a questioner in turn opens up the possibility of hearing a word addressed by God in history. But after having heard such a word—even if that word be considered definitive in itself, as Jesus is in Christianity—the hearer is inevitably inclined to still further questioning; as such, he remains always a philosopher in the literal sense, a lover and seeker of wisdom.

Most of Rahner's contemporary commentators treat him as a theologian. Ann Carr, for example, goes so far as to say that even *Spirit in the World* and *Hearers of the Word* are intrinsically and implicitly theological:

> [W]hile these works appear to be philosophy, it is my conviction that they are, rather, a theology which looks like philosophy . . . the theological method which Rahner has explicated with increasing clarity since 1954 is in fact the method which he himself has been using from the very beginning of his career. It is a philosophical theology which has its foundation in theology itself.[61]

It is not self-evident that Rahner himself would have shared Carr's view. Throughout his own Introduction to *Spirit in the World*, Rahner never refers to his enterprise there as anything but philosophy. Even when he refers to his use of Aquinas in that work, it is philosophy and not theology which is presented as methodologically foundational. Of Aquinas he writes,

> [W]hat we must try to do is grasp his philosophy anew as it unfolds, from its first and often hardly expressed starting point. . . . the living philosophy out of which he wrote his theology was never articulated in its unity and development in any immediately and historically accessible form, but remains hidden in the silence of this thought.[62]

Perhaps it would be more accurate to say that Rahner's theology has its methodological foundation in philosophy and that his philosophy has its experiential foundation in the Christian life lived.

Another student of Rahner also focuses on his theological significance. According to Leo O'Donovan, though Rahner's anthropology always took human experience as its starting point, it was always theological in its inner impulse.[63] Still, as O'Donovan describes the central insights of Rahner's thought, the intimate and intrinsic connection of his philosophy and theology is evident. The "epistemological absolute of imaginative experience to which we must continually turn if we are to understand and act responsibly" and "the religious absolute of a God transcending time who calls us toward eternity"[64] were not two separate discoveries of Rahner which are extrinsically and accidentally related. Rather, they are complementary aspects of a unitary experience, which has been reflected upon from two different points of view, in the light of two different questions.

In a retrospective piece which he wrote on the occasion of Rahner's death, John Galvin also puts the spotlight on Rahner's theological contribution. He claims that Rahner "contributed more than any other theologian" to the twentieth century renewal of Catholic theology,[65] and identifies his work on grace as his single greatest achievement. Rahner, it seems, was able to talk about grace in a manner which was both faithful to the tradition and intelligible to twentieth century men and women. It is significant, however, that in his description of Rahner's contributions on grace, Galvin draws particular attention to the inadequacies of the neo-Scholasticism of the late nineteenth and early twentieth centuries.[66] If Rahner was able to make some headway in the understanding of grace and nature, it was not simply because he found new theological language to communicate the perennial truths of faith. It was also because he had been willing to deal first with the philosophical foundations and presuppositions which were at the root of the problem. As long as neo-Scholasticism was going to be completely defensive in its posture—unwilling to look even at the components of modern thought which were compatible with Christian revelation—no progress could be made. Rahner's genius had something to do with his willingness to look for the possibility of grace in the modern philosophical mind.

Among the handful of commentators who pursue the philosophical side of Rahner's thought, Thomas Sheehan stands out. His recent work, dedicated to an analysis of Rahner's metaphysics, argues from a Heideggerian viewpoint that Rahner did not go far enough in overcoming metaphysics—that, in effect, Rahner was still looking for the ground of rational certitude just as all metaphysicians and anti-metaphysicians had before him.[67]

Andrew Tallon, another student of Rahner's thought who emphasizes its philosophical importance, argues that it is the theme of personization which predominates in Rahner's work even though it is never explicitly mentioned.[68] In another place, Tallon argues for the primacy of love and of the heart in Rahner's metaphysics of cognition.[69] But even Tallon, who treats Rahner's philosophy with the utmost seriousness, admits that the line between Rahnerian philosophy and theology is not so clear:

> To understand human being as [Rahner] does is to grasp the continuity
> between philosophy and theology in such a way that their differences
> diminish without in any way compromising divine freedom. Perhaps
> what has marked Rahner's thought so specially is the metaphysical
> way he understands the human, resulting in a metaphysical
> anthropology which is the foundation of any theology possible to
> created persons.[70]

Inasmuch as theology deals in worldly concepts and speaks in human language, it cannot escape doing philosophy. At the same time, inasmuch as philosophy's attempt to describe human cognition and human action points it beyond finite things in a finite world, it cannot help opening up to theology.[71]

Given what has been said thus far about Rahner's Thomistic lineage, it would be tempting simply to describe him as a transcendental thinker—a thinker who begins with reflection upon the cognitive activity of the human subject and then attempts to derive from this the conditions of possibility for knowing and being. Indeed, Rahner was deeply influenced by Maréchal, the father of so-called "Transcendental Thomism." Still, to describe Rahner this way is to miss something of the considerable subtlety of his method.

Between Rahner's early and later works, there seems to be a shift in methodological emphasis. In the earlier works, his focus is on the structure of the human subject; here he uses the phenomenological discoveries of German philosophy from Kant to Heidegger to flesh out a metaphysical anthropology. This may be referred to as Rahner's *transcendental* phase. In his later works, the subject is treated more explicitly within his/her concrete historical context; this may be designated as Rahner's *historical* phase.[72] Still, to the extent that it may be said that both methodological strains are present from the start, there may be a third strain in Rahner's thought which relates and is related to the others. Rahner is not only a transcendental and historical thinker; he is also a *dialectical* thinker. Commenting on Rahner's last works, O'Donovan writes:

> His method had never been merely transcendental; issues of his time and lessons of the past had always guided his reflections on the dialectical unity-in-difference of time and eternity, worldly figures and sacramental grace, and the ineffable triune God's everlasting love for the world. . . . In these last writings I believe that it is clear that Karl Rahner was preeminently a dialectical religious thinker who came increasingly to recognize theology's mediating role in a culturally pluralistic world.[73]

Hence, Rahner's method may be described as, at once, transcendental, historical, and dialectical.

To describe Rahner's method as *transcendental* is both to say something about his philosophical pedigree and to say something about his own procedure for handling a question, a concept or a text. The former is less important than the latter; still something should be said about Transcendental Thomism as a philosophical school.

Bucking the conventional wisdom, Joseph Maréchal—with a background in biology and psychology as well as in philosophy—tried to come to terms with the thought of Immanuel Kant. In light of his scholastic training, Maréchal was particularly interested in dealing with the Kantian claim that theoretical reason never reaches reality as it is in itself, but only knows reality as it affects the knower. In his famed *Cahier V,* he employs a two-pronged strategy in his debate with Kant. First, he shows the denial of the absolute value of metaphysical affirmations to be self-refuting and points out the aspects of human cognition that Kant had overlooked. Then, adopting for rhetorical purposes the Kantian method—i.e. beginning with the experience of the knowing subject—he shows how the absolute value of metaphysical affirmations may still be vindicated.[74] Maréchal's transcendental version of Thomistic epistemology, "sees the stamp of the Absolute upon the human intellect in the hypothetical necessity which affects every human affirmation."[75]

To be sure, Rahner accepted and built on some of Maréhal's conclusions, but Maréchal's greatest influence on Rahner can be detected on the level of method: First of all, this was a Thomism not narrowly confined to repetition or elaboration of a fixed set of Thomistic theses; it was rather a Thomism which reached beyond itself to other valid historical and cultural frameworks. Secondly, this was an approach to metaphysics which did not take the objectivity of the known world for granted, but sought first of all to uncover the conditions of possibility for this objectivity in the existence of the concrete, individual human subject. Like Maréchal, Rahner was convinced that when one successfully uncovered these conditions of possibility, one would discover a fundamental human dynamism toward Absolute Being as the first of these conditions. Hence, as Carl Peter has put it in his description of transcendental method in theology, "transcendental" really has two senses: 1) Having to do with *a priori,* pre-given conditions of possibility, and 2) pointing beyond the presently known and grasped to that ever-receding horizon within which basic cognitional operations occur.[76]

The implications of this transcendental approach can be seen throughout Rahner's thought, especially in the grounding of the entire philosophical enterprise in metaphysical questioning.[77] This questioning is expressed in myriad ways—ranging from the questions we may ask about the most mundane things ("What is it?") to the questions we ask about that which enables mundane things to be ("What is being?"). What becomes clear when philosophy focuses on the individual human subject is that the human person is a being who questions.

If it can be said that Rahner was indebted to Maréchal for his transcendental focus, perhaps it can be said that he was similarly indebted to

Heidegger for his *historical* emphasis.[78] Surely, Hegel had already talked about human history as the locus for the manifestation of Absolute Spirit. But it was Heidegger who moved beyond the still-abstract notion of pre-determined history's unfolding (a notion which seemed to leave little room for individual human subjects or their freedom) to an appreciation of the inescapable temporality of human existence and the meaning of being.

The Rahnerian emphasis on historicity is fully present in his earliest works.[79] Indeed, the distinctiveness of human spirit in both *Spirit in the World* and *Hearers of the Word* is described at least partly in terms of historicity. Because human knowledge is inescapably worldly, there is no getting away from space and time. Hence, should the human being hear a word addressed to him by God, it will be in space and time, i.e. in human history.

One particularly strong indication that historical consciousness was present in Rahner's method from the start can be seen in the way he interprets a portion of Thomas' *Summa* in *Spirit in the World*.[80] The Heideggerian method of retrieval (*Wiederholung*) which he employs there—an effort to get at what remains unsaid but potentially sayable in a given text—reveals an early convinction that philosophy does not consist merely in the recital of time-less truths but in the search for a truth which can only manifest itself in time.

Still, Rahner's commentators argue that the full impact of this historical dimension to his method is not seen until his later theological works.[81] In his mature Christology, for example, the man from Nazareth (historical) is understood to be the way to eternal life and truth (transcendental). In dogmatics, the inviolable deposit of the faith (transcendental) is expressed in the culture and language of individual men and women, in specific places, at particular times (historical).

Obviously, this emphasis on historicity could be seen as relativizing not only Rahner's own thought but truth in general. What basis will there be, for example, for claiming Jesus as the definitive historical revelation of God, if human experience of God is always "on the way"? As Sheehan frames the problem: "Retrieval takes historicity seriously, and historicity puts us face-to-face with relativism. Terror before relativism is terror before man himself, the radical question that finds no answer."[82] Whether Sheehan's description of the inevitable consequence of historicity is valid is a question to which it will be necessary to return. For the moment, however, there is enough here to point to the paradox and tension built in to Rahner's thought. It is in this sense that Rahner may also be described as a *dialectical* thinker.

In contemporary parlance, dialectic is often identified with the thought of Hegel or of Marx. What may be obscured by this identification are the philosophical roots of dialectic in Early Greek thought as well as the dialectical character of the medieval *disputatio*. In the Hegelian framework, the dialectical succession of historical epochs is a matter of rational necessity. In the Greek and later Thomistic frameworks, dialectic refers to the free play of ideas, the ever deepening penetration into the truth of a matter through successive questions, arguments, objections, and replies. Rahnerian dialectic—though it shares the Hegelian concern for history—also exhibits the grounded freedom which is characteristic of the earlier form. Rahnerian dialectic has its basis, not in rational necessity, but in "the mystery of creative love . . . both in time and in eternity."[83]

The dialectical character can be discerned in the way that Rahner stays with rather than seeks to dissolve all existential tensions and polarities: Freedom and necessity, individual and society, nature and grace, theological exploration and ecclesiastical authority.[84] These tensions and polarities are not to be seen as lamentable testimony to the failure of human reason and, still less, to the unreasonableness, the unintelligibility of God. They are rather to be seen in Rahner's thought as the potentially fruitful arena for a continually growing appreciation of the mystery of human existence as grasped by and reaching for the Absolute Mystery of God. Even at the very center of Rahner's theology one finds not a static principle but a dynamic reality, not an abstract term but a personal relationship which can be reduced neither to its transcendent nor historical dimensions. That center is

the mutuality of love between Jesus Christ and God, his loving origin towards whom we are all invited and into whom their Spirit guides us. Time alone cannot bear this exchange of love, nor can eternity itself simply effect it. Rather, it must be sown in time so as to be harvested in eternity.[85]

It is the dialectical character of Rahner's method which gives particularly strong evidence of the presence of a contemplative component in his thought. In continuity with a strain of thought which reaches back to the early Greeks, includes Christianity's greatest theologian, and receives renewed attention in the aftermath of the Enlightenment, Rahner describes and exercises reason not simply as an active principle whereby the human person tries to impose order on the chaos of sensible experience, but also as a principle of receptivity. In its contemplative dimension, reason enables reality in all its historical, finitely-bounded, and dialectically-related multiplicity to present itself as it is. Only if the human person disciplines the inexorable drive to squeeze experience into the categories with which he is most comfortable, does the human person advance in knowledge and ultimately, Rahner would say, in love.

III

Rationality in the Early Rahner

Having situated Rahner in the context of the post-Enlightenment crisis of rationality and the intellectual life of Roman Catholicism during the first part of the twentieth century, we can now look at the two most comprehensive expositions of his philosophy, *Spirit in the World* (*Geist in Welt*, henceforth referred to as "GW") and *Hearers of the Word* (*Hörer des Wortes*, henceforth "HW"). My purpose here is to cull from them Rahner's operative conception of rationality as he began his scholarly career and to see if there are some preliminary indications of a contemplative dimension.

GW was completed in 1936 and published for the first time in 1939. As Rahner notes in the Preface to the second edition, however, "it fell out of sight rather quickly, and perhaps somewhat undeservedly, because of the disturbances of the war."[1] In 1957, however, a second edition was prepared by Johannes Baptist Metz, with minor revisions and Rahner's authorization. Almost immediately it was translated into several languages, including English, and by the mid-sixties was receiving a fair amount of attention, particularly in Catholic journals of philosophy and theology. The second edition was not superceded.

HW had its genesis in a series of lectures which Rahner gave at Salzburg in the summer of 1937. The first edition appeared in 1941, but it met a fate similar to that of GW.[2] With Rahner's approval, Metz once more undertook a revision—this time more substantial—of the original edition, and it was published in 1963.

Spirit in the World

Rahner's project in GW is not explicitly to expound a particular conception of rationality; it is rather to expound a general metaphysics on the basis of an interpretation of human nature as spirit in the world. How the human being can at one and the same time be capable of reaching out beyond the world and be restricted to the world as the scope of his immediate experience is the central question of GW. Rahner is concerned to show how it is that sensibility and intellect collaborate together in human cognition in such a way as to leave open the possibility for metaphysics.[3]

That a conception of rationality may be culled from such a metaphysics is clear from a comment made by the author early in the work: "If we use the word *animality* instead of *sensibility*, and *rationality* instead of *intellect*, then our question is about the unity of the rational and animal."[4] Hence, in working out a metaphysical anthropology, a metaphysics developed out of a transcendental reflection on the distinctiveness of human cognition, Rahner is implicitly saying something about what it means to describe the human being as rational.

Rahner takes as a basis for his enquiry Question 84, Article 7 of Thomas' *Summa Theologiae*. The issue under consideration there is whether or not the human intellect can know anything without turning to the phantasms. Rahner distinguishes his approach in GW from the typical strategy of neo-scholasticism. His purpose in using this text from the *Summa* is not simply to repeat what Thomas said or to explain what he meant in such a way as to justify already-established conclusions. Rather, he looks to Thomas to provide a stimulus for his own thought in the contemporary situation. Referring to himself, Rahner writes: "[The author] would not know of any other reason for which he could be occupied with Thomas than for the sake of his philosophy and that of his time."[5] It is with this purpose in mind that Thomas uses a hermeneutic of retrieval in his treatment of the text: What is it that remains unsaid but potentially sayable and signficant for our own age in the text under consideration, in this case, Question 84 of the *Summa*?

The Human Person as Questioner

From the very beginning of GW, there is an indication that rationality may have a contemplative aspect. Rahner sees signficance in the fact that Thomas always took as the starting point of any discussion some question, problem, or aporia. To question "belongs so intrinsically to the philosophical event that on its formulation depends essentially whether the truth that is perhaps found will be recognized as such at all."[6] Seeming to echo Aristotle's conviction that philosophy begins in wonder,[7] Rahner identifies questioning as the irreducible starting point for philosophy. If one should try to get beneath the reality of the question, one will inevitably find oneself asking still another question, and so on, ad infinitum; it is the one aspect of human existence which defies further reduction. "Man questions necessarily," and, at the same time, "being is accessible to man at all only as something questionable."[8]

This starting point, the human person seen as a questioner, already provides the framework the metaphysical anthropology to be worked out in the rest of GW. On the one hand, the fact that the human being must question reveals something of his contingency and finitude: The one who asks a question recognizes that he is limited, that he does not "have it all." On the other hand, the fact that the human being must question gives indication of man's openness to and drive toward the infinite. While both of these aspects are present in the questions of any science, in a transcendental science, the questioner is reflexively aware of them. Therefore, while a transcendental metaphysics will strive to know being, it will do so fully aware of the limits of its perspective—aware that for all this science may bring to light, there is infinitely more that remains concealed.[9]

The Modern Problem of Knowledge

Toward the Original Unity. Rahner was well aware that a principal problem for modern epistemology had been to explain how a person can know for himself that which is other than himself. How can a subject grasp an object? But, according to Rahner, this way of framing the question is doomed from the outset, for it will never be possible to explain the subsequent union of that which is understood to have been, from the beginning, completely separate and incommensurable. He appeals to Thomas who approached being and knowing in terms of their original unity:

> The essence of human knowing and that of its object can only be apprehended in a single act of comprehension, because they are reciprocally the ground of their intrinsic possibility and therefore ultimately spring from a single ground.[10]

In fact, the problem of knowledge turns out to be quite different than has been assumed. It is not a matter of bridging the gap between knower and known, but explaining how any gap at all can exist.[11]

There is strong evidence of the original unity of knowing and being in the nature of the human person as questioner. Any question which we might asked already contains, implicitly and pre-reflexively, that which is questioned.[12] One could not question that of which he was utterly ignorant. And so, whenever I ask the question, "What is it?" there can be no doubt that there is some existing "it" which precontained in my question—even should that "it" turn out to be that act of apprehension by which the mind creates a "being of reason."

For Rahner, knowing consists in being-present-to-self (*Beisichsein*). The degree to which a being is present-to-self is indicative of its degree of knowledge and vice versa.[13] And so, for example, in the Thomistic hierarchy of being, pure spiritual being, which is not dependent on the material world for knowledge, is fully present to itself. Material being, on the other hand, having little or no self-presence, has no knowledge either. Human being is a peculiar case in the middle, capable of a certain degree of self-presence (able to return to oneself through thought) and yet dependent on the material world for knowledge.[14] For the human being, to be rational is neither to be entirely delivered over to the materiality of the world, nor is it to have the privileged perspective of a being entirely out of this world. It is to accept one's existence as it is: being in between.

Rahner shares Kant's conviction that there are no intellectual intuitions for human knowers. (Thomas, of course, had also insisted on this.) Knowledge always traces its origin to sense experience of some kind. But the senses are not to be understood simply as passageways through which things enter into us; rather, they are the very "ground on which what is had in consciousness is placed in this process of objectification."[15] It is not so much that something of that which is external to the knower somehow becomes a part of him. It is rather that, in sensibility, the knower becomes present to something other (*Bei-dem-andern-sein*) and, to that extent, absent to self. And yet, the human being is not so totally abandoned to the other in knowledge that it loses the consciousness of its own being.[16] In fact, it is precisely through contact with the other that one establishes oneself as subject. The things which we know are not ready-made objects that we as already-established subjects come upon;

rather, we make an object of something else and subjects of ourselves (i.e. we take our stand over against it as something which is really different and distinct from us) by our complete return to self in thought.

And so, sensibility and intellect are not two distinct moments in the process of knowledge. They are, instead, "two mutually conditioning phases which constitute one human knowledge." Sensibility consists in the abandonment of self to the world and the return to self through abstraction. Intellect consists in the placing of self over against self and turning again to the world; this is what is meant by *turning to the phantasm*.[17] There is no question here of an intellect subsequently trying to make sense out of a jumble of raw sense data. Nor is there any question of the intellect somehow extracting self-subsistent essences from the things it knows. Sensibility is the distinctive way that human intellect knows, and intellect is always directing sensibility.

The Nature of Thought. But how is it possible for a knower who is present to the "other" of the world through sensibility to distinguish itself from this other and return to itself in thought? How is it that the undifferentiated unity of sensibility and sensible object which is had in sensation can become a subject, a differentiated unity, self-possessed over against a world? Rahner claims that the possibility of the return to self in thought can be understood through a consideration of its actual characteristics: *the universal concept, the judgment,* and *the truth of the judgment.* All of them are traditional Thomist themes scored in a new key, and together they reveal something of the distinctiveness of human rationality.[18]

Human thought is characterized by the use of *universal concepts* which, in the language of traditional Thomism, are grasped through simple apprehension. Such a concept is simply "a known intelligibility" that exists in and can be predicated of many: redness, treeness, horseness, and so on. The place of such concepts in thought reveals the differentiation and unity which is characteristic of human knowledge. On the one hand, intellectually there are only universal concepts; e.g. the redness of the flower is only recognizable to the mind as an instance of that which may be said of many red things. On the other hand, universal concepts may only be known through conversion to the phantasm, turning to the world of concrete individuals. Universals can only be talked about as if they were subjects; in fact, they are abstractions from an already-realized concretizing synthesis. For example, redness only exists in the color red, which in turn exists only in red things. Hence, essential to any universal concept is a reference to those possible objects determined by it.[19]

In an affirmative synthesis or *judgment*, the universal concept simply apprehended becomes a predicate. The concept of "redness," for example, predicable of any number of possible red objects, is predicated of this particular object through the affirmation, "The flower is red." One should not be misled, however, into thinking that simple apprehension is temporally prior to judgment. What occurs in judgment is not the subsequent joining of two already-constituted concepts (i.e. that of the subject and that of the predicate). Rather, through judgment it is determined which "this" in particular (the individual flower experienced here and now through sensation) is meant in the concretizing synthesis of the predicate universal (redness) with any "this" whatever. There is no knowledge in human consciousness, not even of universal concepts, except through affirmative synthesis whereby a known concept is referred to an "in-itself" (*An Sich*). Here again, one discerns the the necessity of both the abstractive return to self in thought and of the turning to the phantasm through which the knower is present to the world.[20]

Finally, in any judgment, there is the question of its *truth* or falsity. What is at issue here is not whether the universal concept expressed in the concretizing synthesis is true or false. One would not say, for example, "Redness is false." What is at issue is whether or not the reference of the universal concept in question to the existing reality is successful. There is a kind of comparison which occurs in judgment between the incomplex (the universal) and the complex existing thing, the *An Sich*. Does this flower, in fact, match what is normally meant by "is red"? Truth only becomes characteristic of thought when the concretizing syntheses of subject and predicate are referred to one and the same in-itself through an affirmative synthesis. When the reference in unsuccessful, truth is absent.[21]

In sum, it may be said that whereas sensibility gives the other to the knower (though not yet as something objective about which a judgment can be made), through thought, objectification takes place, i.e. knower and known are placed over against each other. Thought—universal, judgmental, and true—reveals the place of the known in relation to the knower and the knower's return to itself. By relating the universal to something and judging the success of its reference to a "this," the knower thereby differentiates himself from the "this" and distinguishes himself as self-present, as a subject. The prime condition of possibility for the complete return to self is the agent intellect, its power of abstraction, and the unique pre-apprehension through which abstraction takes place.[22]   The heart of Rahner's unique conception of rationality can, in turn, be found in what he retrieves from the Thomistic doctrine in this regard.

Abstraction and Pre-apprehension. There is an interesting paradox in human knowledge. On the one hand, the judgment through which knowledge is expressed purports to be universal, necessary, and true. On the other hand, no universal concept exists except as the intelligibility of a certain existing "this," which in its individuality and contingency falls short of the hoped-for universality and necessity. How can that which is only potentially intelligible (in Aristotelian terms, form in matter) be made actually intelligible? Rahner follows Thomas in arguing that form must, in some sense, be liberated from matter if there is to be any judgmental knowledge. The capacity to do this is described in terms of the agent intellect and its power of abstraction.[23]

This liberation of form from matter which takes place in abstraction is only possible if there is an antecedent grounding knowledge of the contingency of sensible concretion. In other words, only if a form (e.g. redness) is known as limited by a "this" (the redness of this particular flower), can it be known as form, i.e. as that which is predicable of many, ontologically different from matter, and universal in itself. Only by contrast with limit (experienced in the individuation of matter) does the idea of that which is unlimited (a universal concept predicable of an infinite number of individuals) have any meaning.[24]

Accordingly, Rahner rejects the notion of agent intellect as "the power to imprint on the possible intellect a spiritual image of what has been sensibly intuited."[25] Such a description posits the very cleavage between knower and known that was rejected from the outset—not to mention the difficulty of describing the kind of mechanism this peculiar theory would entail. What, for example, would an "intellectual color" be? Redness can only be truthfully predicated of red things, not of immaterial ideas. Moreover, even if the mind could produce an intellectual double of what was given sensibly, it would be as concrete as the sensible model and, therefore, not universal at all. Hence, the agent intellect is the capacity to know the sensibly intuited as limited, as a realized concretion. Only to this extent if the human knower capable of universalizing.[26]

Now if grasping a thing conceptually is not a matter of extracting its essence or manufacturing a mental copy but of recognizing the form of the sensible thing as limited and thus embracing further possibility, then the human intellect must be able to

> comprehend of itself the whole field of these possibilities and thus, in the sensibly concretized form, experiences the concreteness as limitation of these possibilities, whereby it knows the form itself as able to be multiplied in this field. This transcending apprehension of further possibilities, through which the form possessed in a concretion in sensibility is apprehended as limited and so is abstracted, we call pre-apprehension (*Vorgriff*). Although this term is not to be found literally in Thomas, yet its content is contained in what Thomas calls '*excessus*' using a similar image.27

With the identification of the *Vorgriff*, the pre-apprehension of unlimited possibility through which the abstractive grasp of limit takes place, we reach into the heart of Rahner's metaphysics of cognition and begin to feel its contemplative pulse.

As pre-apprehension, this *Vorgriff* would seem to cry out for an object: What is it that I pre-apprehend? Yet, Rahner makes it clear that that toward which this pre-apprehension reaches (its *Worauf*, its "whither") is "not a humanly conceivable object" nor even the totality of all conceivable objects. It is a way of talking about "the movement of the spirit toward the whole of its possible objects." Only against such an unlimited horizon can the limitation of the individual known be experienced. It is "not an inconsequential supplement, but a condition of possibility of any objective knowledge at all."28

Given that the *Vorgriff* has no object as such but is the very movement of the intellect which makes objectification possible, can anything be said about the scope of that movement, the breadth of that pre-apprehension? What precisely is meant by the expression "the whole of its possible objects?" Just how "unlimited" does the "horizon" against which the intellect judges limit need to be?

Could the scope of the *Vorgriff* be the same as the total range of sensible intuition? In other words, are the limits of the mind's reach to be defined in terms of infinite time or infinite space? Rahner argues that this proposal is untenable, since the direct knowledge which sense and imagination have of space and time is only in their limitation. There is no pre-apprehension of their empty possibility and indeterminacy.[29]

If the breadth of pre-apprehension is not the same as that of unlimited space and time, what about the horizon of sense intuition as such? In other words, could it be that the mind reaches beyond the actual experience of space and time inasmuch as it apprehends being, i.e. "mobile, material being, being as the principle of number, the being of the plurality of the same, of the quantitative, of the existent in space and time, the quiddities of material things."[30] In this explanation, the mind pre-grasps not the empty possibility and indeterminacy of space and time, but the full possibility of all that is.

Rahner observes that there is a reciprocal limitation which binds the universal as form to the supposite or subject in which form and matter subsist. The universal (redness) is relatively unlimited in itself; i.e. can be predicated of infinitely many (red) things; but it is limited "by the supposite to which it is referred insofar as, as form unlimited in itself, it becomes precisely this 'this.'" And yet, form also limits; for the matter which it informs is in itself potentially many things when thought of apart from the form which makes the supposite what it is.[31] There are, then, two kinds of infinity and two kinds of limit. There is "privative material infinity," which refers to the infinity of matter considered apart from its limitation by form. This infinity is in the order of imperfection, since it is only through form that matter receives its ontological actuality. But there also "negative formal infinity," which refers to the fact that form, relatively unlimited in itself, may limit matter in any number of possible cases. This infinity is in the order of a perfection; its "negativity" consists in its not having intrinsic limitedness rather than in its lacking ontological actuality.[32] While both of these infinities and their corresponding types of limitation may become objects of knowledge, there is a logical priority to the knowledge of the latter. Only through abstraction of the form (the intelligibility of the thing) can there be knowledge of matter (which is unintelligible in itself). Knowledge of matter is not the condition for, but is conditioned by, the knowledge of the universal.

What, then, is the *Worauf* of the pre-apprehension?

[M]an knows the finiteness and limitedness of a concrete, ontological determination . . . insofar as it is held in the broader 'nothing' of its potentiality; but this broader 'nothing' itself is known only insofar as it itself is held against the infinity of the formal actuality as such (of being), whatever this might be: essence or *esse*.   In the pre-apprehension of this all knowledge is grounded.[33]

That which, in judgment, was affirmed as limited (namely, the objective in-itself of the known) in the pre-apprehension, is affirmed as unlimited—to adapt Rahner's terminology, in-itself-ness as such.[34] This means that the extent of that toward which human intellect strains is nothing less than Being itself, or what Thomas talked about as *esse*.

Esse and Absolute Being.   Thomistically, what can be a said about *esse*? According to Rahner, it has to do with being actual or real—capable of being experienced as an already-realized synthesis antecedent to the affirmative synthesis which the mind accomplishes through judgment.   It is in this sense that what Thomas might have understood in terms of *Wirklichsein* (being real or actual) coincides with what Rahner describes in post-Kantian terms as *Ansichsein* (what I have called "in-itselfness").[35]   Through sensibility, the knower is present to something which is other than himself—something that is or has *esse* in itself.   Although a reflexive awareness of the distinction of this in-itself from the knowing subject requires abstract thinking, the distinction itself is antecedent to the judgment through which it is affirmed.   Apart from an already-realized distinction, the objectification which takes place in thought would have no basis.   This is the case, even when the knowledge claimed pertains to so-called "beings of reason"; the only difference in such instances is that it is not the object of the act of apprehension which has real existence, but the act of apprehension itself.[36]   Similarly, in the case of so-called "ideal being," (e.g. the validity of propositions): the basis for objectivity is also traceable only and ultimately to some really-existing in-itself to which the proposition refers.[37]

This *esse* for which human intellect reaches is not mere presence (*Vorhandensein*), as if it were an indifferent and inert basis on which ideal essences stand or from which they derive their reality. Rahner describes *esse* in dynamic terms:

> *Esse* is not a 'genus,' but appears rather as intrinsically variable, not as statically definable, but oscillating, as it were, between nothing and

infinity. The essences are only the expression of the limitation of this esse, which is limitless in itself, to a definite degree of the intensity of being in this or that definite 'being.'[38]

Hence, just as there is an abstraction through which form (the universal intelligibility of thing) is liberated from matter (which considered apart from form is nothing at all), so too must there be a kind of abstraction through which esse is liberated from that matter-form composite which, by judgment is affirmed as an in-itself. That "abstraction" precedes the abstraction of objective thought and is discussed by Thomas in terms of excessus, by Rahner in terms of Vorgriff.[39]

As the dynamic condition of possibility for abstraction, Vorgriff attains to a universal. In fact, esse exhibits a universality which is both formal and transcategorical. In its formal unity, essence (the kind of thing it is) expresses "the extent to which, in a definite existent, esse, the ground of reality for an existent, can let such an existent really exist." This formal universality, the "repeatability of the same in many" also pertains to esse: The many concrete instances of the same quiddity (e.g. horseness) are apprehended also and only as existing; horseness apart from an existing horse is literally unthinkable.[40]

Esse, however, also exhibits transcategorical universality. As that which brings the form to reality in every concrete instance, esse is not one determination among many (the way redness, or sweetness might determine a flower). It is rather the one ground of all real determinations. Unlike matter, which is empty indeterminateness; esse, if it exists as such, is utter fullness and can receive no further determination whatsoever.[41]

Rahner is careful to emphasize that the esse affirmed in the Vorgriff which accompanies every judgment is not a first order object of knowledge but rather "the expression of the scope of the pre-apprehension itself." Being is never known by itself, but only as the being of some concrete thing which is. At the same time, Thomas had argued that an object does, in a way, manifest itself within the scope of intellect's excessus, in what Rahner refers to as "the whither of pre-apprehension." "Any possilbe object which can come to exist in the breadth of pre-apprehension is simultaneously affirmed."[42] Inasmuch as an Absolute Being would completely fill up the breadth of this pre-apprehension, it may be said that the reality of God (absolute esse) is implicitly affirmed every time the breadth of the Vorgriff is recognized. But to say that God's reality is "implicitly affirmed" is quite different from making God a "first-order object" in a judgment. Absolute Being is given in consciousness of the pre-apprehension itself, and consciousness of this pre-apprehension takes place only in the *a posteriori* apprehension of a real existent as its necessary condition.[43]

To be sure, the metaphysics which Rahner expounds re-opens the possibility which Kant has closed, namely the possibility of attaining knowledge of God. In the Rahnerian framework, however, this knowledge has a distinctive character. At one point, Rahner refers to it as unobjective-unthematic consciousness (*Bewusstheit*), "which of itself, in its pure apriority, cannot be raised to the level of reflexive knowledge at all."[44] Only when this consciousness is thematized (as it is, for example, in Thomas' "five ways"), does it approach the level of a reflexive knowledge. This thematization is nothing more than another instance of *conversio ad phantasmata* which was mentioned at the outset of the present discussion of the modern "problem" of knowledge. Even human thought about God must turn to the world in order to be present-to-self.

Implications for the Rationality Question

In light of everything that has been said of abstraction and of the *Vorgriff* which is said to be the condition of its possibility, we can now be more precise about what "conversion to the phantasm" is intended to express and what it implies with regard to human rationality. Near the end of GW, Rahner describes it as "the unity of intuition and thought in the power of judgment . . . the expression of the original unity of the free spirit with the sensibility into which it forms itself."[45] Hence, it is not to be understood as the referring of a certain concept to a certain "this," as if one could be separated from the other. *Conversio ad phantasmata,* "the turing of spirit to sensibility is not merely a logically prior moment, but the actual movement of the spirit whereby the sensible content is informed by the *a priori* structure of spirit."[46]

Abstraction and conversion, therefore, are really one and the same process looked at from two different points of view. The human spirit, because it is embodied, must be present-to-others (through sensibility) in order to be present-to-self. In its bodiliness, through imagination, and over time, human being is present to the world. At the same time, however, the human being brings to that presence-to-the-world a drive toward Absolute Being, as evidenced in the way the intellect recognizes the limits of every thing it knows. Human intellect is active receptivity.

For Rahner, therefore, rationality has nothing to do with conformity to an abstract criterion of certitude, or to a "standard weight and measure," if what is meant by these expressions is some static principle outside of space and time. Human rationality pertains to a spiritual dynamism. Contemplatively speaking, human reason is driven to ponder and question both the mundane details of human existence and that which transcends the limits of a particular time and place. Indeed, it is the unlimited scope of this drive which makes possible the knowledge of any limit whatsoever. But, in the end, human rationality never escapes the exigencies of the spatio-temporal world, not even in its apprehension of God. Reason may ponder the transcendent, but it never becomes free of its transcendental requirements. Human knowers make the abstractive return to self in thought by way of a turning to the world. The contemplation of that which transcends time and space occurs precisely in time and space, by way of sensibility and imagination.

There is in the Rahnerian conception of rationality something of the same dialectical quality which we saw in the earlier literature (e.g. Clement's *Stromata* and Thomas' *DeTrinitate)* and noted as a principal characteristic of Rahner's method overall. In line with a tradition which originates with the early Greeks, runs through the Middle Ages and is revived in the wake of the Enlightenment, Rahner does not consider the dialectical ambitions of reason as marking fixed boundaries which one may cross only at one's peril. Nor does he attempt to dissolve all dialectical tension in an artificial and undifferentiated unity. Rather, he interprets this dialectical quality—the infinite impulse to question, the partiality of every human judgment—as indicative of reason's insatiable appetite for *esse*, which can and will be satisfied only in the attainment of a fully-saturating object: Absolute *Esse* or God. This dialectical quality, combined with the dynamism and worldliness of his conception of rationality, points strongly in the direction of a contemplative dimension.

Hearers of the Word
Toward an Ontology of Obediential Potency

Presupposing the metaphysical anthropology developed in the earlier work, HW works out its corollaries in the philosophy of religion. The central question which Rahner attempts to elucidate here is whether by metaphysical reflection man may legitimately define himself as possessing a nature capable of looking into his own history, hoping to see there a possible revelation from God who appears to him in human metaphysics as the essentially unknown.[47]

Once more, Rahner contrasts his approach with the customary method of nineteenth century neo-scholasticism. This is not only an interesting historical detail, but helps to bring to light the conception of rationality implicit in Rahner's philosophy of religion. The older fundamental theology exhibited three major weaknesses: 1) It never clarified how man can receive through revelation subject matter which is in itself inaccessible to him; 2) it never discussed the sense in which man's nature compels him to look into history for a possible revelation; and 3) it did not explicitly clarify "why man is disposed toward the fulfillment of his knowledge through free revelation, and through it alone."[48] Like the rational ideal which it sought to overcome, nineteenth century Catholic apologetics was not conscious of the inescapable historicity of reason's activity—even of its activity with respect to Absolute Being. Rahner emphasizes from early on in HW that the conquest of modern historical skepticism "with its natural scientific and technical ideal of evidence" depends on proving

> that an historical foundation of human existence is *a priori* absolutely unavoidable, and that the freedom which manifests itself in such a foundation provides no instance contradicting the empirical evidence of truth but emanates from the nature of man and the specific object of knowledge that is required for the foundation of his existence.[49]

In a way, Rahner is saying that the failure of nineteenth century apologetics was not a function of an inability to conform to the rigorous criteria of the empirical sciences but of the failure to recognize that even these criteria were historically born and historically conditioned. Hence Rahner seeks to make room in fundamental theology for an ontology of *potentia oboedientialis* (obediential potency). Can a metaphysical anthropology show that the constitution of the human person is such that, it is not only possible for him to hear a word of God in his historical experience, but that he must choose to listen for such a word if he is to fulfill his rational nature?[50]

Admittedly, such a philosophy of religion comes perilously close to theology, a circumstance which can be a source of anxiety for philosopher and theologian alike. But Rahner insists that philosophy, if it is to be true its deepest metaphysical promptings, can and must venture into the dangerous frontier land. Should philosophy cease to want to hear any reference to theology, "it would forthwith become . . . a highly academic, existentially indifferent affair." And this can even be the case in philosophy which was nominally Christian: "Whoever is familiar with the common scholastic textbooks of philosophy will already have gained the impression that the Christianity of philosophy in this sense has not always been a prominent characteristic, despite its orthodoxy and much stressed ecclesiasticism."[51]

Likewise, should theology cease to listen to philosophy, it runs the risk of lapsing into fideism or rationalism. A theology no longer connected with a metaphysics always runs the risk of becoming purely negative from an anthropological standpoint. "[A]ll its utterances, which still have to employ human language, can really be nothing but a sheer 'No' to man, an exclusively negative reference to the divine which remains utterly unknown."[52] Or else, unconscious of its indispensable metaphysical underpinnings, theology will be prone to uncritically assume the language and thought structures of the prevailing philosophical trend.[53]

Either way, in denying its connection with philosophy, theology winds up denying itself. Once again it becomes evident that, beneath the reason/revelation problematic, lies the question of what it means to describe the human being as rational. A conception of rationality is not the sole possession of philosophy or of theology or of any other science for that matter. It is rather a set of underlying presuppositions about human existence which is operative in every science, including theology, even if infrequently thematized.

Three Propositions

In the course of HW, Rahner attempts to work out three propositions of a metaphysical anthropology, with the question of revelation explicitly in view:

> a) The basic constitution of man is spirit, i.e. he is the locale of transcendence correlative to being pure and simple.[54]

b) Man is that existent thing who stands in free love before the God of a possible revelation.[55]

c) Man is that existent thing who must listen for an historical revelation of God, given in history and possibly in human speech.[56]

A Reprise of Rahner's Anthropology. To a great extent, the proposition that man is distinguished by a transcendence toward being is a rehearsal of what was already established in GW about the human being as a rational questioner: Namely, the question about man and the question about the meaning of being are intimately related, since man is the one whose nature is to enquire about being. The implicit affirmation of being in every judgment and every question, the centrality of *Vorgriff* as the condition of possibility for abstraction, and the pre-conceptual knowledge of God which accompanies all knowledge of the finite world—these themes are presented again, this time with a view to establishing openness to God as constitutive of human nature.[57]

But some new hints of a contemplative dimension also emerge here. At the beginning of the third chapter, Rahner describes what he takes to be the proper approach to philosophy of religion:

> Only if one is prepared to keep quiet, to hold in check the eager concupiscence of one's subjectivity which always sets out intent upon collecting its dues, and let the object speak for itself, only then does it make sense to enquire what the philosophy of religion is, how it and theology are related, why and how true philosophy of religion in the final analysis is nothing more than the command to man to turn his ear towards his history to discover whether the word of God has been sounded there.[58]

In this statement, the *via* is as important as the *positio*. The only way one can have entry into the kind of philosophical theology or theological philosophy which is described in the first part of the book is by openness and receptivity. In terms reminiscent of Heidegger's call to "let being be," Rahner invites the reader into what can be aptly described as a contemplative attitude. He seems to admit that, to the person who exercises the power of abstraction without the correlative *conversio*, the argument laid out in HW will make no sense.   In another place in the first third of the book, Rahner addresses another contemplative theme: the "negative" dimension of human rationality.

> We cannot avoid but must reckon with the fact that, as far as our mere
> thoughts are concerned we will make the vessell smaller than it has to
> be in order to contain the treasure of divine faith. . . . [The philosophy
> of religion worked out here is] an attempt at a scientific conceptual
> understanding of the being of man as the subject of a possible faith . . .
> which remains open to question . . . which we maintain in a tentative
> and pre-scientific manner, and yet which as believers we already know
> assuredly and properly.[59]

In this statement, Rahner emphasizes, not only the limitations of his own project, but also the limitations of human knowledge in general with regard to God. In the contemplative attitude, there is no room for apodeictic certitude in our conceptual description of God. Inasmuch as our concepts are derived from the world and are intrinsically limited, they will never be able to bear adequately the breadth and depth of the reality which is God. The assurance which the believer experiences is quite genuine; but it has nothing at all to do with comformity to some static and fully-accessible principle.

Man Before the God of a Possible Revelation.   In the second third of the book, Rahner builds on the foundation laid in GW, elaborating the significance of freedom, human and divine. He attempts to show how the human being can be described as obediential potency without necessitating God or man. For if obediential potency is taken to mean that man must hear a word addressed by God, then revelation as such is made impossible.   All things—including God—would be accessible to man by nature, and the grace of revelation would be superfluous. The problem that Rahner tries to resolve here is this: How can human transcendence be described in such a way as not to anticipate the content of a possible revelation?[60]

Rahner finds the key to resolving this problem in a full appreciation of both the necessity and contingency of human existence. From the start, it was recognized that the human being *must* question, must enquire. At the same time, this very necessity reveals man's inescapable limitation; i.e. man must *question*. Hence, it is possible to affirm man's essential openness to the divine without in any way limiting the possibility of the divine's revealing itself in a manner as yet unconceived by man.[61] In this framework, God is not to be seen as an immovable ideal, but as a free autonomous power: "God is the objective of the reaching out of the human spirit, but he is that precisely because he appears as the free power which stands in contradistinction from the finite."[62] There is in Rahner's thought no rigid separation of the metaphysical and moral, the speculative and the practical. For Rahner, man's highest moral good (the best and fullest exercise of freedom) consists in sustained and loving attention to (contemplation of) that which is the very essence of freedom, i.e. God.

Here again, hints of a contemplative dimension emerge. First of all, rationality shows itself not to be the necessary exercise of an impersonal power, but a free act of love. Only when the human knower does not relegate that which is outside him—whether material objects or other persons—to the status of a mere object; only when the human knower recognizes in everything that is some participation in Absolute Being; only then is knowledge fulfilled, for only then has the knower freely given the objects of his knowledge the freedom to be what they are in themselves.[63] Knowledge then is not merely a mental exercise, but has a practical component and consequences. Knowledge involves a certain asceticism:

> a readiness to criticize one's own order of love and to evaluate it in the light of the remainder of this order as it subsists in everybody and to organize it ever anew and more correctly in the growing light of true insight. . . . Only he who, in spirit, lives in temples and cloisters, can be a philosopher.[64]

This is not meant to suggest that genuine rationality is something available only to the contemplative in the narrow sense of that term. Nonetheless, in Rahner's thought, a contemplative posture in the broader sense is a *sine qua non* of the human rational quest.

History as the Locus of a Possible Revelation. As the kind of being that can only know by turning to the phantasms, the human being can achieve knowledge only in space and time. Here, in the final third of HW, the historicity of human knowledge is elaborated explicitly in its connection with the possibility of revelation.

Because temporality, in its original sense, refers not so much to the external measure of duration, but to "the inner extension of the existent thing into the actualized totality of its possibilities,"[65] what is at stake in an affirmation about human historicity is not just that an individual person or human kind in general live through a series of historical epochs. Rather, what is at stake in an affirmation about human historcity is the fact that human beings create history through the way in which they freely choose to actualize their infinite possibilities. Hence, the problem with the abstract and ahistorical conceptions of rationality which were rejected earlier in this chapter is not that they involve abstraction and ignore history. The problem is that they attempt to exercise abstraction in isolation from its correlative foundation in sensibility and that they conceive of history in a purely external and superficial way; i.e. as a mere sum of events in temporal succession rather than as the creation of human freedom. An ascetic rationality like that described in the second section of HW is aware that knowledge and sensibility are inextricably linked, and that there is an internal development to history which takes place through freedom.[66] Hence, should God reveal himself at all, should he freely choose to speak, it will inevitably be in a human language and a human history:

> In order to stand before being, man must turn to appearances . . . not simply particular sensible objects of external sense perception, but the whole of mundane existence, including a man's own history and insofar as a man is always one of humanity, the history of humanity also. Turning toward history is thus not an attitude for man to adopt as he pleases, but is imposed upon man by his specifically human spirituality . . . Hence all rationalism, as the attempt to give human existence a non-historical foundation, is to be rejected as non-human and therefore unspiritual as regards the human spirit.[67]

As we saw in the development of the Enlightenment criterion of rationality and the Catholic reaction to it, rationalism is not the exclusive possession of the philosopher. Whether as a philosopher or as a theologian or as any other kind of thinker, it is always possible for a person to be non-contemplative, i.e. inattentive to that which constitutes his fullfillment. In Rahner's philosophy of religion, the human person is already spiritual, i.e. always oriented toward God. He/She can only *choose* not to be. If philosophy has not been entirely successful at working out a conception of person, perhaps it is not simply because of the din caused by the conflicting claims of the various schools; perhaps it is also because of the accompanying unwillingness to listen for, to be attentive to, the word of Being as it is spoken in space and time. At the same time, if theology has not been entirely successful in making faith's message intelligible for contemporary men and women, perhaps it not simply on account of the resistance of contemporary culture to a word spoken by God; perhaps it is also theology's occasional unwillingness to listen to how it is that God may be speaking in culture and history. Rationality, whether exercised by the theologian or the philosopher, has a contemplative dimension; as a taking-time-with, con*temp*lation will always entail historicity.

And so, though it must be left to subsequent chapters to work out with greater precision rationality's contemplative dimension, an overview of the conception of rationality operative in *Spirit in the World* and *Hearers of the Word* has at least brought to light a certain constellation of characteristics which may be described as contemplative:

1) Reason finds the source for its activity in the irreducible status of the human person as a questioner and the necessity which which the human spirit reaches out for that which transcends it.

2) Knowledge, as a prime achievement of reason, is inescapably linked to sensibility and, therefore, can be fully attained and expressed only over time.

3) Reason's activity is made possible through freedom; it is the disciplined exercise of that freedom in love which constitutes reason's fullest expression

In Rahner's earliest philosophical works, then, there are indications of a dimension in his thought an appreciation of which could illuminate the distinctive way in which he handles the reason/revelation problematic and a number of related issues. In order to bring out this dimension with greater clarity, it will be necessary first to return to some of the principal formative influences in Rahner's thought (Part II) and then to look at some of his later works through a contemplative lens (Part III). As Rahner once retrieved from

Question 84 of Thomas' *Summa* a metaphysical anthropology which provided a new basis on which to do theology, it is also possible to retrieve from Rahner's work an appreciation of contemplation which provides a basis on which to work out the reason/revelation problem in its contemporary form

Part Two

Contemplative Influences on Rahner

IV

Retrieval and Rahner

The complementarity of reason and revelation is grounded in a more primitive and original unity experienced in contemplative thinking and living. Employing the hermeneutics of retrieval, I will argue that this principle stands unthematically but indispensibly at the center of Rahner's conception of rationality. In order to do this, it is necessary first to describe the hermeneutics of retrieval, to justify its use in the interpretation of Rahner, and to explain how specifically it is to be carried out in the present context.

Retrieval as a Hermeneutic Principle

Philosophically, the word *retrieval* is an effort to translate the German *Wiederholung*, a compound formed from the adverb *wieder* (again, afresh, once more, anew) and the verb *holen* (fetch, get, go or come for). Although some translators of Heidegger's works, for example, have chosen to render *Wiederholung* as *repetition*,[1] the term *retrieval* seems to capture more fully the idea that *Wiederholung* means to convey. In his commentary on Heidegger, Richardson explains that the word *retrieve*, taken from the French verb *retrouver* (find again, recover, rediscover, remember), is "more faithful to the sense of *Wiederholung* than the possibly misleading *repetition*."[2] Even MacQuarrie and Robinson who opt for *repetition* in their version of *Being and Time,* are careful to distinguish Heidegger's meaning from the simple "repeating" or "doing over again." For Heidegger, "*wiederholen* does not mean either a mechanical repetition or an attempt to reconstitute the physical past; it means rather an attempt to go back to the past and retrieve former possibilities, which are thus 'explicitly handed down' or 'transmitted.'"[3]

The concept of retrieval did not originate with Heidegger. Husserl and Kierkegaard before him already had some appreciation of the potential significance of repetition to human thought and endeavor.[4]   Even Thomas' reading of Aristotle may be characterized as a retrieval of sorts. Still, there is no gainsaying the fact that Heidegger was the first to self-consciously utilize retrieval as such as an interpretative tool with respect to experience as well as to texts.

In his great early work *Being and Time,* Heidegger's discussion of *Wiederholung* is actually a small part of a much larger discussion of human existence (*Dasein*) as temporality.   In the first part of *Being and Time,* Heidegger undertakes a preliminary analysis of *Dasein* in an effort to work out the question of the meaning of Being. Although he contends that care or concern (*Sorge*) is "the totality of the structural whole of *Dasein's* constitution," he concludes that the description of human existence in terms of care can lay no claims to primordiality.[5] Temporality is the possibilizing condition for care and the primordial ontological basis for *Dasein's* existentiality.[6] Only because man is temporal through and through can he, in the present moment, take up his past and project himself into a future and toward death. Accordingly, in the second part of the work, Heidegger tries to confirm concretely his temporal-existential analysis of *Dasein* by "lay[ing] bare in their temporal meaning the ontological structures of *Dasein.*"[7]

According to Heidegger, historicality is one such ontological structure which takes its meaning from temporality. *Dasein* is not temporal because it stands in history; "on the contrary, it exists historically and so exists only because it is temporal in the very basis of its Being."[8] Only a being directed toward a future (ultimately, death) and rooted in a past (created out of given circumstances and free choices) can be said to have "authentic historicality." It is out of inherited possibilities and toward the inevitability of death that man creates history and chooses his fate through decisions made about an always-receding now.[9] Historicality thus described is worked out precisely through *Wiederholung.* It is worth quoting Heidegger verbatim on this point:

> The repeating of that which is possible does not bring again something that is "past," nor does it bind the "present" back to that which has already been "outstripped."   Arising, as it does, from a resolute projection of oneself, repetition does not let itself be persuaded of something by what is past, just in order that this, as something which was formerly actual, may recur.   Rather, the repetition makes a

reciprocative rejoinder to the possibility of that existence which has-been-there . . . Repetition does not abandon itself to that which is past, nor does it aim at progress. In the moment of vision, authentic existence is indifferent to both these alternatives.[10]

What significance might Heidegger's remarks have for the present project? The retrieval which is to be used here as a hermeneutic principle in textual analysis is primordially a hermeneutic principle for human life and existence. What is at stake is not simply a question of exegetical method, but also and more fundamentally a question about the nature of humanity in its temporality. Because human existence is not just a series of disconnected perceptual experiences artificially charted according to a linear or even cyclic pattern, we are never simply "getting rid of the past" and thus "making progress" (which would merely amount to cleverness). Human existence is a unitary process whereby the future—its possibilities limited only by choices previously made and by the inevitability of death—draws each free being forward through innumerable "now's." Hence the opportunities latent in the so-called past may be recovered for present actualization. Only if this is the case, does it make any sense to talk about retrieval as a way of understanding the writings of an earlier thinker.

In his *Introduction to Metaphysics*, Heidegger insists that *Wiederholung* is no mere improvement in a given situation nor a continuation of things as they are. Related as it is to the question of being, retrieval has to do with the transformation of one's spiritual existence through the asking of fundamental questions—questions which return us to the very beginning of things, where nothing is taken for granted, questions like "Why are there existing things rather than nothing?" "Repetition as we understand it is anything but an improved continuation with the old method of what has been up to now." It implies rather the willingness to face "all the strangeness, darkness, insecurity that attend a true beginning."[11] Heidegger, as we shall later see, makes extensive use of this method in his reading of the history of Western philosophy in general and ancient Greek thought in particular. His objective, stated in many different ways, is the same throughout: Not simply to repeat what someone else has said or to maintain some dogmatic position, but to allow what others have thought and written to "[awaken] the energies of independent questioning out of and for the sake of our own history in the present hour."[12] It is not difficult to hear an echo of Heidegger in the words of Rahner as he writes at the beginning of *Spirit in the World*: "[The author] would not know of any other reason for which he could be occupied with Thomas than for the sake of his philosophy and that of his time."[13]

However, Rahner was not the only twentieth century Christian philosopher to follow Heidegger in the use of retrieval as a hermeneutic principle. The German Thomist Josef Pieper is explicit about his debt to Heidegger in *The Silence of St. Thomas*. In that work, which aims to lay bare the doctrine of creation as the largely implicit but decisive presupposition for Thomistic metaphysics and epistemology, Pieper situates retrieval in the context of the difficulty that accompanies all textual interpretation. Because an author may choose not to express certain assumptions or presuppositions which to him seem self-evident, the reader who does not share these same assumptions or has not brought them to conscious awareness may face difficulty in interpreting the text at hand. Pieper claims that it is important—though by no means easy—"to grasp those basic assumptions, which, remaining unexpressed, nevertheless permeate all that is actually stated; to discover the hidden key note that dominates whatever has been explicitly said."[14] So important is this grasp of *das im Sagen Ungesagte*, that an interpretation which never uncovers the hidden key "must remain in essence, a misinterpretation."[15]

More recently, John Caputo has made very extensive use of retrieval in his work on Heidegger and Aquinas. He links the concept of retrieval with the concept of deconstruction (*Ab-bauen*):

> To retrieve or deconstruct is not to destroy but to shake loose from a text its essential tendencies, tendencies which the text itself conceals. [Deconstruction is] not the leveling or wrecking [of] a text, but rather. . . taking a text apart in order to find its most essential and enlivening insights and then reconstructing the whole around it.[16]

In this conception of *Ab-bauen* Caputo owes a debt to Jacques Derrida's *Of Grammatology*.[17] Using deconstructive method, Caputo proceeds to argue that, even for the greatest of Christian metaphysicians Thomas Aquinas, the task of metaphysics is not fulfilled until metaphysics and its complex ratiocinations wither away, leaving an opening for a new dispensation of Being to be given in mystical experience. Admittedly, there is a certain "violence" to such an interpretation; it is radically different from that proposed by mainline twentieth century Thomism, not to mention that of sixteenth century scholasticism. Its violence, however, is not a function of some arbitrary textual mutilation or antipathy toward previous interpreters. Its violence is a consequence of the fact that the recovery of the enlivening insight of any given text "cannot proceed except by clearing away the superficial and commonplace understanding of things which systematically obscures our view and subverts the understanding."[18] Does this mean that all previous and standard interpretations of Thomistic metaphysics are wrong in Caputo's view? Not necessarily. But, at the very least, they must be judged as partial and perhaps inadequate for our own age and situation.

In his more recent book on hermeneutics, Caputo devotes a significant portion of the work to explicit reflection on repetition or retrieval. Two characteristics stand out.

First of all, retrieval is not an individualistic and therefore idiosyncratic reading of a text. Because, in Heideggerian language, *Dasein's* ontological structure necessarily includes being-with-others who share the task of living authentically with given possibilities in the face of death, retrieval can never be a "purely personal" affair.[19] Other persons enter into the matrix of our individual existence neither accidentally nor marginally, but necessarily and fundamentally as co-makers-of-history. "Together, fate and destiny, the heritage of the individual (the narrative of one's own life) and the heritage of the community (the history of the time) make up 'the full authentic historicizing of *Dasein*.'"[20] In fact, it would seem that even where the interpreter is not conscious of the collaboration of his interpersonal experience in the retrieval, that collaboration is nonetheless operative and significant. One's culture, heritage, upbringing, and present relationships have an undeniable impact on the way one interprets existence itself, let alone a text which intends to break open its truth. A recognition of this communal component makes it less likely that one will absolutize any single interpretation under the title of "pure reason" and makes it more likely that the individual interpreter will bring his own perspective into fruitful dialogue not only with other contemporary viewpoints but also with more ancient traditions in thought.

Secondly, Caputo relates retrieval to the theme of anticipation—a theme which is not unrelated to the Rahnerian notion of the *Vorgriff*. Husserl had already brought to light the anticipatory nature of human cognition in his phenomenological account of the genesis of meaning where the categorial constitution of reality takes place through certain forestructures. The precise nature and origin of these forestructures is, of course, a matter of debate; but this much is clear in Husserl's thought: "the work of phenomenology consists in unpacking the prereflexive, prethematic, or as he puts it, the 'horizonal' structures which are at work in the 'wakeful cogito.'"[21] Retrieval in Heidegger was yet another expression of this anticipatory component in human cognition. The human mind may well be a *tabula rasa* to the extent that it has been given no glimpse of the forms, enjoys no intuition which is not in the first instance sensible. But this does not mean that a human knower comes to experience without any structure of receptivity whatsoever:

> To understand means to project a certain horizonal framework within which the being is to be understood. Entities can appear only insofar as a certain horizon of Being has already been laid out for them in advance. We can learn something new only on the condition that we have already been appropriately oriented to begin with. We can understand only if we already pre-understand. There are no pure, uninterpreted facts of the matter but only beings already set forth in a certain frame, projected in their proper Being.[22]

And so, if it can be said that retrieval bears a communal character, even when the interpreter fails to advert to it, perhaps it can also be said that knowledge bears a "retrieved" quality, even when such a quality is denied. Philosophers, whether proponents of hermeneutics or of some species of positivism, cannot escape the fact that they are already retrieving from some prior experience or some prior text a notion or framework which is brought to bear on the current interpretative task. The question is not whether or not I shall execute a retrieval; the question is whether I shall do so reflectively and daringly, or else unconsciously and carelessly.

If some justification is sought for the use of retrieval in the reading of Rahner, perhaps it is contained in this last observation. Still, Rahner himself has given us reason to think that the explicit employment of this hermeneutic principle is a strategy which he endorsed. His reading of the concept of *excessus* in Thomas in terms of *Vorgriff* represents a case in point.[23] If Rahner saw some value to executing a retrieval with respect to Aquinas, there is no reason to believe that he would have rejected the employment of a similar strategy in regard to his own thought.

Hence, though Rahner nowhere says explicitly that rationality has a contemplative dimension, the appreciation and exercise of which is essential to the complementarity of reason and revelation, I hope to show by way of a retrieval that this notion is present and operative in his thought as it is expressed in various genres and on many themes.

Early Influences on Rahner's Thought

What were the major early influences on Rahner which together helped to constitute the particular conceptual horizon which he brought to his philosophical and theological thinking? If we can identify what these influences were and the extent to which they possessed contemplative significance, we will have established the basis for our retrieval. In the present section, I will identify these sources; in the next three chapters I will examine each in turn.

A valuable source of information about Rahner are the hundreds of interviews which he gave, particularly during the last ten years of his life.[24] These interviews reveal a more spontaneous, conversational, and transparent Rahner than is accessible in his formal academic writings. Most importantly for our purposes, these interviews provide the clearest indication of who Rahner himself judged to be the most significant influences on the development of his thought. Obviously, one could surmise from his writings, his choice of themes and his method of proceeding, which thinkers had the greatest impact; but in the interviews, he is explicit about this.

He mentions a number of classical spiritual authors: Bonaventure, Teresa of Avila, and John of the Cross. He also credits a number of his own contemporaries with significant spiritual influence: Peter Lippert, Erich Przywara, Dunin Borowski, and Marcel Viller (with whom he wrote a work on asceticism and mysticism in the Fathers)[25] However, there are three figures who are mentioned repeatedly in the interviews and deserve particular attention: Thomas Aquinas (ordinarily mentioned in connection with his twentieth century transcendental interpreters Rousselot and Maréchal), Ignatius of Loyola, and Martin Heidegger.

Given the fact that he dedicated his doctoral dissertation in philosophy to an interpretation of a text from Thomas' *Summa*, it is not surprising to find

Rahner expressing, in a 1982 interview, the hope that his theology "has inner authentic and living connections" with that of Thomas Aquinas.[26] Earlier on, he had expressed a conviction which he shared with Metz that Thomas was, in a sense, the first modern anthropocentric thinker—at least to the extent that Thomas recognized the impossibility of speaking about God or the human person in isolation from eachother.[27]

Rahner was intrigued by the possibility of connecting Thomas' strategy with that of more modern thinkers:

> If one analyzes St. Thomas in proper perspective, it is quite clear that he is a *penseur moderne*. There is certainly a conformity, affinity, and correspondence between the modern method of proceeding and that problem which may be called transcendental. Even in the work of St. Thomas this can be found. To grasp that fact is very important for any genuine mutual understanding of the modern concept of man and the Thomistic concept of man.[28]

Hence, if it can be said that the thought of Thomas Aquinas was a primary influence in the development of Rahner's thought, it must also be said that it was not the thought of Thomas pure and simple (indeed, Rahner was sceptical that such a thing ever existed save in Thomas himself[29]), but that of a transcendental Thomas—the Thomas known to Pierre Rousselot and Joseph Maréchal.

Rahner mentions both figures as having "exercised a great influence" on his philosophy.[30] Perhaps because of the small size of the Rousselot corpus and the fact that Rousselot's untimely death prevented a more extensive development in his thought, Maréchal looms larger in the interviews. In 1974 Rahner comments on Maréchal's influence together with that of Heidegger: "I have to confess . . . that I would not have done philosophy in a transcendental manner had I not studied the philosophy of Maréchal and of Heidegger."[31] Maréchal and Heidegger are mentioned together again in a 1979 interview, though here Rahner emphasizes that the Belgian Jesuit had a more significant impact.

> I have to say that I owe my most basic, decisive, philosophical direction, insofar as it comes from someone else, more, in fact, to . . .

Joseph Maréchal.   His philosophy already moved beyond the
traditional neo-Scholasticism. I brought that direction from Maréchal
to my studies with Heidegger and it was not superceded by him.[32]

In 1980, Rahner repeated his strong conviction about the importance of
Maréchal to the constitution of the conceptual horizon which he brought to his
work in philosophy and theology: "Discovering Maréchal was a major
breakthrough for me; it expanded my horizons somewhat beyond the scholastic
philosophy of the manuals."[33]   Hence, an effort to retrieve a contemplative
component from the Rahnerian conception of rationality will have to include a
return to the thought of the transcendental Thomists.

If Rahner's debt to Thomas seems quite obvious and natural, his
philosophical debt to Ignatius of Loyola may seem more dubious at first. One is
not apt to be surprised by Rahner's attributing specifically spiritual importance
to Ignatius—after all, Rahner was a Jesuit. But one may well be taken aback by
his talk of Ignatius' epistemological contributions.   In fact, Rahner's
discernment of philosophical significance in the thought of an ascetical thinker
itself constitutes an important clue in deciphering Rahner's distinctive
conception of rationality.

Rahner is unhesitating in giving Ignatius first place among the various
persons whose thought influenced his:

> I do think that in comparison with other philosophy and theology that
> influenced me, Ignatian spirituality was indeed more significant and
> important.   There, too, to be honest, I cannot say that individual
> Jesuits, spiritual directors, retreat masters, and so forth made an
> overpowering impression on me . . . . But I think that the spirituality
> of Ignatius himself, which one learned through the practice of prayer
> and religious formation was more significant for me than all learned
> philosophy and theology inside and outside the order.[34]

To Rahner's way of thinking, Ignatius challenged the epistemological
assumptions on which traditional theology rested.   He moved beyond the
essential and narrowly rational theories of knowledge which predominated in
the early sixteenth century to what Rahner calls "the logic of concrete
individual knowledge." According to Rahner, Jesuit theologians up until the

present, "did not use the greatest and most important riches from the *Spiritual Exercises* to fertilize their own theology."[35] He evidently sought to correct that error.

There is a great deal more to be said about Ignatian epistemological assumptions, but here a few preliminary observations may be made. Whereas manual theology tended to be satisfied with its own rational concepts and formulations about God, Ignatian mysticism presupposed a distinction between these concepts and the experience they sought to express. Ignatius realized that, beyond the important but limited conceptual grasp of God which could be communicated in words, is a more comprehensive and foundational grasp which defies clear conceptualization but is a species of knowledge nonetheless. That is why, argues Rahner, a genuine Christian spirituality "cannot be kept alive and healthy by external helps, not even those which the Church offers . . . but only through an ultimate immediate encounter of the individual with God."[36]

Even the famous *Spiritual Exercises* of Ignatius do not themselves constitute this immediate encounter but seek only to create the condition of possibility for such an encounter to take place. Still, Rahner believed that there was something distinctive about the *Exercises* as a help to persons in their quest for God. They were and are more than theological instruction. They cannot be identified even with Eastern meditation or mysticism, which are at best first steps in opening an individual to an experience of God. Rahner believed that the exercises provided an outstanding way for a person "to find God and not just talk about him," a way that retains its validity even four hundred years after its inception.[37] Accordingly, our effort to retrieve a contemplative component from the Rahnerian conception of rationality will also have to include a return to the spirituality of St. Ignatius, particularly as it is expressed in his *Spiritual Exercises*.

Finally, there is one more name that is repeated with some frequency in Rahner's interviews, and that is the name of Martin Heidegger. As we have already seen, Rahner mentions Heidegger together with Maréchal as influential with respect to the development of his philosophical method. In several places, Rahner makes mention of his participation in Heidegger's seminars at Freiburg for two years.[38] And though he ended up writing his dissertation under the traditional neo-Scholastic Martin Honecker, it is clear that Heidegger exercised the dominant influence on Rahner while at Freiburg. He explains the fact that he did not write under Heidegger in this way:

> J. B. Lotz and I were not anxious to throw in our lot with him for good or ill. [Heidegger was the first university rector in the Nazi period.] So we enrolled with the professor of Catholic scholastic philosophy, Martin Honecker. On the other hand, our meeting with Martin Heidegger was the truly decisive, impressive experience. So I arrived at a dissertation which dealt with Thomas on the one hand and attempted to view Thomas, I might say, from the point of view of a modern philosophy on the other . . . [39]

That Rahner saw Heidegger as having had an important role is his intellectual formation is unmistakable; but the precise nature of that role appears to have been a point of ambivalence for Rahner. It is true, as Sheehan notes in his recent work on the philosophical foundations of Rahner's thought, that Rahner once referred to Heidegger as his only true teacher.[40] And in a 1980 interview, he refers to Heidegger as "the only teacher for whom I developed the respect that a disciple has for a great master."[41] However, just a year earlier he had expressed an unwillingness to identify any individual as a singular influence: "I would not really say that I have met the great master to whom alone in one way or another, I was bound in a blazing discipleship."[42]

The reason for Rahner's ambivalence about Heidegger's influence seems to have been three-fold: For one thing, Rahner found it impossible to follow Heidegger to certain conclusions about the nature of human existence and the history of metaphysics. Of Heidegger's well-known opinion of the history of Western metaphysics as a history of *Seinsvergessenheit*, Rahner remarks laconically, "I cannot share this opinion. I consider it false."[43] Another factor was the fact that their specific areas of inquiry were different; quite simply, Heidegger was a philosopher; Rahner was first and foremost a theologian.[44] The third, and perhaps most important, factor seems to have been Rahner's disdain for systematic dogmatism. If human understanding of existence, the world, and God is always incomplete, always developing, then it can make no sense to attach oneself immovably to any one thinker's position on everything. Rahner is unyielding in proclaiming his right to differ from Heidegger even while honoring him as a teacher: "[I] refuse to be condemned . . . to being subject exclusively to a completely determined philosophical system."[45]

What, then, did Rahner take from Heidegger? Here again, it is best to let Rahner speak for himself:

> One may perhaps say that it is not specific doctrines that I have taken from Heidegger, but rather a style of thinking and of investigating which has proved most valuable. This may be described as a method or approach by which one does not examine dogmatic truths merly as evidence derived from the positive sources, but one seeks to construct a synthesis.[46]

In another place, Rahner indicates that he was particularly impressed by Heidegger's way of handling a text: "He taught us how to . . . ask what is behind a philosopher's individual texts and his statements that wouldn't immediately strike the ordinary person . . . "[47]

Moreover, it should be noted that the Heidegger from which Rahner learned this style of thinking and investigating was the Heidegger who was his teacher from 1934-1936. "That was the Heidegger with whom I learned to think a little bit, and for that I am grateful."[48] And so, our effort to retrieve a contemplative component from the Rahnerian conception of rationality will have to include a return not only to a transcendental Thomas and to the Ignatius of the *Exercises*; it will also have to include a return to the Heidegger of the 1930's.

V

A Transcendental Thomas

The first of the important early contributions to the development of Rahner's contemplative conceptual horizon was the Thomism of Pierre Rousselot and Joseph Maréchal. With the writings of these two transcendental Thomists, we detect a shift from the preoccupation with concepts and their empirical content which characterized early twentieth century scholasiticism and philosophical positivism to a concern for the conditions of possibility for conceptualization and the meta-empirical dynamism of the human spirit. In this context, it is contemplation rather than conceptualization which is considered epistemologically decisive

Pierre Rousselot

The sole major work of the Parisian priest and theologian, Pierre Rousselot S.J., (1878-1915) was *The Intellectualism of St. Thomas*, an effort to forge a metaphysics of knowledge which could respond to both the anti-intellectualism and the hyper-rationalism which marked the university scene at the start of the twentieth century.[1]

According to Rousselot, intellectualism typically signifies "a rather naïve confidence in intelligence and, in particular, in deductive reasoning." He contrasts this with Thomistic intellectualism which he describes as

> a doctrine which goes beyond the theory that all being is capable of being explained, and . . . just the reverse of a system which would conceive the life of mind on the pattern of human reason. . . . Intelligence for St. Thomas, is the faculty of the real, but it is the faculty of the real only because it is the faculty of the divine.[2]

The entire work is given over to the elaboration and demonstration of this thesis.

The reason that this thesis is so important for our purposes is that it suggests that chief among the elements missing from a conventional understanding of Thomist intellectualism is an appreciation for the contemplative dimension. Critics and disciples of Thomas alike interpret Thomistic metaphysics in such a way as to make Thomas seem an excessive dogmatist and an idolater of abstraction. Even where the primacy of contemplation in Aquinas is recognized, little or no importance may be attached to it. For Rousselot, however, the principle of the primacy of contemplation "is the really deep and central thing in [Thomas'] system." Rousselot is emphatic on this point:

> It is by setting out from [this principle] that one may hope to reach the very heart of the Thomistic metaphysic most easily, for no one can study this principle with out seeing it expand and grow and finally develop into an affirmation of the absolute value of the act of intelligence. Arrived at this point, one is in possession of the master-idea which introduces unity everywhere and which links up philosophy and theology in an indissoluable synthesis.[3]

It is not that Rousselot ignores the importance of abstraction in Thomas' metaphysics of knowledge; clearly, it is the only means by which the human being can attain knowledge in the present life. Rousselot's objection is to the absolutization of abstraction to the detriment of human intellectual becoming. "Not to take account of what as a whole is simultaneously one and multiple is to ignore becoming and to be out of touch with reality"—that reality which is the very goal of intelligence.[4] Typical scholasticism, by the exaggerated importance it gives to abstractive intellect, amounts to "a rationalization of the divine." It attributes to the human formulations about the divine (i.e. dogmas) the kind of stability which only the divine itself can enjoy.[5] Though this strategy is intended to protect the truth claims of revealed faith, it ironically undermines those claims by subordinating the divine-as-revealed to the categories of human rationality narrowly-construed. If a Christian philosophy or theology were, instead, to conceive of God as a "spiritual personality" as well as a supreme idea, it would be more faithful to Thomas and less likely to absolutize mere human concepts.[6]

This conviction of Rousselot about the primacy of contemplation and the relative importance of abstraction becomes more clear when one understands his conception of knowledge:

> To know is primarily and principally to have within the self a non-self which in its turn is capable of seizing and embracing the self: it is to live with the life of another. Intelligence is the faculty of the divine, because in this way it is capable of embracing God; and if we are to have a correct idea of it, we must grasp the fact the the function of intelligence is not to fabricate concepts or adjust its propositions but to enrich itself with realities . . . [7]

Note the resemblances between this and the Rahnerian conception of knowledge discussed in Chapter III: The conception of knowledge as self-presence, the relative importance given to concepts and propositions, the implication of an original unity of being and knowing. In particular, Rousselot's overall assessment of the power of human intelligence—an assessment which is, at once, disparaging and laudatory—also finds strong echoes in Rahner. As "spirit in matter" human beings must employ concepts in their thinking, but in no way do these concepts constitute a direct grasp of the essences of things. They simply represent an attempt to "solidify" the being of things for human apprehension. For Thomas, this solidification is "the essential blemish of our mind, but it is at the same time the indispensable condition of its functioning."[8]

Rousselot is careful to explain that, on a theological plane, this realistic assessment of the limits of human intellect should not be thought to completely undermine the value of dogma. It is true that dogma cannot "exhaust the divine fact which it translates in human terms." At the same time, however, dogma is more than "merely a useful symbol for conduct" in life. A moral order somehow distinct from an order of being (one may assume Rousselot had Kant in mind here) would be unintelligible.[9] In Rousselot's framework, judgments of value and judgments of reality cannot be completely differentiated because, as we shall see, they are both a function of the overall dynamism of the human being toward the real, the most fully real, Absolute Being, i.e. God.

94

Contemplation, therefore, must be seen as having a practical as well as speculative aspect.

Rousselot admits that the preliminary description which he has given of Thomas' metaphysics of knowledge is not always supported by the primary texts:

> Here and there [Thomas] has attached too much importance to formulae; in his explanations of texts, he has too frequently substituted a conscious finality for the historical mechanisms of psychology; he betrayed a tendency to conceive perfection, even this world of corruptible things, in terms of constancy and repose.[10]

Nonetheless, Rousselot is convinced that these are but minor deviations from the overriding trajectory of Thomas's thinking. Contemplation and not conceptualization is the highest achievement of human intelligence this side of the grave. And the fulfillment of human intelligence in its highest aspirations, the acquisition of reality in its fullness, depends on supernatural activity.[11] Thomas' metaphysics of knowledge only makes sense if this fundamental principle is understood.

The Distinctiveness of Human Knowledge
In the first of the three major divisions of the book, Rousselot elaborates on his description of the human intellectual process as the activity of spirit in matter. Because human beings are spiritual, they possess the capacity for self-presence; because human beings are material, that self-presence is always exercised by way of sensible experience. As capable of self reflection, human beings occupy an exalted place among material beings; as subject to the conditions of sensibility, human being occupy the lowest place among intellectual beings.[12] So far there is nothing new here. What may be new in Rousselot's interpretation of Thomas is his conviction that an examination of human intelligence must also lead to an affirmation of Absolute Mind. The human soul's capacity and appetite for all that has being is indicative of human participation in and directedness toward the supremely intelligible source of being.[13] Hence, the proper terminus of human intellectualism is neither the judgment nor the concept, but "a real grasp of reality, given . . . in the form of ideas and principles."[14] Although this direct grasp can never be attained by

man without supernatural assistance (viz. human reason is inescapably discursive), human knowers are always reaching for such a goal.[15]

It is in this context that the significance of angelology for epistemology can be seen. Not only does the Thomistic description of angelic knowledge prevent one from reducing or limiting intellectual knowledge as such to discursive reason, it also brings to light the original unity of reality and idea, being and knowledge:

> If . . . we are anxious to resuscitate the idea of this ever-youthful spiritualism, let us cease to represent the 'intelligible world' as a system of laws and axioms and principles. Beings come before laws: it is intellectualism that says so. Let us try, following St. Thomas and his contemporaries, to have an adequate idea of 'spiritual substance,' be it angel or soul, in its exquisite grandeur and its subtle purity.[16]

If the philosopher can make intelligible for himself such an idea, then both the limitations of human knowledge in its present state and the greatness of the goal for which it aspires come to light. What happens more often than not, Rousselot seems to be implying, is that philosophers treat laws, axioms, and principles as if they were the ulimate measure of human intellectual activity.

For human beings (as opposed to angels) a non-discursive grasp of reality lies in the future in the form of what has been traditionally spoken of as beatific vision. But this is not to say that beatific vision is an experience wholly discontinuous with man's present intellectual functioning; indeed, it is made possible by the very same faculty which is responsible for human concepts and rational deductions in the present order.[17] Evidence for this may be seen in the necessity and universality attributable to at least certain human judgments, e.g. the first principles of logic:

> If reason is capable of forming judgments that possess an absolute value and of perceiving laws from which not even God can derogate, if the indivisible certitude of its clear assertions puts all intellectual subjects, as it were, on the same level, the reason of this is to be found in that potential participation which makes intellect to be what it is and in that capacity for the divine which God will fill up in the beatific vision.[18]

This vision of the real does not abrogate the finitude of human intellect; otherwise, the individual intellect would cease to be itself and would be utterly swallowed up in the being of God. What happens in the beatific vision is that, by means of supernatural assistance, materiality no longer proves inimical to the human intellect's possession of reality in its fullness, i.e. God himself.[19]

In the meantime, the human being strives for this full possession of reality through volition. The dynamism or movement of intellect, Rousselot seems to be suggesting, is a function of human desire, described in terms of will.[20] In knowledge, the human intellect attains (at least to some limited extent) possession of reality. But this is not something which is simply given whole and entire, but is the achievement of some process which begins, first of all, as a desire to know. It is true that, for Thomas, volition is said to be subordinate to intellect; the desire of the end subordinate to its attainment. This is because the dynamism and movement of human intellectual becoming has some definite term, i.e. Infinite Being, understood as God.[21] (As we shall later see, Rahner's adoption of this position makes it impossible for him to follow Heidegger completely.) At the same time, however, it is love which is viewed as pre-eminent where God is involved as end or object.[22] Such a love—which is more than mere desire—seeks not only to grasp but to be grasped:

> Love . . .as it arises in me is a principle of activity which has for end and object something outside of me, something that forms part of a whole, which surrounds me, goes beyond the self, and subjects me to its empire.[23]

With God as the object of such a love, love surely takes ontological precedence over knowledge. It is in this sense that it may be said that genuine knowledge finds its fulfillment in love.

In the first part of Rousselot's work, then, one may already find the basis for a description of the contemplative dimension of rationality: The highest of material creatures, the human person possesses a capacity for self-presence and an appetite, as it were, for all being, for all that is real. In his ability to form judgments of absolute value the human knower gives implicit affirmation to the existence of Absolute Mind. Still, limited by the materiality of his present condition, the human being cannot attain a full and direct vision of God but awaits a future time when this vision will be given. This waiting is not a state of utter passivity, but a kind active receptivity, whereby the person is moved by the desire for God (whether implicitly or explicitly) to acquire knowledge. In its highest and purest form, this movement (which is a relative, not endless, dynamism) is contemplation.[24] In the second part of his dicussion, Rousselot makes more clear what the contemplative entails.

Contemplation: *Ratio* Converging toward *Intellectus*

There is in Aquinas a distinction to be drawn between *intellectus* and *ratio*, a distinction which nicely summarizes everything which Rousselot has said to this point about the glory and shortcomings of the human intellect and points ahead to a fuller appreciation of contemplation. What is being discussed here is the antithesis between intellectual activity in its purity (*intellectus*) and the human exercise of intellect (*ratio*) whereby "the perfection of intelligibility as such" is disintegrated by the process of reasoning which human beings must employ in order to achieve knowledge . Whereas *intellectus* involves intimate penetration of the truth, the best *ratio* can achieve is research into the truth. Whereas *intellectus* begins with a simple truth from which many things are grasped, *ratio* must traverse around objects to obtain simple knowledge. Whereas *intellectus* is the underlying priniciple of reasoning and the very source of reason's certitude, *ratio* converges toward *intellectus* and is the very sign of the poverty of human intellectual activity.[25] If Rousselot is correct in his interpretation of Thomas on this score, then it must be said that a version of the Thomistic conception of rationality which attributed ultimate value to *ratio* (i.e. to the concepts and judgments of reason in its discursive mode) would have to be considered false. To some extent, the critique which the Rousselot-inspired Rahner makes of conventional neo-scholasticism hinges on this fundamental interpretive issue.

In order to make up for its own deficiences, the human intellect has devised several "substitutes" for the direct grasp and intimate penetration of the truth which it lacks: These are concepts, science, system, and symbol.[26] There is nothing wrong with human employment of these substitutes, as long as their use is accompanied by critique. Consider, for example, the issue of our knowledge of God. Obviously, there is no human knowledge of God which does not involve the use of concepts; but these concepts always fall infinitely short of the reality they seek to grasp and convey. We speak of God as a being, albeit a Supreme Being, but in a sense,

> of God such predication is impossible. He is pure Act and subsisting Being from whom all duality is excluded. He is above and beyond genera or categories and for that reason he transcends every created concept of Him that we can entertain.[27]

Even where finite things are involved, concepts are far from adequate. Because they are formulated precisely by abstraction from the sensible particular which they seek to grasp, the particular as such is never grasped in its essence, but only as an instance of a kind. The problems associated with concepts arise not from their limitation but from our tendency to overlook this limitation. As Rousselot metphorically describes man's plight, "Intellectually desirous of such diamonds [i.e. the essences of spiritual substances], he does not take the trouble to assess the value of the copper treasure he believes he possesses."[28] Parallel problems arise with respect to science,[29] system,[30] and symbol.[31]

While we cannot elaborate on the manifestation of the limitation of *ratio* in these areas, what must be noted is how each substitute moves progressively closer to *intellectus*, culiminating in contemplation. Man's penchant for systematization, for example, gives evidence of the human mind's indefatigable aspiration to grasp the totality of things in the unity of a single idea.[32] And at the limit of systematic construction, where a single idea can no longer bear the weight of the totality in question, emerges symbolization—a metaphorical, figurative, or poetic expression of that which wholly transcends the power of concepts to convey. In symbolization, the rigor of scientific demonstration is sacrificed to the desire for the unity of the Idea in its purity. Thomas' reliance on analogous language to explain sacred realities, his use of sensible images to explain the super-sensible, is an instance of this principle.[33]

> The whole question is to introduce harmony into man, to evoke his belief by means of images and to reach his mind by reasons aided by the grace of God. Even if the speculative value of the symbol is negligible, and not adequately distinguished from its usefulness for man . . . even if it is primarily intended to influence the animal part of

man and prevent it from warring against the spirit, yet it is natural to link it up with system and with our other instruments of knowledge, the aim of which is to simulate the Idea.[34]

In fact, suggests Rousselot, Thomas' use of symbolization may be more significant on the whole than all the logical structures which he seems to have preferred.[35] In any event, it is evident that Rousselot's conception of rationality not only takes its ultimate meaning from intellectus, but includes the whole range of "substitutes for the pure idea"—from scientific concepts to symbols appealing to the imagination. Rationality is not primordially a matter of deductive demonstrability but of maximal openness to the real and a consciousness of the inescapable limitations of human intellectual activity in its present state.

Obviously, such an account of rationality implies a certain clash between "intransigent intellectualism," on the one hand (i.e. the human desire to grasp the Idea in its purity) and the limitation of human intellectual activity on the other. How can any happiness or fulfillment be possible for man in the natural order of things, if he is constantly striving for something which he cannot reach? Rousselot's answer is two-fold:

[St. Thomas] seems to have regarded a kind of aesthetic beatitude. . . possible in the purely natural order. Secondly, this beatitude which he considered satisfying in its own order would not . . . exhaust man's full capacities for love and knowledge. The value of human speculation, then, may be considered with reference to the two domains, that of the possible order of 'pure nature' and that of the actual order of grace which prepares man for the vision of God.[36]

What Rousselot appears to have in mind with regard to "aesthetic beatitude" is the contemplation which Aristotle described as man's highest activity. Contrasting contemplation to any activity which is not an end in itself, Rousselot points out that "all speculative activity is intrinsically something more than a means to to an end and that it is already an installment of the absolute end itself."[37] Contemplation on this first and purely natural level consists in wonder about reality, a questioning attitude which is not directed toward any useful or practical end, but finds satisfaction simply in the acquisition of the truth.

However, the very power of human knowledge itself—and not simply considerations arising from revelation—propels the man who is open beyond this first level of contemplation. The limitations of human knowledge which become evident contemplatively, as well as the desire for a more complete and direct vision of reality in its ultimate foundation, which grows when one is in the contemplative attitude, have the potential to move the person to a second and deeper level of contemplation informed by faith.[38] When Rahner wrote of obediential potency in his *Hearers of the Word*, he was at least partially drawing on Rousselot's conviction on this matter. "The 'obediential capacity' of intellectual natures, according to St. Thomas, is not something independent of their natural capacity [as the fideist might suggest]; it is rather to be identified with the intellectual nature as such."[39] The human person is disposed by nature to hear the word of God spoken in history; hence beatitude—ultimately supernatural as well as natural—is universally attainable. Whether a person in fact hears such a word depends on a host of factors, not the least of which is the person's own attitude.

Knowledge and Freedom

Rousselot's comparison between religious and philosophical contemplation brings out the attitudinal factor nicely:

> For St. Thomas, religious contemplation is more calculated to attract man than philosophical contemplation, because the love of such contemplation is not distinguishable from love of the object to be contemplated. Further he ascribes more liberty to religious contemplation, since he regards religious obedience as a sacrifice of practical and comparatively unworthy scientific pursuits, those namely which are concerned with things of the body and with the regulation of everyday affairs, in favor of a complete giving of oneself to the highest part of the soul to union with the One Thing Necessary.[40]

Hence, one is not surprised to find Rousselot, in the final and briefest section of the book, returning to the interpenetration of the speculative and the practical which he emphasizes at the book's beginning. This third section is largely a polemic against both voluntaristic and deontological ethics.[41] Presupposed throughout the argument is this crucial principle: What we in fact come to know is in large part a function of what we choose to know and how we choose to seek it out. At the same time, what we choose to do depends in large part on what we have come to know—about ourselves, about others, about our world, and about God. *Contemplation thus involves the free modification of the mind's intentionality, the choice made by an individual in freedom to open oneself up to and to move in love towards that which he or she already knows implicitly as the principle of all knowledge, that Spiritual Personality and Supreme Idea, which believers name God.* It has to do, not simply with the way a person thinks, but also with the way a person lives.

In this sense, contemplation does not presuppose, but simply opens up to, divine revelation. As such it may even lay claim to validity within a philosophy that is not explicitly Christian. For St. Thomas, contemplation is not only a valid, but an essential component of human rationality, even considered apart from revelation. For the man sometimes referred to as the "Angelic Doctor," mysticism and an integral intellectualism were synonymous. According to Rousselot, Thomas' entire corpus, in all its systematic grandeur must, in the final analysis, be read in the light of the judgment which he said to have pronounced upon it at the end of his life: " . . . all I have written now appears to me as so much straw."[42]

Joseph Maréchal

Our interest in the possibility of a contemplative dimension to rationality naturally leads us to two works of the Belgian Thomist Joseph Maréchal. One is the landmark *Cahier V* of his *The Starting Point of Metaphysics*, wherein he attempts a conversation between Thomistic metaphysics and the critical philosophy of Kant. The other work is his less widely-read *Studies in the Psychology of the Mystics*, which offers a singular opportunity to see how Maréchal applied his own epistemological principles to the analysis of contemplation.

Cahier V: Aquinas and Kant in Conversation

Maréchal's aim in the fifth section of his massive work on the history of metaphysics in the West is to provide a double demonstration. First, he wants to show that, starting out from "the basic realism of direct and reflexive intellectual knowledge," it is possible to discover in the ontological relations between subject and object the logical characteristics of the various human faculties. This would constitute a metaphysical critique of knowledge. Secondly, he wants to show how, by using the Kantian starting point—i.e. an analysis of the subjective conditions of possibility for objective knowledge—one may arrive at conclusions identical to those of the metaphysical critique. This second part of the demonstration, the transcendental critique, "will first go along with Kant in order to proceed beyond him."[43]

The metaphysical critique is distinguished by three aspects: 1) It presupposes the absolute value of its first principle in the necessary synthesis of being with every datum which may be affirmed. 2) It discovers the distinction between subject and object in the progressive diversification of affirmations of being. 3) It integrates voluntary action within the system of reason, linking knowing and willing.[44] It is in the context of this last point that contemplation emerges as an explicit theme for Maréchal. Like Rousselot, he argues for the fundamental interpenetration of the speculative and the practical:

> The analysis of the data of consciousness reveals the initial indigence of our speculative action, since it depends on outside data of knowledge for its exercise. On the other hand, it shows how our practical activity is always busy reaching out for and appropriating these outside data so as to reduce the distance between potency and act in our faculty of knowledge. In this way, by steadily expanding our knowledge, it makes us strive in a groping fashion towards the fullness of theoretical activity: the intellectual intuition of being, the contemplation of the supremely intelligible—*contemplatio optimi intelligibilis*, as St. Thomas says after Aristotle (ST, II, II, 180, 4)[45]

Hence, the unity between thought and action is not something constructed subsequent to some original duality; rather, it is derived from the primordial unity of that end toward which the human spirit is directed by its own very nature. As we shall see, the transcendental analysis of human cognition gives strong evidence of the fundamental dynamism of the human intellect.

As for the transcendental critique: It "holds the realistic affirmation in abeyance and concentrates on the apparent content of consciousness in order to consider it in itself." In place of the ontological absolute which provided the starting point for the metaphysical critique, the transcendental critique begins with "an ordered diversity of contingent 'phenomena' present to the mind, whose eventual relation to an ontological absolute must be evaluated." It is interesting to observe that, while the first principle of thought (the principle of identity) is observed here, just as it is in the metaphysical critique; in the transcendental critique, it is viewed as a logical norm without any ontological meaning being attributed to it.[46]

Now, according to Maréchal, when Kant employed this transcendental method, he correctly identified the inner dynamism of human knowledge: An object becomes present in consciousness as a totality of 'determinations' or 'conditions' which actively affect some matter coming from the senses."[47] Where Kant erred, according to Maréchal, was in his failure to move beyond the static and purely formal unity of pure apperception to the dynamic ontological unity of the thing-in-itself. He was too influenced by Cartesian and Wolffian rationalism, to see the full ontological import of his transcendental premises.[48] One purpose of *Cahier V* is to correct that error. The position for which Maréchal argues is that both the more ancient metaphysical critique and the more modern transcendental one—if correctly carried out—converge toward the same result.[49]

It should be noted that it is not the case that Maréchal understood the two methods to be serving the same purpose. Clearly, he saw the metaphysical method as necessary and foundational and the transcendental one merely as "precisive." His point was that, if Kant had followed his own method to its logical conclusions, he would have agreed with Thomas in his identification of God (and not the mere *idea* therof) as the *telos* of the human intellectual dynamism. Whether Maréchal is correct on this score is obviously a moot point. It is indisputable, however, that Maréchal never sought the overthrow of Thomistic metaphysics, but only its transposition into a form which would be intelligible for post-Kantian European philosophy.[50]

An analysis of human cognition.   Maréchal's analysis of human cognition begins by emphasizing the original proportion of subject and object. Knowledge does not consist of a subject having in mind an immaterial copy of a radically distinct external object, a copy which is judged to be faithful or unfaithful to the original according to some otherworldly standard. Subject and object, knower and known are originally proportioned to one another as lock to key:

Through its very design, the lock represents the previous rule of the shape of all the keys which are to fit, whether made of gold or of iron. Hence we shall not say that it would be unwise to look in the subject for some *a priori* knowledge of the objects. Every objective knowledge lower than an intellectual intuition, arises at the meeting of *a priori* exigencies (which outline *a priori* some of its features) and of empirical *a posteriori* data (which provide it with a content). A knowledge which should be wholly *a posteriori*, wholly "alien" . . . to the subject, is an impossibility.[51]

From the outset, then, it is evident that Maréchal will be opposed to any kind of epistemological reductionism—subjectivism or objectivism, empiricism or rationalism. What remains to be seen is how precisely Maréchal will describe the basis for the proportion, the common term.

Not surprisingly, the relationship of sensibility and intellect takes center stage in the discussion. The human intellect clearly requires sensibility as the material basis for its knowledge; as spirit in matter, human being possess no pure intellectual intuitions. But this is not to say that sensibility independently acquires data which is only subsequently organized by the intellect.

[The intellect] insinuates itself continually into sensibility as a cause insinuates itself in the effect which it shapes into its resemblance. Under this permanent influence, the senses will be radically finalized towards the intellect. The end of sensibility as moved by the intellect will coincide in this respect with the very end of the intellect, will be an "intelligible end."[52]

Hence, the intellect in its activity (agent intellect) is a participant from the very outset in the process by which knowledge is achieved: Asking questions, directing the attention of the senses, providing a framework of receptivity for perceptual experiences. In this regard, Maréchal detects a signicant difference between Thomas and Kant. Kant reserved to meta-empirical Reason (*Vernuft*) what Thomas attributes to agent intellect. Agent intellect is more than a mere quantitative synthesis which takes place subsequent to sensual experience (*Verstehen* in Kant). Through an abstraction made possible by an *a priori* principle of unification, the agent intellect devises the very concepts required for objective knowledge.[53] The dynamic principle of unification which Maréchal argued was co-present in every knowing act, forms at least part of the foundation for Rahnerian *Vorgriff.* How did Maréchal conceive of this anticipatory aspect of human intellectual activity?

Affirmation and Anticipation. Conceptualization—the identification of an object of knowledge as limited—is only possible if human intellect possesses some dynamic finality. Both Kant and Aquinas would seem to agree on this; the bone of contention between them is the scope of the dynamism. Clearly, the intellect must have some kind of pre-conceptual orientation toward that horizon against which the differences between types and kinds of things will be evident. So too must the intellect be capable of distinguishing one particular of a kind from another particular of the same kind. But what about things in their transcendental status—their Being, their Truth, or their Goodness? Do these lie within the reach of the human intellect or are these merely ideas of reason with no necessary ontological correlate?[54] Maréchal argues that an analysis of human affirmation must lead one to conclude that the ambit of the human intellectual dynamism is nothing short of Absolute Being, and that Kant—if he had followed his own premises to their logical end—would have arrived at the same conclusion.

Through careful argumentation, Maréchal establishes the following with regard to affirmation: 1) It is through affirmation that a certain datum is constituted as an object; viz. it is when a subject takes its stand vis a vis some sensible thing that such a thing is constituted as an object. 2) Every affirmation expresses the repose of the tendency of an intelligent subject toward its end. That repose is achieved either through the nature of the datum itself or by subordination of the datum in question to a truly saturating object. 3) The only adequate object for an intelligent subject lies beyond any static conceptual representation. "Since . . . the universal object of the affirmation must be imprinted in some way in our intellect, it should be imprinted dynamically, as an end which is anticipated in a tendency." 4) Affirmation, which is a moment in the movement of the intellect, serves as a substitute for the objective function of intellectual intuition in a non-intuitive intellect.[55] (The parallel with Rousselot on this last point is striking.) In other words, the assent which the intellect gives in any affirmation (e.g. "The tree is green") represents the attainment of a subordinate end (i.e. the being of the thing in question) in the intellect's pursuit of its ultimate end (i.e.the attainment of the only object that will satisfy it fully, Being itself).

> Thus we see that the affirmation stands at the common boundary of the two orders of intellectual finality whose meeting point in us is called understanding. It is both the result of a previous exigency and the starting point of another one, a "formal" acquisition and a value for possible action; in a word, a partial quieting and an immediate awakening of the very desire which constitutes the core of our intellectual nature, the deep and never resting desire for Being.[56]

The Unity of Intellect and Will. In the dynamic tendency of the human being toward Being pure and simple, the original unity of the volitional and intellectual comes into view, for will and intellect are reciprocally related and dependent on a first and universal cause, namely, God.[57] Likewise related and interdependent are all those acts which emanate from intellect and will.[58] Hence, Maréchal did not interpret the intellectualism of St. Thomas (his conception of rationality) as abstract or impractical. For him, as for Rousselot, true knowledge is related to and terminates ultimately in love. The desire to know is a distinctively spiritual or intellectual expression of the fundamental human desire to acquire reality, to grasp being—the restlessness of a spirit that seeks, even if only implicitly, the source of its being.[59] Because an intuitive knowledge of God (the only thing that will satisfy our deepest longings) is beyond our finite nature, the perfection of that beatitude lies in the future and depends on supernatural assistance.[60] Nonetheless, even in the present order of things, a certain "inchoate beatitude" is available to the human being in the contemplation of the divine.[61]

In this light, Maréchal argues, that Kant's failure to secure the speculative necessity of the existence of the noumenal order was a result of his radical separation of the practical from the speculative. Had Kant attended instead to "the very genesis of the object as object, within the implicit and still undifferentiated dynamism whence derive both speculation and action," he may have come to a different conclusion.[62] Although it is not within the scope of the present project to engage Maréchal on this question, his point helps to locate the the place of the contemplative dimension within a Thomistic metaphysics of cognition as it is expressed in dialogue with transcendental philosophy. Contemplation emerges at that point where intellect and will, thought and action, are experienced in their interdependence and common origin. We have already seen in Rousselot that it is *a free modification of intentionality*, a choice made by an individual out of freedom to open oneself up to and to move in love towards that which he or she already knows implicitly as the principle of all knowledge. In Maréchal, the nature of this intentional modification is further elaborated: *A human person adjusts his intellectual and moral orientation from the myriad finite particulars, concepts, and systems which normally command his attention to that inner dynamism whereby all knowledge is attained and all action is accomplished. In this attitude, the contemplative attititude, a person comes to recognize the utter poverty of all that is normally included under the title of knowledge and the limits of every good that he can achieve or acquire and opens himself up to infinite possibility.* When that dynamism is identified and the absolute transendence of its end and term has been discerned, something approximating a philosophical affirmation of God's existence has been achieved. This interpretation of Maréchal on the nature of contemplation is confirmed in his analysis of mysticism.

Studies in the Psychology of the Mystics
Maréchal's scholarly interests were extraordinarily broad and varied. In addition to his work in philosophy (logic, epistemology, metaphysics, and history of modern philosophy), he also taught experimental psychology, biology, physiology, nervous and mental pathology as well as legal psychiatry. For him, these were not just so many disparate disciplines; rather, he discerned "a certain unity in this diversity," a unity which culminated in mysticism. In a letter quoted in the Foreword of the English edition, Maréchal comments: "Mysticism has always attracted me as the crowning achievement of metaphysics and psychology; it is from below, as a philosopher and as a man of science, that I have wanted to view it and have tried my best to achieve some modest understanding of it."[63] And so, Maréchal prepared a collection of essays on various aspects of the topic of mysticism. Although we shall focus primarily on the essay concerning Christian mysticism specifically, his introductory comments about the nature of positive science are worth noting, for they give some indication of the wider implications of the metaphysics of cognition which he worked out in his *Point de départ*.

The Metaphysical Underpinnings of Positive Science. When science limits itself strictly to the phenomenal order, it becomes involved in a concomitant "renunciation of the act of judgment on the integrality of an objective fact." Only a strict scientific agnostic or pragmatist would fail to recognize the insufficiency of science thus construed. According to Maréchal, scientific method, "demands, in order to make contact with reality, the complement of some metaphysics or other."[64] He substantiates this position through a summary of his analysis of judgment. The cohesion of three elements is implied in every judgment: 1) Phenomena, those empirical elements (whether of internal or external experience) which are organized in space and time; 2) the meta-empirical mode of synthesis, the compenetration of groups of phenomena according to the superior unity of concepts; and 3) absolute affirmation. "In this third stage . . . we detect the proper movement of the human spirit, the expression of its intimate nature, effecting and affirming unity, because it points fundamentally toward the unity of Being, its inaccessible object, the end which ever escapes it."[65] It is not necessary for the positive scientist to work out the precise nature and function of absolute affirmation (that is the work of the metaphysician); but he should, at the very least, be aware of its integral role in scientific judgment. Such an awareness constitutes a kind of critique of knowledge.

In the article which is of specific interest to us, "Features of Christian Mysticism,"[66] Maréchal makes an implicit criticism of conventional neo-scholastic method based on his presuppositions about the proper place of positive science. He distinguishes his own essay from those "admirable scholastic treatise[s] . . . which painstakingly expose the mechanism of human activity, in order to give ourselves the somewhat artificial pleasure of contemplating the scattered pieces, arranged motionless, under suitable labels in our conceptual pigeonholes." Because a penetrating analysis of human cognition reveals man to be "an activity at superimposed levels," science practiced in typical scholastic fashion must be judged superficial and incomplete.[67] Here, as in *Cahier V*, an awareness of the interpenetration of practical and speculative reason proves essential to realistic judgment. Ontologically expressed, the interpentration amounts to this:

[T]hat the Absolute Being pure and simple, beyond all determination,
is at the same time the latent mover, the ideal form of unity, and the

last end of the strivings of the human soul; at the term of these latter, at their perhaps inaccessible point of convergence, the One and the Good are mingled in the intuition of Being, for only in this intuition, the limiting activity of every created mind, will the soul realize at once the supreme unity of speculation and the unmixed possession of love.[68]

This intuition of Being (really, an anticipatory pre-conceptual grasping , not a pure intellectual intuition) both "surpasses the limits of human psychology" and "command its whole perspective." In light of this fact, the question which the essay must attempt to answer is whether or not mysticism amounts to anything more than "a hypostasizing of the form of the mind, in order to project it into the ontological order."[69] In other words, is mystical experience merely the mind's intensified consciousness of its own dynamism or does it have some transcendent correlate?

Maréchal carries out his investigation through a phenomenology, as it were, of the spiritual life. Outward religious practices (e.g. ritual and vocal prayer) and various modifications of interior life (e.g. interior prayer, various ascetical practices, etc.) all serve as context and preparation for contemplation as such.[70] Contemplation is not identical to intuition; sense intuition, for example, is not necessarily contemplative. It is, perhaps, "inchoative intuition." Maréchal explains: "There can be no contemplation without sustained attention . . . Perhaps the characteristic of contemplation is rather a *deep orientation* of the human being *in* an intuition or *towards* an intuition."[71] The meaning of these cryptic words becomes more clear as he delineates the various types and levels of contemplation.

A Typology of Contemplation. Maréchal's typology differs from Rousselot's. Whereas Rousselot makes a distinction between religious and intellectual contemplation, Maréchal is more interested in the degrees of possible intensity of contemplation. All of his examples are religious, but he does not exclude the possibility that there could be parallel contemplative experiences without explicitly religious content. At the lowest level, there is sensible contemplation. Through a given sensible object, or set of objects, the attention of the contemplative person is directed to the creator symbolized in it. Francis of Assisi's attitude toward the world of nature and Ignatius of Loyola's attitude toward creation as a whole are instances of this species of contemplation.[72]   At the second level, there is imaginative contemplation, whereby the mind sympathetically ponders the mysteries of faith—visualizing, for example the key events in the life of Jesus or his mother. At this stage, the external presence of a sensible object is not required, but the mind is still directed toward the data of sense.[73]   However, there is a still higher contemplation, "not directed towards any product of the sense-life, however noble, but in closer touch with the fundamental, intelligent, and loving tendency of the mind towards God." This is what Maréchal refers to as intellectual contemplation.[74] This level entails an interior movement which tends toward the unity of mind and the simplification of its content. What needs to be further clarified is the distinction between a simplification which is impoverishing (as may be observed in mental illness, for example) and that which is enriching.

In an impoverishing simplification, an apparent unity of mind is accomplished through the suppression of the true personality in all its diversity. One who is schizophrenic, for example, may be momentarily calmed by a certain religious suggestion; however, the profound fragmentation of his personality has not been corrected but merely concealed. But one need not be mentally ill to be in a state of impoverishing simplification. "Even the state of scholarly distraction, when it it is not brought about by the contemplation of an object worthy to lay hold of the whole soul, is a mark of a lack and a weakness . . . "[75] Hence, this kind of simplification cannot be considered an indication of a contemplative attitude.

In an enriching simplification, by contrast, the unity of mind is more than merely apparent and it is not accomplished through a concealing of a person's authentic self. Maréchal draws an analogy with art appreciation. An amateur and an artist may be contemplating one and the same art object. However, their apparently similar silent and simple admiration "is diversified by the depth and richness of the echoes whose awakening [the object] prepares. The two contemplations, then, differ immensely in their potential symbolism and their latent dynamism."[76] Religiously speaking, an enriching simplification is occuring and the summit of intellectual contemplation is being approached in a person when the following conditions prevail:

God has become the keystone of the arch of his Ego, the point from which he views all his proceedings, the pregnant symbol, the assimilative force of all his experiences, the ideal of all his dreams, the centre of all his affections, the dominating principle of all his actions—in short, the centre of equilibrium and the vital impulse of his whole psychological being.[77]

But when that summit is achieved, contemplation as such gives way to mystical union, which is distinguished by certain "negative notes of pure intellectual unity": the abadonment of discursiveness, reduction to the state of subconscious potentiality of mental imagery, and the loss of all consciousness of the fundamental dualism of Ego and non-Ego.[78]

The Epistemological Value of Mystical Experience. Obviously, from a limited psychological view point, the above description of the mystical state poses a serious problem which Maréchal himself recognized: "After images and concepts and the conscious Ego have been abolished, what subsists of the intellectual life? Multiplicity will have disappeared, but to the advantage of what kind of unity?"[79] There are several possible solutions: Perhaps the absence of multiplicity is merely apparent. Or perhaps the negativity of mystical ecstasy amounts to total unconsciousness. Or else, maybe mystical union consists in a synthesis of an empirical negativity and a transcendent positivity.[80]

Maréchal chooses the third option. The negativity by which mystical union is distinguished from other subjective states—abandonment of discursiveness, imagery, and ego/non-ego distinction—may certainly be empirically substantiated. But this negativity is not absolute. And admittedly, the one who has had such an experience "uses forced metaphors, embarks on a series of contradictions, and excuses himself for his inability to express the ineffable." But the impossibility of adequately conceptualizing such an experience belies the vivacity with which the mystic himself can recall "a state which had nothing in common with an absolute 'void' of consciousness."[81] Accompanying the empirical negativity of the experience, therefore, is a certain transcendent positivity. What has occurred is not a total loss of consciousness but a radical expansion and intensification of consciousness which so far outstrips the capacity of human concepts to convey it, that they are rendered at least temporarily useless[82]

Does this explanation entail a violation of the epistemological principle of *conversio ad phantasmata*? Are we positing an intellectual intuition the possibility of which Thomas and Kant alike rejected for human knowers? Maréchal never addresses this question directly, but he does give two indications of what might be involved in formulating a satisfactory reply. First of all, it is beyond the scope of empirical psychology as a positive science to provide a satisfactory resolution of such a problem. In its account of mystical union, positive science must yield ultimately to philosophy and theology.[83] Hence, we would have to look to the kind of metaphysics of cognition which both he and Rousselot developed to be reminded of that human intellectual activity, even in its ordinary and wholly discursive operation, is always tending toward a simple and direct grasp of the Idea as such; to be reminded that *intellectus* is the standard against which *ratio* is to be measured and not vice versa.

Secondly, however, a fully adequate response to the problem raised above—a response which would bring to light not only the trajectory of the intellect toward a pure intuition but also the possibility of its actual achievement even under present conditions—would have to include some notion of supernatural grace. Here, theology is called upon to elaborate, on the basis of revelation and in systematic fashion, what it means to say that God might gratuitously gift a person with a mystical experience which is anticipatory of the beatific vision to be given in the future.[84]

While it is true that a theology of grace as such is not only beyond the competence of positive science, but also beyond that of philosophy, there need not be anything in such a theology which does violence to the concept of nature properly understood:

> Grace completes and crowns Nature by transforming into an end properly so called what was only the superior and inaccessible limit of a radical tendency, or, if you prefer, by building up into efficacious means of attaining an explicit end psychological activities which, by themselves, were but the impotent expression of a hidden tendency. The unifying development of the psychological life in natural ascesis, and the intimate development of the religious life in supernatural ascesis, then, work in parallel fashion, in conformity with a single ideal of unity; it may be said that they are identical save in value.[85]

Likewise, it would be wrong to conclude that the theology of grace required to explain mystical union as such is also necessary in the explanation of contemplation; for contemplation is not itself identical to mystical ecstasy, but is *that free modification of intentionality which serves as the indispensable condition of possibility for mystical experience.* Whether such an experience in fact occurs and how precisely it is to be explained cannot concern us here. What is important to see, however, is that such an experience is certainly possible and that its possibilizing condition, namely the contemplative attitude, is not something completely discontinuous with ordinary human intellectual activity but is its highest expression in the natural order. Hence, from a transcendental perspective at least, a conception of rationality and revelation which does not take account of the contemplative dimension must be considered something less than complete.

VI

Ignatius of the *Exercises*

The effort to see what Ignatius of Loyola may have contributed philosophically to Rahner's conceptual framework presents a unique challenge. To begin with, Ignatius was neither a philosopher nor a theologian. He was a priest, missionary, and mystic whose written works are of genre quite different from the scholarly tracts of a university professor. Moreover, we will not find him directly taking up the epistemological and metaphysical issues which are the preoccupation of the present project. Therefore, in order to discern a possible contribution to the development of Rahner's philosophy, it will be necessary to reason from what he says explicitly to the philosophical assumptions which are implicit in and the philosophical implications which follow from what he says.[1]

Ignatius was born of Basque nobility in 1491. His time was one of profound upheaval in Europe in general and in the Roman Church in particular. The Reformation, the invasion of the Turks from the East, the discovery and exploration of foreign territories all had a destabilizing influence on the old and, heretofore, firmly-established order of life.[2] The personal history of Ignatius is similarly marked by tumult. As an adolescent, Ignatius is said to have been both courtly and raucous. His training as a young knight and traditional upbringing emphasized both family honor and external religious piety. His natural disposition was optimistic, his personality powerful, and his tastes elaborate and cultivated. But all of this began to undergo transformation while, in 1521, he was recovering from serious battle injuries. This transformation culminated the following year when, at Manresa, he underwent a mystical experience which had a singular impact on the overall direction of his life from that point on.[3]

The years 1524-1535 are of particular interest to us in the present project, for it was during this time that he undertook higher studies at first at

Barcelona, then at Alcala, Salamanaca, and Paris. Although he seems to have taken his studies seriously, there is no evidence that his intellectual training had a direct influence on his distinctive spirituality. According to Harvey Egan, "no more than the slightest traces of the philosophy and theology he studied can be found in his writings."[4] During this period, he also taught catechism and undertook charitable works. Most importantly, it was during this time that he began giving his famous spiritual exercises. Several times, he was charged and convicted by the Inquisition for a lack of orthodoxy, but these experiences did not alienate him from the Church. Together with a band of companions, he took religious vows and eventually established his order, the *Compañia de Jesús*, and dedicated it in a particular way to the ministry of the Roman pontiff. Ignatius of Loyola died in 1556.[5]

Although many contemporary portraits of Ignatius depict him in primarily worldly and active terms—he was, after all, a courtier, soldier and gentleman, a religious preacher, founder, and administrator—Egan argues that he was also a mystic.[6] As we have already seen in our discussion of Rousselot and Maréchal, mysticism is not unrelated to what we are identifying as the contemplative dimension in rationality. My objective, therefore, is to provide some indication of the philosophical significance of the mysticism represented by the *Spiritual Exercises* of St. Ignatius.

Ignatian Mysticism and the *Exercises*

Radical fidelity to the demands of daily life, even if only through implicit, hidden, or anonymous faith, hope, and love—in short, self-surrender to the Mystery that haunts one's life—grounds the mysticism of everyday life.[7]

Obviously, Egan's description of mysticism already carries a great deal of philosophical freight—not the least of which is the preeminently Rahnerian conviction that the human person is always already oriented toward God and can only choose not to be.[8] But even without begging the fundamental question of this book (i.e. by using a Rahnerian concept to explicate the mysticism of Ignatius which will, in turn, be called upon to explicate the thought of Rahner), it is possible to achieve somewhat greater precision with respect to Ignatian mysticism.

Egan and Joseph de Guibert alike appeal to a traditional distinction in ascetical theology between acquired and infused contemplation.   Aquired contemplation is the highest level of prayer which, as its name suggests is attained and worked at by a person by means already at the disposal of a person in relationship to God. Infused contemplation is mystical prayer in the strict sense, attainable solely through a new and special intervention of God in a particular individual's experience:

> God gives the person something new: the explicit awareness that God
> is present and that the person clings lovingly to him.   By actual
> experience the person becomes directly and mediately aware of God's
> loving, purifying, enlightening, and unifying presence.   The person
> realizes that something totally new is occuring.[9]

When when we refer to Ignatius as a mystic, we have in mind not only the first and more general sense in which any reasonably contemplative person may be called a mystic, but also the more strict and intense sense described above. Both Ignatius's own autobiographical writings and the testimony of his companions make it clear that this was the case.[10]

To say that the mysticism which Ignatius lived and taught was partly a function of a new and special intervention by God is not to say that it was other-worldly or disembodied. Jerónimo Nadal wrote this of his companion Ignatius: "[He was able to] see and contemplate in all things, actions, and conversations, the presence of God and the love of spiritual things . . . to remain a contemplative in the midst of action."[11]   Unlike a Dionysian mysticism which would have sought "disengagement from the sensible" and "flight ever more complete from the corporeal," Ignatian mysticism was that of a spirit in the world.[12] (The Ignatian echo in Rahner on this point is loud and clear.) And unlike a mysticism which focused on primarily on infused gifts pertaining cither to the intellect (traditionally referred to as cherubic) or to the will (seraphic), Ignatian mysticism entailed the transformation of will as well as of intellect, as is evident from its emphasis on decision and its trajectory service.[13]

This volitional/intellectual emphasis is yet another case of the dynamic interpenetration of the speculative and practical which was found to be crucial in the thought of the Rousselot and Maréchal and so pivotal in our definition of contemplation.   Likewise is the "worldliness" of Ignatian mysticism philosophically kindred with the transcendental emphasis on the sensible origins and discursive character of all human knowledge which we have also already discussed. These connections are not accidental; they point in the direction of an essential definition of rationality in its contemplative dimension. However, since our demonstration of the worldly and dynamic character of Ignatian mysticism is to be founded in a reading of the exercises, some general remarks specifically about these are in order.

Just as a game cannot be equated with the set of rules by which it is played, and the liturgy cannot be reduced to the rubrics by which it is celebrated, so too would it reflect a fundamental misunderstanding if one were to equate the *Spiritual Exercises* of St. Ignatius with a book bearing the same name. The exercises are meant to be lived and practiced and not read. Still, even from the book a limited number of conclusions about Ignatian mysticism may be drawn, for the book itself is a conpendium of directions and resources for the one (the director) who is leading another person (the exercitant) through the experience.[14]

Ignatius himself defines the exercises through analogy with the bodily training: "In just the same way all methods of preparing and disposing the soul to free itself from all disordered attachments, and, after their removal, of seeking and discovering God's will regarding the disposition of one's life for salvation, are called spiritual exercises."[15]   Surely, the provision of a methodology for contemplation was not original; William of Paris and Bonaventure had already done this during the thirteenth century. What was unique in the Ignatian exercises was the gathering together of elements from several traditions for one specific end.[16] Although Ignatius himself may be identified as a mystic in the strict sense explained above, the proper end of the exercises is not infused contemplation. A fair and faithful interpretation of the exercises depends on an appreciation of this fact above all: For Ignatius, the most important aspect of the Christian life, the true certificate of its authenticity, is not an experience of infused contemplation but the service of God and neighbor.[17]   The practice of acquired contemplation is the indispenable preparation for the decision to serve; but, while it is possible for this contemplative experience to be raised to a higher level, infused contemplation is not an end in itself.

The exercises are organized into four "weeks"—which are distinguishable movements rather than precise chronological units. The First Week begins by encouraging in the exercitant the proper foundational attitude for the discernment of God's will and the making of an election. It counsels an "indifference to all created things" which should not be confused with thoughtlessness, denial of the world, or a caricatured version of Stoic apathy. The indifference recommended here entails a change in focus not unlike the adjustment of moral and intellectual orientation which we saw in Maréchalian contemplation. Egan explains it in this way:

> The "indifference to all created things" sought in this exercise must be seen in the light of a passionate love and service of Jesus Christ, the Creator and Lord of all. The proper horizon and context for grasping the "Principle and Foundation" exercise must be Jesus Christ, the creator from whom everything comes and to whom it will all return. "Indifference to all created things" is actually an Ignatian mysticism of joy in the world, because it was created in, through, and for Christ.[18]

The Principle and Foundation are followed by the individual's meditation on his or her own sinful situation in the context of a cosmic historical drama of sin and redemption.[19]

The Second Week constitutes the heart of the exercises, inasmuch as it is during this time that the exercitant enters into proximate preparation for the making of an election or choice. A series of meditations—on the Kingdom of Christ, on the Two Standards of Life, on the Three Classes of Men, etc.—are intended to lead a person toward an intimate knowledge of Christ and of His Father's will, and thus to make possible a correct decision.[20] The knowledge of God's will involved here is more than a simple rational application of universal principles to the situation of an individual's life. What is hoped for here is a direct, immediate, individual encounter between exercitant and God, so that one may find God's specific will for him or herself.[21] As we shall shortly see, this aspect of the exercises raises a number of epistemological issues relevant to a discussion of contemplation as an aspect of human rationality.

The Third and Fourth Weeks involve a deepening and solidifying of the election made in the Second Week. This is accomplished through guided Meditations on the events surrounding the passion, death, and resurrection of

Jesus.[22]   Also included in the exercises are Rules for the Discernment of Spirits, Rules for the Sharing of Wealth and Possessions, Notes on Scruples, and Guidelines for Thinking with the Church.[23]

Having established the overall movement and direction of the exercises seen as a unitary experience, I now want to look at particular parts of the exercises to elaborate the two philosophically relevant keynotes of Ignatian mysticism which we have thus only identified: its worldliness and its dynamism.

Philosophical Significance
Worldliness and the Role of the Imagination

The mysticism of the exercises is first and foremost worldly. The meditations which they involve make conscious and explicit use of the imagination and the application of the senses.   The directions given in the course of the First Exercise emphasize that the exercitant must come to this experience as a whole person and not as a disembodied spirit. It is worth quoting Ignatius at length:

> [W]hen the contemplation or meditation is about something visible, such as when we contemplate Christ our Lord, the composition will consist in seeing with the imagination the physical location of the object contemplated. I said the physical place such as the temple or mountain where Jesus was according to the subject matter of the contemplation.

> In the case in which the subject matter is not visible, as here in the meditation on sin, the composition will be to see with the imagination the soul as a prisoner in the mortal body, and one's whole being on earth as an exile among brute beast. I said my whole composite being, body and soul.[24]

The use of the emphatic form "I said" preceding each reference to corporeality is evidence that Ignatius is convinced that something like the Thomistic *conversio* principle is operative even when the knowledge being sought is of the individual and direct kind to which the exercises aspire: The intellect can know nothing without turning to the phantasm.

The same principle seems to be implicit when in the Fifth Exercise on hell, for example, a systematic use of the senses is recommended. The exercitant is counseled to see the greatness of the pain experienced in hell; to hear the wailing, screaming, crying, and blaspheming of the damned; to smell the stench and ugliness of death; to taste the bitterness of tears, sorrow and guilt; and to feel the isolation of the condemned.[25] These directions may be offensive to the modern mentality, hesitant as the contemporary mind is to entertain the real possibility of something like hell. And yet, they ironically reflect a peculiarly "modern" recognition that a even something like the metaphysical concept of damnation cannot be understood without recourse to physical experience. And lest the impression be given that the exercises are wholly negative in the application of the senses, directions for a repetition of a contemplation on the birth of Jesus suggest a more pleasant and comforting sensual experience: "This is to smell the infinite fragrance and taste the infinite sweetness of God. Likewise, apply these senses to the soul and its virtues, and to all else, according to the character of the person contemplated and draw some profit from this."[26]

Related to the use of the senses and the imagination are regularly repeated directions aimed at the personalization of the experience. In other words, though the book of exercises represents a common rule of sorts, the exercises as experienced are expected by Ignatius to be different in every case. For example, in the preliminary instructions, the director is reminded that the purpose of the exercises is not the communication of abstraction information but personal appropriation of the mysteries of Christ's life. Hence, the director is urged to be brief in his guidance of the exercitant and to attune himself to way in which the individual, precisely as an individual, is being affected by the experience. The objective in all of this is

> that the one who is contemplating, taking a true foundation of history,
> and personally reflecting and reasoning upon it, may discover
> something that makes it more meaningful or deepens the experience of
> it . . . .For it is not much knowledge that fills and satisfies the soul, but
> the interior experiencing and savoring of things.[27]

Accordingly, the exercitant is repeatedly instructed to end his exercises with a "colloquy" or conversation with the Lord, "speaking exactly as one friend speaks to another, or as a servant speaks to a master, now asking a favor, now expressing sorrow for a wrong deed, now sharing concerns and seeking advice."[28] Likewise is the exercitant explicitly instructed to place himself in the imaginative scene being pondered. One is not asked to visualize the nativity of Jesus, for example, as an omniscient, invisible, and disinterested observer, but as "a poor, unworthy little servant, and as though present, [to] look upon them [Jesus, Mary, Joseph], contemplate them, and serve them in their needs with all possible respect and reverence."[29]

The worldliness and concomitant personalism of the the exercises is also revealed in the numerous instructions for adaptation given to the director. Time and again, the director is told to take into account the age, education, health, and abilities of the exercitant.[30] Similarly, the director is cautioned against too easily encouraging the interests of an exercitant in the religious life. While it is quite possible that the person making the exercises will find God's will in the pursuit of the religious life, the one giving the exercises is not to let his or her own enthusiasm for such a prospect interfere with a sober estimate of the individual's circumstances and qualities.[31] Here again, we see ample evidence that this is not a mysticism which aims to transport the person out of this world to some wholly abstract and undifferentiated state of being, but is intended to help the person to see precisely in his or her own concrete experience in the world, the presence and power of a personal God.

Finally, further evidence of the worldiness of the exercises (and, it may be profitably noted, a counter weight to their intense personalism) may be found in their emphasis on the communal dimension of an authentic experience of God. Admittedly, the ecclesial emphasis in the exercises may appear to be somewhat exagerrated. In explaining the virtue of docility to the Church, for example, Ignatius resorts to hyperbole and suggests that, even if the Church were to say that white is black and black is white, one is bound to submit to the Church's teaching.[32] Still, a more careful reading of the exercises—one which takes into account the circumstances of counter-reformation Catholicism—corrects the impression of sychophancy which the above admonition conveys. Egan's comments on the Rules for Thinking with the Church are helpful in this regard:

These rules stress a mystical felt knowledge of and being at home in the visibe, tangible, historical community of Jesus Christ, not the purely invisible Church of some reformers. Ignatius' felt knowledge, therefore, is neither a subjective, pious sense of an invisible Church nor an extrinsic, voluntaristic attachment to an ecclesiastical bureaucracy. It is is the genuine Christian experience in the mystical, or spiritual senses of full union with every dimension of a Church that is inseparable from the incarnate Christ.[33]

Hence, one is not expected to submit mindlessly to authority or to deny the obvious complexity of the theological issues which the teaching authority of the Church sees fit to clarify. Indeed, there is provision in the exercises both for a responsible way of challenging the decision of one's superiors[34] and for acknowleding the difficulty of definitively resolving troublesome doctrinal issues.[35] The operative principle at stake may be something like this: The nature of the human person as spirit in matter, together with the understanding of Jesus as God incarnate, dictate that man's continued experience of God's presence will be sensible, historical, and thus discernible in the visible and living community of the Church. Although Ignatius himself never elaborates such a principle, it is certainly not inconsistent with the conclusions he has drawn.

Dynamism and the Purpose of Asceticism

In addition to exhibiting a certain worldly character, the mysticism of the exercises also reveals the now-familiar dynamic interpenetration of the intellectual and volitional. To begin with, the contemplation which the exercises seek to cultivate is initiated through a modification of mental and moral attitude freely undertaken. The exercitant is asked to enter upon the exercises "with magnanimity and generosity toward the Creator and Lord, offering God all one's will and liberty, letting God dispose of oneself and all one possesses according to the most holy divine will."[36] Hence, the First Week begins with the adoption of the attitude of indifference mentioned earlier: "[We] should not prefer health to sickness, riches to poverty, honor to dishonor, a long life to a short life."[37] Given what we have already said about the worldliness of the exercises, the purpose of this admonition to detachment cannot be to cultivate a disdain for the good things of this life. Rather, its purpose must be to promote in a person maximal openness—both on the intellectual and moral level; i.e. to render a person capable of seeing his life perhaps in a way he has never seen it before, of making a choice or decision of which he has perhaps never been capable. Only when a person is free of an inordinate attachment to any one aspect of creation can that person be disposed to do what God wants.[38] The discipline or asceticism of the exercises is devised precisely to secure this freedom.

Likewise, if one were to view the exercises in terms of their end and goal, this same unified movement of intellect and will would come to light. "Our one desire and choice should be what will best help us to attain the purpose for which we are created," and all the various meditations are intended to help us to discern that purpose and the means by which it may be attained.[39] The exercises do not culminate merely in a singular intellectual enlightenment, no matter how exalted such an outcome may seem; properly practiced, the exercises culminate in an insight which leads to action.

From one point of view, there appears to be a kind of alternation between knowledge and action throughout the process: A person, for whatever reason, is prompted to undertake the exercises and thus freely chooses to dispose himself to a deeper knowledge of God's will, (in transcendental terms, to modify his intentionality). In this initial phase, the will is prominent. Eventually, through the asceticism of disciplined prayer and patient waiting, the knowledge hoped for is attained. In this phase, the intellect assumes prominence. When knowledge of God's will emerges with enough clarity—and Ignatius indicates that this takes place at a more or less definite moment—the person must then make a decision or election with regard to what God is thought to be asking. Once more, the will assumes the lead. This apparent alternation should not mislead us into thinking that Ignatius envisioned two completely distinct faculties in extrinsic communication with each other. What is more likely is that Ignatius conceived of the whole person—"memory, understanding, and entire will" as the oft-quoted "Take Lord" prayer puts it—as standing before the power of its Creator to whom it longs to return as to the source of it original unity and integrity.[40]

Ignatius indicates that there are three times when a sound election may be made, i.e. three sets of circumstances under which the exercitant is capable of making a good decision about the future direction of his or her life:

1) When God our Lord so moves and attracts the will that a devout soul, without any doubt, or even the possibility of doubt, follows what has been revealed to it.

2) When sufficient clarity and understanding have been derived from experiences of desolations and consolations and from the discernment of different spirits.

3) This is a time of tranquility, during which one first reflects on the purpose for which human persons are born . . . a time when the soul is not disturbed by different spirits, and has free and peaceful use of its natural faculties.[41]

First of all, it should be noted that, despite the differences among them, all three cases are understood by Ignatius to be instances where an individual person has been given a knowledge of God's will for him or her (even if the last case should appear, at first, to be the least complicated epistemologically). The goal of the exercises is stated explicitly at their beginning and is left unmodified throughout: the discovery of God's will regarding the disposition of one's life for salvation.[42] Rahner himself has argued that this "logic of concrete individual knowledge" constitutes an implicit critique of the epistemological presuppositions of conventional Catholic theology (as represented in typical sixteenth century scholasticism). The essentialism of Suarez and even of scholastic Thomism—with its emphasis on universals and deductive certitude—tended to leave the individual element in human knowledge and action untreated.[43] The average theology of the schools, Rahner argues, is not adequate to the task of uncovering "the ontological and gnoseological presuppositions" of Ignatius in the exercises.[44] Rahner provides some indication of what an adequate epistemology would supply:

It would recognize the universal nature and the subsumption of the particular under the general, for in the human sphere there is the common nature of man and general principles of morality with positive content (a universal material value-ethics). Yet it would have to recognize that the universal alone does not determine man, that within it there is and must be the unique, the unrepeatable that belongs to history, what is individual and inexpressible. And all that must be known in a different manner from the norms that are inferred from a universal essence.[45]

Secondly, if Ignatius can be said to have envisioned any one of the three cases outlined above as the "normal" one, judging from the amount of guidance given to the director with regard to discernment, it would probably be the second case. This is the case of a person who, through the course of the meditations leading up to the election, finds himself alternately consoled and unsettled by various images and thoughts. These interior experiences, which are rather difficult to describe, are taken to be significant indicators of the person's present spiritual condition and possible guideposts to the person's future. At first, there may be too much inner upheaval for a person to know clearly the direction in which he or she ought to move. Together with the director, the exercitant is to employ carefully the understanding in the exploration of these feelings, until sufficent clarity is gained for a decision. At no point does Ignatian mysticism degenerate into mindless enthusiasm, nor is the Ignatian mystic counseled to wholly suspend his or her critical faculties. There is no "cloud of unknowing" in the exercises; quite to the contrary, the exercitant is urged to use every positive means at his disposal arrive at a deeper knowledge of God and God's will.[46]

Occasionally, a person may experience what is referred to as a "consolation without cause"; i.e. a feeling of consolation which, even after painstaking reflection, can be traced to no previous act of the person's own intellect and will:

> God alone can give consolation to the soul without previous cause. It
> is for the Creator alone to enter into a soul, leave it, act upon it, and
> draw it totally toward divine love.[47]

In this regard also, Rahner himself has detected epistemological significance in the Ignatian doctrine: The intelligibility of something like an election or choice which is divinely assisted depends on securing the possibility of a non-conceptual experience of God, which is not, at the same time, merely reducible to psychic processes or an individual's emotions:

> [I]f there is such an experience carrying with it an intrinsic certitude
> of its purely divine origin, it cannot consist in a knowledge of God by
> way of particular concepts in which God is known discursively by

thinking a thought about him. God's presence must be of another kind. And this different way of his being involved must *eo ipso* possess intrinsically an irreducibly self-evident, self-sufficient character.[48]

In the exercises, this non-discursive experience is described in terms of consolation *sin causa,* i.e. a sense of interior tranquility that cannot be explained either by the exercitant's state or identifiable factors outside of him or her. This special form of consolation is closely related to that which Rahner had described in terms of *Vorgriff.* In its lowest form, the consolation consists in the recession of the conceptual object into the background combined with an intensified awareness of that dynamism which the human person brings to every knowing act—the dynamism whereby every sensible object is constituted against the limitlessness of Absolute Being toward which the human spirit is always already directed.[49]

> If this transcendence is present in this way in its purity and as itself the focus of awareness, without being mediated by the conceptual object and so hidden, and if this occurs not only in cognition but also as the pure dynamism of the will in positive affirmation and receptivity, in love that is to say, then we have the lowest stage of what Ignatius is probably referring to, without metaphysical and theological terminology when he speaks of the consolation *sin causa.*[50]

It is as if one, in gazing at the moon, no longer saw the moon but the light of the sun which is reflected in it and by which alone it may become visible. The acsceticism of the exercises is intended to make such vision possible.

Underlying Philosophical Assumptions

There is no escaping the fact that the *Spiritual Exercises* of St. Ignatius of Loyola are more a masterpiece of religious and ascetical wisdom than of philosophy. Still, they are laden with assumptions and principles pertaining to human existence in its ontological, noetic, and practical dimensions. Many of these share a great deal in common with both the Thomism that preceded the exercises and that which has evolved in our own time: The dynamic teleological thrust and the insistence on the sensible foundations of human knowledge—these are themes with which we were already familiar as we began our discussion of Ignatian mysticism. Other elements, if not particularly original in themselves, certainly represent an original emphasis: The extraordinary role given to the human imagination as a locus for revelatory experience and the insistence on the possibility of an individual attaining a concrete knowledge of God's will through non-conceptual experience.

However, in the final analysis, what may prove to have been most influential on Rahner in the exercises is nothing which we have specifically noted here but something more important than everything we have seen taken together: Rahner both lived and gave these exercises; in other words, he experienced them and was deeply affected by the experience of God which was made possible through them. Such an influence is obviously incalculable and, to that extent, cannot be easily incorporated into a philosophical argument. And yet, it does not seem implausible that a man who himself attained knowledge of God through something like the exercises would attribute a certain importance to contemplation specifically and to contemplative living in general. In the final analysis, the indifference of the exercises—as well their unique asceticism devised precisely to cultivate that indifference—is not so different from the condition on which all knowledge in its highest aspirations depends: Never to be so attached to anyone or anything or any particular point of view that one is no longer free to see what there is to see—and, ultimately, to be what one is called, in the depths of his or her being, to be. This may have been the methodological principle above all others which determined Rahner's direction in the practice of philosophy and theology.

And so, to the transcendental notion of contemplation as a modification of intentionality we may now add that *its character as a specifically human activity requires that it always occur in space and time. As such, contemplation involves both the collaboration of sensibility and imagination in an individual and the kind of asceticism which leaves the individual open in principle to that which is more than or beyond the world of space and time—the very context, source, and goal of human being and thinking.* In Heidegger, we will see the notion of contemplative asceticism radicalized.

VII

Heidegger During the Thirties

Rahner claims to have taken from Heidegger "a way of thinking." What then was the character of Heidegger's thinking during the period Rahner was exposed to him? What elements prominent in Heidegger's thought during the thirties provide a light in which the contemplative dimension of Rahner's thinking may emerge with greater clarity?[1]

It is well known that Heidegger wanted to raise the question of the meaning of Being in an entirely new and fresh way. I have derived the principal themes for our discussion from this description of his problematic: First of all, Heidegger is raising the *question* of the meaning of being; hence, we will begin by considering the importance that Heidegger attributed to questioning as the prime mode of human access to being. Second, Heidegger is raising the question of the meaning of *Being*; thus, we will want to consider what he meant by "Being" and the way in which the peculiarities of the Being concept demand a distinctive investigative strategy. Third, Heidegger is raising the question of the *meaning* of Being; viz. an effort is being made to establish what Being is for us, in relation to our questions, concerns, situation. Therefore, we will want to consider Heidegger's analytic of human existence, *Dasein*. In that analysis, the question of the meaning of Being finds its ontological basis, not in some kind of highest being or super entity, but in temporality. This result places Heidegger in opposition to the Western metaphysical tradition and prompts him to call for a return to a more radical philosophical questioning that will open a thinker up to a primal experience of Being. Although contemplation is not an explicit category in Heidegger's thought, the fundamental ontology which he develops has a decidedly contemplative quality the influence of which may be detected in the development of Rahner's conceptual horizon.

Questioning

Heidegger's concern is the meaning of Being, but Being is not "out there" ready-made, and able to be grasped whole and entire. Being is basic, at least to the extent that it is implicated everytime we say of a thing, "It is . . . ." But Being is accessible to man only as something questionable. We can experience the ground of our *Dasein* "in its dignity and rank only if we question it."[2]

The questioning in which man engages is not just another thing we do or function we perform. Questioning is more than the interrogative sentence through which it is enacted.

> To question is to will to know. He who wills, he who puts his whole existence into a will is resolved . . . . Re-solve is no mere decision to act, but the crucial beginning of action that anticipates and reaches through all action. To will is to be resolved.[3]

Questioning, therefore is neither a thing nor the indifferent starting point of a cognitive process mechanistically understood. It is a free decision to dispose oneself in a particular way, and the particular way which is chosen makes a profound difference.

Does this mean that our questioning determines what is? Obviously not. Things have a givenness about them which cannot be modified simply by placing them in question. And still, inasmuch as things reveal themselves to us only in answer to our questions, we may expect a thing's meaning for individual persons to differ according to their interests. A building engineer, an historian, and an architect, for example, may all have questions to ask about a particular old building. But their rather different interests will determine the kinds of questions they ask and, in turn, the kinds of answers they get. For the first, the structure may represent a major safety hazard; for the second it may have profound significance as the site of a critical event; for the third, it may be an example of a particular architectural style. One and the same building presents different profiles to different persons precisely as function of their questioning. "Our questioning only opens up the horizon in order that the essent may dawn in such questionableness."[4] Here, Heidegger is indebted to

Edmund Husserl, for in the Husserlian notion of intentionality, the essence of consciousness is not to enter into relationship with a ready-made external object but rather to constitute objects of thought through the giving of meaning.

Now philosophy, for the early Heidegger, represents a peculiar form of questioning, a distinctive intentionality. Unlike the positive sciences, for example, "philosophy has no object to begin with. It is a process which must at all times achieve being (in its appropriate manifestness) anew."[5] As Heidegger describes the situation in his inaugural lecture: The sciences as they are usually practiced have a decidedly ontic intentionality; they are concerned with particular beings and nothing else. Hence the rootedness of the many sciences in their essential ground is obscure to the sciences themselves. Philosophy's interests, on the other hand, are decidedly ontological; for only philosophy transcends particular beings, even all beings conceived of as a whole, to ask the most fundamental question, "Why are there beings at all, and why not rather nothing?"[6]

Philosophy is also different from the practical sciences in that its questioning is not particularly useful. In his *Introduction to Metaphysics* (EM), Heidegger grants that one cannot "do anything" with philosophy; but he insists that this is not the final word. "For the rejoinder imposes itself: granted that we cannot do anything with philosophy, might not philosophy, if we concern ourselves with it, do something with us?"[7] Philosophy is more than a mere exposition of what certain experts called philosophers have held down through the ages. It is rather,

> a thinking that breaks the paths and opens the perspectives of the knowledge that sets the norms and hierarchies, of the knowledge in which and by which a people fulfills itself historically and culturally, the knowledge that kindles and necessitates all inquiries and thereby threatens all values.[8]

In short, philosophy is the most radical kind of questioning possible, and this radical questioning bears a strong resemblance to the basic modification of intentionality which have already seem described in terms of contemplation.

Historically, two misinterpretations of philosophy's task have predominated. One asks too much of philosophy; the other distorts its proper function. By some, philosophy is expected to provide a foundation for the renewal of a whole nation's historical life and culture. It is expected to supply a program, of sorts, for renaissance. Although Heidegger's complicity in the National Socialist movement remains troubling, in 1935, he can be found rejecting in strong (if somewhat elitist) terms the subordination of philosophy to nationalistic aims:

> Philosophy can never directly supply the energies and create the opportunities and methods that bring about a historical change; for one thing, because philosophy is always the concern of the few . . . the creators, those who initiate profound transformations. It spreads only indirectly, by devious paths that can never be laid out in advance, until at last, at some future date, it sinks to the level of the commonplace; but by then it has long been forgotten as original philosophy.[9]

The other misinterpretation is not quite as ambitious as the first, but is equally problematic. Philosophy may be looked to for a comprehensive and systematic view of all things, so as to make life in the practical sphere easier, more predictable, less ambiguous and disordered. But then, philosophy would betray its own nature as the most radical kind of questioning possible—the kind of questioning which sees every answer, every concept, every rule and system as more or less provisional. "[It] is in the very nature of philosophy never to make things easier but only more difficult."[10]

The status of Being as the fundamental topic for questioning and the fact that such a question can only be addressed in terms of human existence—these become evident only when one has reached the most radical of radical questioning, the question about questioning. "Inquiry is a cognizant seeking for an entity both with regard to the fact that it is and with regard to its Being as it is. . . . The inquiry does not become transparent to itself until all these constitutive factors of the question have themselves become transparent."[11]

Being

"Why are there entities rather than nothing?" or "Why are there things which are rather than nothing at all?" Heidegger says from the outset that this is the primordial question, not because it is the first question asked by a person chronologically; indeed it may be asked only in peak moment, or asked not at all.[12] It is primordial in that it is at once the widest, deepest and most fundamental question: It is the widest, because "the range of this question finds its limit only in . . . that which simply is not and never was."[13]   It is the deepest, because in seeking a "why" it seeks a ground, a foundation for all that is.[14] It is the most fundamental, because it seeks not simply a particular or even a multitude of particulars, but that which simply is, without any special preference or differentiation.[15]

But what is the nature of this ground after which the question searches? The precise form of the question as asked excludes the interpretation of ground as simply another entity—even a "super entity"—which explains everything else there is. "Why are there entities rather than nothing at all?" The inclusion of the second part to the question does not simply serve to contrast that which is with that from which it may have obtained its being. Rather, the question holds out entities over the abyss of non-being. "Why is the essent torn away from the possibility of nonbeing?   Why does it not simply keep falling back into nonbeing?"[16]

> [A] ground is sought which will explain the emergence of the essent as an overcoming of nothingness. The ground that is now asked after is the ground of the decision for the essent over against nothingness, or more precisely, the ground for the oscillation of the essent, which sustains and unbinds us, half being, half not being, which is also why we can belong entirely to no thing, not even to ourselves . . . [17]

According to Heidegger, the mood or state of mind in which one is brought before nothingness is that of anxiety or *Angst*. Unlike fearfulness which implies a more or less determinate object; anxiety is distinguished precisely by its indeterminate character. One becomes anxious not because of some thing, but rather because there is no thing to hold on to. Paradoxically, this encounter with the Nothing is the very condition of possibility for the knowledge of any being whatever: "In the clear night of the Nothing of anxiety, the original openness of beings as such arises: that they are beings and not nothing." Only in the contingency and aloneness of anxiety, does human existence encounter beings in their radical otherness.[18]

Here again, though contemplation is not invoked explicitly, it is evident that what Heidegger is describing is a contemplative intentionality. Although we are rarely aware of it, anxiety is always present in us—even if "asleep." "In secret alliance with the cheerfulness and gentleness of creative longing . . . it can awaken in existence at any moment. It needs no unusual event to rouse it. Its sway is as thoroughgoing as its possible occasionings are trivial. It is always leading, though it only seldom springs, and we are snatched away and left hanging."[19] The place occupied by the speculative/practical dynamism of human spirit within the framework of transcendental Thomism seems in Heidegger to be occupied by the concept of *Angst*. But in Heidegger, it should be noted, the nothingness which brings about dynamic *Angst* pertains primarily to the sphere of freedom—that which, in Thomism, is considered under the category of will rather than intellect.

Heidegger also notes that this primordial question presumes that a preliminary question has been answered. He does not express this preliminary question as might be expected from a common sense viewpoint: "What is Being?" Rather he asks, "How does it stand with Being?" His intention seems to be twofold: First he wants to avoid all entitative and reifying notions of Being, since they tend to conceal the fact that we are not seeking a "super entity" to put an end to all our questioning, but entertaining the possibility of there being or having been nothing at all. Secondly, Heidegger wants to make it clear that there is no direct trajectory to Being; like every other aspect of experience, Being is meaningfully constituted only in the human relation to it. Hence, the best we can do is to determine how it presently stands with Being and our understanding of it.[20]

As metaphysics has traditionally been practiced in the West, the question of Being, more often than not, has been forgotten or trivialized. The very theme which provided a stimulus for the thought of Plato and Aristotle has paradoxically receded from view, overshadowed by a preoccupation with their doctrines rather than than with the effort to engage Being itself.[21] In the wake of logical positivism, the one who inquires about Being is "charged with an error of method," because he is trying to delimit the most universal concept, to define what is indefinable, and to explain what is self-evident.[22] Heidegger grants that an understanding of Being is already included in any apprehension of an entity, but he argues that the universality at stake here is not that of class or genus. Rather, the concept of Being has a transcategorial universality which is *sui generis* and makes it "the darkest of all [concepts]" and hence the most needful of further questioning.[23] Likewise, Heidegger grants the indefinability of Being which flows from its universality; he is simply unwilling to accept this as an excuse for the prohibition against raising the question of its meaning.[24] And as for its alleged self-evidence, there is no doubt that man regularly employs the concept of Being in his cognitive activity. But this fact does not point to a kind of self-evidence which settles a question once and for all. There is something enigmatic about our employment of the concept of Being in the cognition of entities: "The very fact that we already live in an understanding and that the meaning of Being is still veiled in darkness proves that it is necessary in principle to raise this question again."[25]

These peculiarities of the concept of Being are not taken by Heidegger as indicative of the futility of asking the question about Being. Rather, they are indicative of the fact that the way of access to Being will differ in some sense from the way of access to entities. In a sense, involvement in the world of entities is a necessary, but by no means sufficient, precondition for access to Being.[26] If we are correct in associating the encounter with the Nothing which takes place in Heideggerian *Angst* with the contemplative dynamism identified by the transcendental Thomists, then the one who is entirely absorbed by the world of entities and fails to recognize the need to treat Being differently may be thought of as non-contemplative. It remains for us to see the precise sense in which the access to Being differs from access to entities.

Dasein

If our intention is to get to the meaning of Being, we need to look at the Being of that entity which is asking about Being.[27] The selection of human existence as the locus for the discovery of the meaning of Being is not based on a naïve or exagerrated sense of man's importance in the universe. In terms reminiscent of the eighth psalm, Heidegger emphasizes man's smallness:

> For what indeed is man? Consider the earth within the endless darkness of space in the universe. By way of comparison it is a tiny grain of sand; between it and the next grain of its own size there extends a mile or more of emptiness; on the surface of this grain of sand there lives a crawling, bewildered, swarm of supposedly intelligent animals, who for a moment have discovered knowledge.[28]

The basis for the selection of human existence is not its relative greatness, but its distinctiveness: It is distinguished by the fact that, among known entities, human beings are the only entitities for whom Being is an issue. In other words, constitutive of human being is an interest in Being—construed, of course, in many different ways. This interest indicates the presence of a pre-reflexive disposition on the part of human beings toward Being.[29]

And so, Being is to be sought after through an analytic of human being understood specifically as *Dasein*. This expression, literally "to be there," makes clear that the analytic to be pursued will be no mere accounting of material conditions and psychological processes unique to an animal rationale interpreted in a wholly abstract sense. Rather, the analytic of *Dasein* will be pursued through a painstaking phenomenology of human existence designed to reveal the basic structures of human existence and, hopefully, their ontological basis.[30] In fact, the only source for a truly fundamental ontology can be found in the existential analytic of *Dasein*. Unlike ontotheology, which resorts to theology for the resolution of its problematic—positing a highest entity to explain the being of all other entities—fundamental ontology stays with human existence in all its worldliness and temporality.[31]

The analytic of *Dasein* is executed in two movements: 1) The phenomenological description of human existence as Being-in-the-world is 2) brought into relation with its ultimate meaning, i.e. Being-in-time. As Being-in-the-world, the human person is always seeking to restructure his power to be through understanding (*Verstehen*) and, at the same time, must cope with the givenness of his concrete situation (*Geworfenheit and Verfallenheit*). In other words, *Dasein* cannot forgo intercourse with the mundane; hence, the structural whole of human being in *Sorge*, i.e. care or solicitude. But, as we noted in our earlier discussion of retrieval, the description of human nature in terms of *Sorge* can lay no claims to primordiality, but itself presupposes a more fundamental ontological foundation, namely, temporality. Therefore, if Being can be known only in its relation to *Dasein*, and *Dasein* has as its ontological foundation temporality, then Being can be known only in time, and all claims to have completely grasped Being must be judged, from the outset, to be false. Hence, even after we have determined that the primordial ontological principle in *Dasein* is temporality, there is infinitely more to be said about Being. In other words, between the Being, the meaning of which we seek to discover, and the Nothing, which is the abyss over which we hold ourselves in the asking of a fundamental question, is the Appearing of Being which takes place in human thinking and activity over time. As long as such thinking continues, we can never claim to have fully grasped the meaning of Being—or of Nothing, for that matter.[32] Being remains, in a sense, largely concealed.

Now let us be clear about what Heidegger is saying here. It is not simply that the human intellect is too limited to handle Being in its totality. Rather, concealment belongs to Being essentially. In his interpretation of a fragment from the writings of Heraclitus he brings this out explicitly:

> Since being means emerging appearing, to issue forth from concealment—concealment, its origin in concealment, belongs to it essentially. This origin lies in the essence of being, of the manifest as such. Being inclines back toward it, both in great silence and mystery and in banal distortion and occultation.[33]

In his later essay, "On the Essence of Truth," Heidegger emphasizes that concealment is not an undesirable and avoidable exigency of human knowledge; it is—along with the unconcealment which complements it—the unavoidable and essential character of Being itself. "Letting be," which is what one must do if she hopes to attain the truth of things, is "intrinsically, at the same time, a concealing," because letting be always lets Being be in a particular way."[34] In a sense, this concealment is more original than any particular disclosure of being, and thus holds sway throughout human existence.[35] This concealment is mystery, which may be rightly called "the proper non-essence of truth" (provided that "non-essence" is not invested with the connotation of inferiority).[36]

In light of all this, then, it is not the original concealment of Being which is problematic for Heidegger; what is of greatest concern to Heidegger is the extent to which Western man has forgotten that all this is the case, and has put his all-too-limited conceptions of being in the place of gods. Western metaphysics is forgetful of its origins. In the absolutization of "tradition," one or another of the limited ways in which Being has been understood is presented as "self-evident," effectively "block[ing] our access to the primordial sources from which the categories and concepts handed down to us have been in part quite genuinely drawn."[37] This is why Heidegger puts so much emphasis on the etymology of the various Greek terms which eventually become traditionalized in Western metaphysics. There was in the Ancient Greek experience of Being something basic and primal which we have lost and must recover. We have fallen away from what the word "Being" says, "and for the moment cannot find our way back." He goes on:

> [I]t is for this and no other reason that the word "being" no longer applies to anything, that everything, if we merely take hold of it, dissolves like a tatter of cloud in the sunlight. Because this is so—that is why we ask about being. And we ask, because we know that truths have never fallen into any nation's lap.[38]

Symptoms of *Seinsvergessenheit* are everywhere, according to Heidegger. He speaks passionately about the spiritual decline of the earth, diagnosing the world's greatest powers as metaphysically bankrupt. His assessment of the global socio-political situation in the thirties is not irrelevant in the nineties:

> From a metaphysical point of view, Russian and America are the same; the same dreary technological frenzy, the same unrestricted organization of the average man. At a time when the farthestmost corner of the globe has been conquered by technology and opened to economic exploitation; when any incident whatever, regardless of where or when it occurs can be communicated to the rest of the world at any desired speed . . . when time has ceased to be anything other than velocity, instantaneousness, and simultaneity, and time as history has vanished from the lives of all people; when a boxer is regarded as a nation's great man; when mass meetings attended by millions are looked on as a triumph, then yes then, through all this turmoil a question still haunts us like a specter: What for? Whither?—And what then?[39]

Heidegger was convinced that nihilism (the epithet sometimes used to describe various species of existential philosophy) was not the outcome of an ontology which saw temporality as fundamental, eschewed all final answers and solutions, and did its work through deconstruction. The true nihilism is satisfaction with what today passes for knowledge: A preoccupation with particular entities and a rejection of the question of Being as unimportant. Treating Being like a Nothing (*nihil*)—this is the true nihilism which can only be overcome, not simply by persuing the question of Being, but by pursuing it to the very limits of nothingness.[40]

Fundamental Ontology as a Contemplative Exercise of Rationality

Since it is a "way of thinking" above all which Rahner claims to have taken from Heidegger, a couple of clarifications should be made about his procedure. Heidegger was aware that his method might be criticized for its apparent circularity. There is something slippery about seeking the meaning of Being in the being which has been defined precisely in terms of a comportment toward Being. He responds to this argument in two ways. First of all, what has been detected in such an objection is not circularity but facticity: In his very Being-in-the-World, man finds himself concerned with Being. One may take this fact as a starting point without yet having in mind an explicit concept of the meaning of Being. Being, however it may eventually be worked out, must be presupposed if the investigation is to make an progress at all. Indeed, without some at least vague anticipatory grasp of Being, no being, no entity at all could be articulated.[41]

However, Heidegger provides a second and, in some ways, more telling response to the circularity objection. Such an argument has no force in the assessment of a concrete way of investigating, since it is founded merely on an abstract first principle.[42] It is not that one may casually abrogate the basic laws of formal logic. Rather, Heidegger's point seems to be that, prior to and more fundamental than the first principles we use in argumentation, is the concrete experience in which those principles are forged or come to light. As opposed to an ontical inquiry which takes those principles for granted in the consideration of particular entities and kinds of entities, a truly ontological inquiry must start in the primal experience where even these "self-evident" principles are no longer taken for granted. Real scientific progress is made not through the mere collection of data according to laws everyone accepts; real scientific progress is made through reflection on the constitution of meaning.[43]

This methodological point is of profound significance for our effort to bring out the contemplative aspect of rationality in Rahner by the light of a Heideggerian influence. With Husserlian phenomenology in the background, Heidegger could not content himself with a purely deductive approach which presumes the possibility of subsuming discrete bits of pristine sense data under abstract rules which apparently bare no intrinsic relation to sensibility. To begin with, such an approach can never really account for the unification of thought with the world which takes place in knowledge, because it starts out with a fundamental duality.[44] Moreover, by treating sense experience in its first occurence as if it were wholly innocent of and separate from the intellect, the purely deductive method overlooks the highly significant way in which all experience reveals movement and direction in its very genesis.

The goal of a fundamental ontology, then, is not to ground something by a deductive derivation; "it is rather one of laying bare the grounds for it and exhibiting them."[45] Whatever serious differences must be admitted between the thought of Heidegger and that of Ignatius, Rousselot, and Maréchal, this much at least may be said to held in common: *To get to the truth in some ultimate and fundamental sense—whether that truth be identified as the ground of all things in Absolute Being, the will of God for this or that individual, or the meaning of Being—one must adopt from the outset an attitude of radical openness and receptivity, the attitude which I have called contemplative.* Although these four figures would have disagreed with each other as to the extent the others had followed this largely implicit but absolutely essential principle, it is evident that a similiar intentionality characterizes them all.

At the same time, it is important to be cognizant of what is distinctive in Heidegger's thought: For him, the attitude of radical openness is not merely an initial posture or an occasional methodological exigency; rather, it characterizes the analytic of *Dasein* from beginning to end:

> [The analytic of *Dasein*] merely brings out the Being of this entity, without interpreting its meaning. It is rather a preparatory procedure by which the horizon for the most primordial way of interpreting Being may be laid bare. Once we have arrived at that horizon, this preparatory analytic of *Dasein* will have to be repeated in a higher and authentically ontological basis.[46]

This attitude, according to Heidegger, is the polar opposite of dogmatism. No matter how self-evident some particular idea of Being may seem, no matter how useful the familiar categories for talking about Being may be, one "must choose such a way of access and such a kind of interpretation that this entity can show itself in itself and from itself."[47] This way "is directly opposed to the naïvté of a haphazard, immediate, and unreflective 'beholding.'"[48] Hence the movement which Heidegger detects in Being is not a relative dynamism, as it had been for the Thomists and for Ignatius—the comprehension of which is limited simply by the metaphysics of human cognition. Heidegger's is an absolute dynamism, a dynamism without term which holds out human existence over the abyss of nothingness.

Are we thereby condemned to sheer relativism? Does his method simply amount to "shaking off of the ontological tradition"? Not necessarily. "We must, on the contrary, stake out the positive possibilities of that tradition, and this always means keeping it within its limits; these in turn are given factically in the way the question is formulated at the time and in the way the possible field for investigation is thus bounded off."[49]

However, it would be a mistake to identify the limits of which Heidegger speaks with the affirmation of Absolute Being we have seen elsewhere. One consequence of the radical dynamism of philosophical questioning is the exclusion of the possibility of a "Christian philosophy." To *really* ask the question, "Why are there entities rather than nothing?"—that is, to ask it in such a way that the "Nothing" is genuinely and not just hypothetically confronted—"is to push our questioning to the very end."[50] For the person of Christian faith, says Heidegger, this kind of radical questioning is impossible, since God's existence is already affirmed by a believer with absolute certitude. From the Christian point of view, philosophy is sheer foolishness and "Christian philosophy" an oxymoron.

Still, even if Heidegger is correct with regard to the impossibility of a Christian philosophy, there is no *a priori* reason why other aspects of his methodology could not be brought to bear within the arena of religious thought. There is a historicity and an asceticism about Heidegger's way of thinking which is reminiscent of and compatible with the historical and ascetical emphases we have seen in our Christian sources.

In terms of historicity, Heidegger was convinced that no purely abstract and deductive analysis could shed light on the question of being. *Only an analysis of human existence explicitly aware of its own roots and articulation in the world and in time can hope to make progress in its inquiry into being.*[51] It is not difficult to see the connection between this requirement and the transcendental emphasis on the roots of knowledge in sense experience and the Ignatian emphasis on the imagination.

With regard to the ascetical element: With Heidegger, we end up where we began, namely *in question.* At the start of this chapter, we saw how questioning expressed the human will to know, the state of being resolved (resoluteness). In *Being and Time*, resoluteness is elaborated in relation to conscience as "authentic Being-one's-self" as opposed to exercising an "empty *habitus.*" Heidegger associates a unique kind of discourse with each of these contrasting notions of conscience. In the latter case, where conscience is equated with doing what "they" say is best, discourse amounts to "loud, idle talk." But for one who "wants to have conscience"—i.e. to have conscience in the sense putting one's entire existence into a will—the characteristic mode of discourse, paradoxically, is reticence:

> [T]he discourse of the conscience never comes to utterance. Only in keeping silent does the conscience call; that is to say, the call comes from the soundlessness of uncanniness, and the *Dasein* which it summons is called back into the stillness of itself, and called back as something that is to become still.[52]

Only in the reticence of wanting to have a conscience can one be ready for that *Angst* which brings one before the Nothing, and therefore, Being. As he puts it in his *Introduction to Metaphysics*: "To know how to question means to know how to wait, even a whole lifetime, . . . [for] the essential is not number; the essential is the right time, i.e. the right moment and the right perseverance."[53]

Hence, if we are correct in identifying the Heideggerian confrontation with the Nothing as the contemplative dimension in his unique brand of rationality, then it is clear that asceticism is as integral to Heideggerian contemplation as it was to the Ignatian variety. For Heidegger, *the asceticism of a careful thinking which refuses to allow itself comfortable repose in any particular concept or system—even the concept of God or the system of religion—safeguards the freedom of the human being to know whatever there is to know and to be what he is called in the depths of his conscience to be, the freedom of everything which exists to be and to be in precisely the way that it is.* Notwithstanding the Heideggerian ambivalence about Christianity, there can be no doubt that his strongly ascetical emphasis also contributed significantly to the development of the conceptual horizon which Karl Rahner brought to philosophy and theology.

Part Three

The Contemplative Dimension
of Rationality

VIII

Contemplative Method:
A Question about Human Existence
as a Totality

Executing the Retrieval: An Introduction to Part III

In the first part of this study, we established the reason/revealtion problematic
in contemporary form and provided some preliminary indications as to the
contribution which the twentieth century theologian and philosopher Karl
Rahner may have to make to the discussion. In the second part, we proposed
the hermeneutics of retrieval as a way of bringing out with greater clarity the
contemplative aspect of Rahner's thought and provided the basis for that
retrieval in an overview of three dominant influences on the development of his
conceptual horizon.

Notwithstanding the significant differences among the influences
considered, a certain agreement was found to exist among them with respect to
the nature and importance of contemplation. Whereas in Part I the
contemplative dimension emerged as a certain constellation of characteristics
discernible in human intellectual activity as it is described by Rahner, in Part II
contemplation itself emerges as a prominent theme in the writings of those
thinkers who were most important to him: *It is a free modification of
intentionality, whereby a human person adjusts his intellectual and moral
orientation from the myriad finite particulars, concepts, and systems which
normally command his attention to that inner dynamism whereby all knowledge
is attained and all action is accomplished. In this attitude, a person comes to
recognize the utter poverty of all that is ordinarily included under the title of
knowledge and the limits of every good that he can achieve or acquire and
opens himself up to infinite possibility. As a specifically human activity,*

contemplation is always exercised in space and time, involving the collaboration of sensibility and imagination in an individual. But because human knowledge also involves a preconceptual affirmation of that which is more than or beyond the world of space and time, contemplation involves the kind of asceticism which is necessary to safeguard freedom—the freedom of the human being to know what there is to know and to be what he/she is called to be, the freedom of everything which exists to be and to be precisely in the way that it is.

What remains to be accomplished in the third and final section of this study, is to execute the retrieval prepared for by Part II and then to work out the implications of our findings for the resolution of the problematic which was described in Part I. That which follows is based on a careful reading of several texts representative of Rahner's later thought (1974-1984), through the lens of the notion of contemplation described above.[1] Among the works considered, one in particular assumes pride of place, because its expressed purpose, to give "an intellectually honest justification of Christian faith,"[2] dovetails nicely with the objective of the present project. This work, *Grundkurs des Glaubens* (the English is entitled *Foundations of Christian Faith*) was, as its German title suggests, based upon a basic course in the idea of Christianity which Rahner gave first in Munich, then in Münster. Though the external stimulus for the course was the desire of the Second Vatican Council for "a better integration of philosophy and theology" in priestly formation to be effected through "an introductory course of suitable duration,"[3] the course and the book based upon it addressed a concern present in Rahner's thought from the beginning of his philosophical career. The task of Foundations does not, in the final analysis, differ dramatically from what Rahner described in the late 1930's as the goal of Christian philosophy in general, namely to be a *praeparatio evangelii*—the formation of a person capable of hearing a word addressed to him by God which does not offend or violate his human existence but completes and fulfills it.[4]

In the context of the present project, *Foundations* is a particularly valuable source, because it seeks to provide a rational justification for faith explicitly in light of the changed historical situation of the post-modern West. No mere repetition of the traditional proofs for God's existence, for example, will suffice in the contemporary setting, if for no other reason than on account of the extraordinary pluralism—both interdisciplinary and intradisciplinary—which exists in contemporary thought and could not have been foreseen and is not addressed by the authors of the scholastic manuals or still less by Aquinas himself.[5]   Rahner writes rather of "situat[ing] Christianity within the intellectual horizon of people today."[6]   The relevance of such a project to our concern, the reason/revelation problematic in its contemporary form, is self-evident.   Accordingly, in the discussion which follows, our retrieval of a contemplative dimension from Rahner's late writings, will proceed according to the general outline of the Introduction and first two chapters of Rahner's *Foundations*.[7]   The other material which I have considered for retrieval—interviews, devotional writing, and essays—will be treated primarily in connection with themes raised in this text.

From the outset it must be noted that the project of retrieving a contemplative dimension from Rahner's thought poses a peculiar difficulty. It is not as if contemplation were itself a theme which is identified and worked out neatly at one point in *Foundations*, for example, and then systematically applied to other dimensions of the discussion there. Quite to the contrary, contemplation, or the contemplative dimension of life and thought, is present everywhere in the book, even though it is nowhere explicitly identified. In fact, when *Foundations* is read in light of the notion of contemplation which was elaborated in Part II of the present project, it may be seen as implicitly operative on at least three different levels.

First of all, contemplation may be seen as characterizing the very path by which Rahner proceeds through his investigation. We have already seen the importance of questioning as a distinctively human activity and prime mode of human access to Being.[8]   What Rahner does in his "primary plane of reflection" amounts to the raising of *a question about* human existence as a totality. The very raising of such a question reveals a contemplative dimension to rationality which is concealed by and to be clearly distinguished from any kind of rationalism. Hence, I will argue in the present chapter that the very method which Rahner describes and employs, as well as the epistemological principles which underlie it, may aptly be described as contemplative.

Secondly, contemplation may be viewed as an implicit but essential component of a complete definition of the human person. In terms of the questioning which we have identified as a distinguishing mark of humanity, contemplation consists not only in the raising of *a question about* human existence but also in the remarkable capacity of the human being himself *to be placed in question*. Hence, in the next chapter, I argue that weaving in and out of everything Rahner has to say about the situation of the human person in the world is an unnamed but omnipresent contemplative capacity. Contemplation will be recognized as characterizing, not only Rahner's methodology, but also his anthropology.

Finally, contemplation may be seen as presupposed within the Rahnerian model of revelation. In the language of questioning: Contemplation is the only modality in which the human person may experience himself *as questioned*, i.e. as addressed in such a way by others, his world, and ultimately by God, as to require a response. The myriad questions and one great question which are addressed to a human being throughout his/her life may not be heard except by one who is in a contemplative posture. Hence, in the final chapter, I will argue that, for Rahner, revelation itself does not occur—nor does it even make sense as a concept—apart from contemplative thinking and living. In short, the contemplative dimension of rationality is a condition of possibility for revelation.

Method: A First Level of Reflection
The Asceticism of Careful Intellectual Reflection

The project undertaken in *Foundations* had as its external stimulus the call of the Second Vatican Council for an introductory course which would demonstrate the credibility of Christianity's central idea. Rahner is careful to remind his reader that establishing credibility is no simple undertaking, whereby one is merely inspired by the attractiveness of Christianity, makes a personal decision to believe, and then returns to his or her normal activities without further ado. *Foundations* "is meant to be an introduction within the framework of intellectual reflection." If it is to be successful, the undertaking will be "patient, laborious, and at times tedious."[9] The introduction to the idea of Christianity will involve an asceticism not unlike that for which Heidegger called in his rethinking of the question of Being: Control of the desire for quick results and easy answers and a willingness to be engaged in a reflection upon human existence which is neither so abstract as to exhibit no connections whatsoever to the concrete experience of individual persons, nor so delivered over to the immediacy of isolated human experiences that it loses sight of its object in the absolute and incomprehensible mystery of God.

Rahner self-consciously strives to remain with and not reductionistically to resolve the tension between human finitude and the infinite term of its intellectual and moral dynamism. Although his method here as elsewhere may be described as transcendental—at least to the extent that he assumes an anthropological starting point and proceeds by way of reflection upon human existence—it should be noted that such a starting point and procedure do not *a priori* exclude the transcendent but actually precontain the transcendent as origin and goal:

> For a Christian, his Christian existence is ultimately the totality of his existence. This totality opens out into the dark abysses of the wilderness which we call God. When one undertakes something like this, he stands before the great thinkers, the saints, and finally Jesus Christ. The abyss of existence opens up in front of him. He knows that he has not thought enough, has not loved enough, and has not suffered enough.[10]

These words of Rahner suggest more than typical methodological restraint. They are not merely a *pro forma* admission of the limitations of the author's competence or of the scope of his work. They are instead an important indication of the very nature of project which *Foundations* undertakes. No one can show or hope to be shown that it is possible to be a believer with intellectual honesty who has not first recognized the radical limitations of his own situation and perspective and the infinite possibilities for thought, action, and existence which lie before him. *Foundations* is a contemplative work intended for the contemplative reader.

Rahner is careful to contextualize his investigations historically, and to show how such historical consciousness is essential to exhibiting the intelligibility of the idea of Christianity. There is, he says, a "permanent and insurmountable difference" between the original Christian actualization of existence and any reflection upon it.[11] The latter will never be wholly adequate to the former, because the former is is always taking place in space and time, is never complete, and is directed ultimately toward that which lies outside of space and time. Hence, even if something like an introduction to the idea of Christianity has already been worked out in Thomas' *Summa Contra Gentiles,* for example, it will still be important to make fresh efforts at such reflection upon the whole of Christianity. All such efforts "are always conditioned, since it is obvious that reflection in general, and all the more so scientific theological reflection does not capture and cannot capture the whole of this reality which we realize in faith, hope, love, and prayer."[12]

The reflex consciousness of the conditioned quality of all knowledge which Rahner's thought exhibits is not merely an exigency of contemporary hermeneutics but also has ancient and venerable evangelical motives. In his "Ignatius Speaks to a Jesuit of Today," for example, Rahner does not hesitate to place on the lips of his spiritual forebearer an encouragement to study Marx, Freud, and Einstein, so as "to evolve a theology which can touch the ear and heart of men today."[13]   One cannot expect the contemporary person to listen for or to hear a word addressed to him by God in history if that word cannot be shown to have something to do with his concrete situation.

The Situation Today: Recognizing the Pluralism of Knowledge
What is it that characterizes the contemporary cultural situation relative to the possibility of being a believer with intellectual honesty? In contrast to the Catholic religious milieu of the first part of this century (not to mention the religious milieu prior to the Enlightenment) where the faith, religious existence and prayer of the theology student, for example, could be taken for granted; the contemporary addressee of theology does not feel so secure in his or her faith or feel supported by a homogeneous religious milieu common to everyone.[14] Surely, there have always been elements of secular thought and experience which could not be easily integrated into a Christian world view; the situation at the University of Paris during the thirteenth century is a case in point. "But in former times," says Rahner in an essay from the *Schriften* on faith, "such relics of an experience subjectively already existing but not yet positively integrated into a homogenous Christian world-view were comparatively slight, if only because people knew nothing at all about many secular facts relevant to faith but difficult to integrate."[15] A theology which does not take into account this prior attitudinal or dispositional factor will never fulfill its objectives—and this is precisely what Rahner believed was beginning to happen in theology in late twentieth century Catholic theology:

If theology students today live in a situation of crisis for their faith, then the beginning of their theological studies must help them, so far

as this is possible, to overcome this crisis of their faith honestly. . . .
[The theological disciplines are] too much scholarship for its own
sake, . . . too splintered and fragmented to be really able to respond in
an adequate way to the personal situation of theology students today.[16]

What Rahner has to say about the addressee of contemporary theology also
applies *mutatis mutandis* to the situation of the addressee of the Christian
message in general. To say that Rahner's own method in *Foundations* is
contemplative is to say, in part, that it is reflective about its own starting point
and the extent to which that starting point corresponds to that of the person
whose experience it seeks to clarify.

Rahner admits that he is not the first one to attempt to achieve the
synthesis of an otherwise fragmented situation in theological studies. The
Tubingen theologians attempted something of the same sort during the
nineteenth century. Encyclopedists like Staudenmaier "wanted to make the
difference between theology and philosophy and between reason and revelation
intelligible in the light of their equally original interrelationship."[17] Their
original and quite valid intention was to show how a coherent theology could be
reconstructed out of the plurality of theological disciplines by starting from
their original unity. Where Rahner says the encyclopedists failed—and where
we must not—was in the loss of contact with theology's content.[18] By
neglecting the origin of all clear conceptual knowledge and faith affirmations
in a primitive and unencompassable human experience, these early attempts at
synthesis lapsed into formalism. *In a contemplative method, by contrast, the
synthetic unity of theology is not the human achievement of a subsequent and
artificial unification of the radically plural on a purely formal level. It is
rather an effort to dispose oneself to an original experiential unity which
ontologically precedes but does not obliterate the inescapable pluralism of
ordinary human knowledge and existence.* And so, instead of quickly
dispensing with the staggering pluralism which seems inimical to
demonstrating the unity and intelligibility of the idea of Christianity, Rahner
takes the time to remain with (i.e. he conTEMPlates) the pluralism for awhile,
probing its depths and its implications.

Pluralism in Theology and the Secular Sciences. To begin with, there is
an overwhelming pluralism within theology itself, both in terms of method and
material. For example, it is by no means certain that a systematic theologian, a

biblical exegete, and church historian will meet with much greater success in an interdisciplinary discussion than would a physicist, chemist, or biologist. In addition to the virtual impossibility of one's attaining a comprehensive grasp of a field other than one's own, the various branches of theology face a problem peculiar to the human sciences, a problem which the natural sciences, for the most part, escape: "[I]n the human sciences the real understanding of an assertion and the evaluation of its validity depend upon one's personal participation in the discovery of what is asserted. And it is precisely this which is no longer possible in theology for the representative of another discipline."[19]

Moreover, theological pluralism inevitably assumes new dimensions in the situation of a world church. Certainly, Roman Catholicism has always been, in intention at least, a universal religion. But theoretical and technological advances, particularly in history and anthropology, in transportation and communication, have brought about a fuller realization of that universalizing intention. In a world where people are more aware of the immense cultural variation which occurs around the globe, where those who were once assumed to be "primitive peoples" assume greater importance in the international scene, where Western European culture can no longer make an undisputed claim to normative status—in such a world, it will not do simply to cultivate a uniform Euro-American theology for export to the rest of the Church. "A certain pluralism in theology must exist simply because we are multidimensional human beings, and because the historical and cultural situations in individual countries are not the same . . . theology must adapt to these culturally, historically, and even ethnologically different situations."[20]

Parallel and, to some extent, related to this situation within theology is a staggering philosophical pluralism. We have already seen that the Enlightenment project of developing a "standard weight and measure" actually met with further fragmentation in professional philosophy.[21] If the way in which one works out the reason/revelation problematic (in *Foundations*, the question of whether one can today be a believer with intellectual honesty) depends on one's operative conception of rationality, then the chances of arriving at a single satisfactory resolution are remote in the contemporary scene.

More significant than even this pluralism within philosophy, however, is the fact that philosophy is no longer "the only and obvious juncture where theology comes into contact with secular self-understanding."[22] Whereas, at one time, philosophy could be counted on to provide a more or less comprehensive statement of man's self-perception or, at the very least, to mediate the discussion among several different participants in an interdisciplinary dialogue, today the situation is radically changed.

In sum, the once modest pluralism with the field of knowledge as a whole has multiplied exponentially: Theology itself is divided into a number of disciplines, each with its own peculiar method and object, and is worked out differently in a host of cultural settings. Philosophy, theology's traditional secular dialogue partner, itself is fragmented into a wide range of approaches, from traditional metaphysical Thomism on the one hand to ardently anti-metaphysical and positivistic forms of language analysis on the other. Complicating the situation further is the enormous growth of sciences which are no longer fully encompassed by philosophy, the natural sciences and even the social sciences. And, as if this were not enough, there are also the myriad non-scientific manifestations of the human spirit accessible in the fine arts and in technological and political life.[23] Clearly, then, pluralism with the field of real and possible knowledge is not just a trivial fact which may be noted and then left aside in the effort to work out a rational justification for the idea of Christianity. In Rahner's thought, this pluralism is the irreducible and unavoidable character of the field in which the idea of Christianity today seeks to establish itself.

Pluralism and Agnosticism. In an essay on the justification of faith today, Rahner describes the effects of pluralism in terms of agnosticism: "The enormous amount of knowledge offered leads to uncertainty. The speed at which the sciences are racing into the future makes every individual element of knowledge already acquired appear to be temporary and subject to revision."[24] Such agnosticism must be clearly distinguished from atheism or nihilism which are mistakenly assumed to be its inevitable by-products. Agnosticism, as Rahner describes it, is the unavoidable situation of the human person today with respect to knowledge. One cannot know individually all that is known, one cannot easily fit into the body of one's present knowledge every experience which one has; nor can all knowers know collectively and presently that which will be known eventually. The experience of agnosticism cannot be denied without detriment to the human spirit: "Can one abstain from the experience of this agnosticism without falling into a suffocating banality? Can one do this without losing the ability to take other people and the terrible things that have happened to them really seriously anymore?"[25]

> We no longer live in solid houses of absolutely sound convictions accepted by society at large and everywhere taken for granted, but in tents hastily pitched for a journey into the unforseeable, simply because we know so much and discover new things so quickly and each individual by himself becomes increasingly stupid in face of the range of what as such is immediately knowable or can be 'looked up.' .
> . . [The result is] a diffuse but everwhere prevailing sceptical relativism.[26]

Human knowledge is inescapably partial and provisional, and this fact must be faced squarely by one attempting to give an intellectually honest account of her faith in the contemporary setting.

There are, says Rahner, three different ways in which one can be disposed with regard to this agnosticism. First of all, one can repress this agnosticism by indifference; one may choose to ignore the element of the unfathomable which surrounds all knowledge, "let the matter drop with a certain uneasiness or . . . declare with a certain testiness that things that cannot be spoken of clearly should be left as they are . . . "[27] Secondly, one can read in the agnostic situation evidence of the ultimate meaningless of human existence. An instance of this approach would be "the false and banal agnosticism of the philistine and self-important philosopher," or the atheism of the nineteenth century which, says Rahner, amounts to "bourgeois cleverness." Or else one may adopt that atheism characteristic of the present moment, which is really a practical attitude engendered by "today's rationalistic and technological society," which does not give a negative answer to the question of God but sees no importance in the question itself.[28] Finally, one may discern in the agnostic situation evidence of life's mystery which, on account of its incomprehensibility, is accepted as salvific. This disposition toward agnosticism Rahner identifies as "the essence of faith":

> [O]ne really accepts the incomprehensibility of one's existence, and one does this as a meaningful act of acceptance, one that contains in itself hope. But if one really does this, then God is already basically

accepted, and this actually is what is meant by this word and is ultimately understood only in an acceptance of this kind[29]

We will have more to say about incomprehensibility in the following chapters. It suffices here simply to note that the agnosticism experienced through the consciousness of the radical pluralism and temporality of all knowing—far from being inimical to faith—is taken up within Rahner's contemplative method as a prime opportunity for faith in contemporary culture.

Faith Giving an Account of Itself
How then might we discover that principle of unity according to which the intelligibility of the idea of Christianity may be shown, given the pluralism and agnosticism which mark the contemporary situation? Inasmuch as the accumulated contents of all scientific pursuits theological and secular are continually expanding and evolving, exhibiting no particularly law-like character in themselves, it is evident that these contents alone will never deductively yield such a unifying principle. But this does not mean, therefore, that there is no possibility of giving a justification of the faith in the contemporary setting. Rahner appeals to the traditional Thomistic exemption of the *rudes* from having to reflect thoroughly upon all of the intellectual grounds of credibility on their way to faith:

> In today's situation all of us . . . are and remain unavoidably *rudes* in a certain sense, and . . . we ought to admit that to ourselves and also to the world frankly and courageously.[30]

Therefore, the exemption from having to examine exhaustively the intellectual grounds of credibility (a task which, as we have seen, is impossible in principle) applies today to all believers—theologians and non-theologians alike. This is not a warrant for intellectual laziness and sloth, but an indication of the necessity for an alternative strategy: A justification of the faith on a first level of reflection, where faith gives an account of itself.[31] It would not seem to be going too far to interpret the "first level of reflection" which Rahner urges and undertakes in *Foundations* as a kind of guided contemplation: A basis on which one might freely adjust his intellectual and moral focus from the myriad finite particulars, concepts, and systems which normally command his attention to that inner dynamism whereby all knowledge is attained and all action is accomplished. A more careful consideration of what Rahner means by a "first level of reflection" sustains this interpretation.

To begin with, unlike contemporary "scientific" reflection, the strategy suggested here is focused primarily on the reflective subject and upon the reflecting itself, not on a particular object of reflection. If, therefore, one were to term this first level of reflection "unscientific" and mean by this that it fails to treat comprehensively every last component among the objective contents of faith, one would be justified. If, however, one meant by the term "unscientific" that the investigation was somehow less than careful, rigorous, or exact, one would be mistaken.[32] Rahner compares the first level of reflection to what Newman had described as the "illative sense," whereby knowledge and freedom collaborate in the making of a decision to believe which is honest and responsible even though it is not preceded by an exhaustive scientific survey having a deductively certain outcome. "[A first level of reflection] makes possible, to put it paradoxically, the scientific nature of being legitimately unscientific in such vital questions . . . life and existence require such a level."[33]

On the primary plane of reflection, justification does not consist in proving the objective truth of this or that dogmatic formula or the coherence of all dogmatic formulae taken together. Such a highly formalistic strategy, which prevailed in Catholic theology until the middle of this century and to some extent can still be seen in some utterances of the hierarchical magisterium, is ultimately ineffective. After all, the goal of justification is to give one the confidence that the very content of Christian dogma may be believed with intellectual honesty, not simply that a set of affirmations which have not been shown to bear any necessary connection to one's experience are true in some highly abstract and ahistorical sense.[34] In an essay on the phenomenon of atheism today, Rahner is highly critical of the traditional approach to justification:

In our average textbook philosophy and theology, which forms the basis of our ordinary proclamation, where is there to be found a painstakingly and serious worked out chapter containing a mystagogy which deals with the experience of an inescapable question about God? Among us Christians the traditional teaching of the schools—in contrast to a Pascal, a Newman, or a Gabriel Marcel and others—continues on its merry and rationalistic way to proffer us the traditional proofs of the existence of God which, however objectively unassailable they may be, give us no clue as to how one might go about expressing these rational paradigms in a way that they can be understood as the verbal objectification of an existential process in human beings whereby they silently experience the unfathomable grounding of their existence in the mystery of God.[35]

Although the motivating concern in *Foundations* is not the practical atheist but the new theology student, the operative principal in both cases is the same: On the first level, justification is obtained and mystagogy is pursued through reflection upon Christian existence and its foundations. In the acknowledgement of the poverty of human knowledge and the openness to infinite possibility which inevitably form part of a first level of reflection, may be found that secure basis on which to confirm that one may be a believer today with intellectual honesty. On the first level, it is acknowledged that even religious dogmas, important as they are, cannot fully emcompass religious experience or inspire faith—that one must be led first of all to identify that mystery which one is and that Holy Mystery which is its origin and goal.

What is particularly significant in the context of the present project is the fact that this kind of approach to justification puts us at a level where, says Rahner, there is still a unity of philosophy and theology:

> [W]e are reflecting upon the concrete whole of the human self-realization of a Christian. That is really 'philosophy.' We are reflecting upon a Christian existence and upon the intellectual foundation of a Christian self-realization, and that is basically 'theology.' We are theoretically, practically, and didactically justified in philosophizing here within theology itself, and this 'philosophy' nccd not have any scruples about the fact that it is constantly stepping over into areas that are properly theological.[36]

This seems to turn the usual way of framing the reason/revelation problematic on its head. No longer are we trying to establish a subsequent relationship between two principles or sciences which are originally separate and perhaps contradictory. Rather, by reflecting on the whole of human and Christian existence and its foundations we find philosophy and theology, reason and revelation in their antecedent unity. In such a context, the question is not so much, "How may these two different spheres of knowledge be related?" but "How is it that these spheres of knowledge can be distinguished at all?"

According to Rahner, philosophy and theology are in a differentiated unity which may be seen as entailing three moments. First, there is reflection "upon man as the universal question which he is for himself." It is this man-in-question, as it were, which constitutes the condition which makes hearing the Christian answer possible. Secondly, there is reflection on "the transcendental and historical conditions which make revelation possible." In other words, some effort is made within the paramenters of a first level of reflection to determine the point of mediation between question and answer. Finally, there is reflection on "the fundamental assertion of Christianity as the answer to the question which man is." This last moment is really theology properly speaking.[37]

While we objectify these three moments as separate and distinct, attentiveness to the experience in which they are based shows them to be mutually conditioned and originally united. "The question creates the condition for really hearing, and only the answer brings the question to its reflexive self-presence." Rahner admits that there is a certain circularity to the first level of reflection described in such terms; but in a foundational course, he insists, this circle "is essential and is not supposed to be resolved."[38]

The Contemplative Aspects of Rahner's Method

Beginning with his stated goal in *Foundations*, running through his sustained reflection on pluralism and agnosticism in the field of knowledge, and terminating in his description of that first level of reflection on which philosophy and theology are experienced in their original unity, we have seen then that Rahner's own method is thoroughly contemplative.

As an introduction within the framework of careful intellectual reflection, his method exhibits that asceticism which, as we have seen is an integral component of contemplation. Through the disciplined exercise of freedom, one opens oneself up as fully as one can to what is, assiduously avoids the temptation to facile reductionism of any kind, and allows what is to present itself out of the unfathomable depths of human experience.

In his reflection on the pluralism and temporality of human knowledge, he gives evidence of an awareness of the dynamism of the human spirit, a dynamism which comes into clear view only for one who is in a contemplative posture. That is, we have seen in the opening pages of *Foundations* an actual instance of that free modification of intentionality whereby one is no longer delivered entirely over to finite particulars, concepts, or systems but makes that infinite process by which the finite world is known the object of one's own awareness.

Finally, evidence of a contemplative notion of rationality may also be found in Rahner's contention that faith today can only be justified on a first level of reflection, the level at which one focuses on the totality of one's human and Christian existence and its foundations, rather than on the particular objectifications of faith. In order for faith to be both free and responsible, it must be possible to demonstrate that one is intellectually justified in being a believer. But, in the face of the overwhelming pluralism and contingency which mark the field of knowledge today, such a demonstration cannot consist in finding reason outside of faith to justify faith's affirmation. Rather, the justification of faith in the contemporary situation consists in facing squarely the utter incomprehensibility, the mysteriousness of human existence, and showing that one can trustingly accept and act in accord with this incomprehensibility without doing violence to one's rationality. The ultimate unity of the sciences and of the human experience upon which they reflect cannot be found in any one of these sciences—not even in metaphysics or theology—but only in the incomprehensible God:

> The ultimate unity to be granted to man seeking knowledge pluralistically—already present and yet remaining also a task that is continually new—is the surrender of all knowledge in a *docta ignorantia* to the eternally abiding mystery of God and his underivable will. This unity also, granted and not produced in the entrusting of all pluality to the only radically one God, is part of the task of integrating the pluralism of our knowledge into a unity.[39]

An analysis of Rahner's epistemological presuppositions brings this out the contemplative side of his own procedure with even greater clarity.

Epistemological Foundations: Moving Toward Mystery

At this point, it may seem that Rahner's emphasis on the irreducible pluralism and contingency of human knowledge reflects a kind of subjectivism or, at the very least, a form of idealism.   If so, not only would Rahner's position represent a radical departure from the realism which is thought to be the hallmark of traditional Thomism, but it would also be susceptible to all the critiques which plague classical idealism. Although Rahner attempts, in the Introduction to *Foundations*, to head off some of these epistemological difficulties; what he succeeds best at doing is sketching a conception of rationality which steers clear of any sort of rationalism.

The Real and the Ideal

Ostensibly, the epistemological problematic is raised in this text by the fact that the *Grundkurs* purports to be an introduction to the idea of Christianity (*Begriff des Christentums*). Obviously, this way of describing his task involves Rahner in an implicit distinction between the ideal and the real. "We are dealing with the idea, not the reality immediately; here as nowhere else idea and reality are incommensurate with each other."[40]   Rahner's problem is to show how this distinction can be maintained without leading inexorably to the reductionism characteristic of most dichotomous thinking. Hence, he hastens to add, "on the other hand, nowhere does the idea require turning to the reality itself in order to be understood as much as it does here."[41]

Behind this, of course, is the famous Kantian problem of the *Ding an sich*, the thing-in-itself. In his mature epistemology, Kant rejected the possibility of obtaining knowledge of a thing as it is in itself. Things are known to human knowers only insofar as they affect us through sensibility. In other words, I do not know the tree, but only my experience of the tree. The necessity and universality which is characteristic of a true judgment was not, for Kant, a function of the correspondence between an idea in the mind and a stable reality outside the mind, but of the *a priori* laws of mind by which a subject makes a coherent whole of his experience. Kant described his approach as "critical idealism." This is an idealism only in the sense that it seeks to establish what it is about the mind that makes objective knowledge possible. It neither reduces everything to psychological impressions as Berkeley had done, nor attempts to wholly transcend appearances to get to a God whose existence will undergird the existence of the world, as Descartes had attempted. Rather, it "concerns the sensuous representation of things" in space and time and the laws according to which sensuous representations may be put together.[42]

Unlike Kant, Rahner argues that there is a unity which is antecedent to the relationship between "the purely objective 'in itself' of a reality" and "the 'clear and distinct' idea of it." This unity is located in the knower himself; it is the unity of the reality of a human person's existence and that person's "self-presence." In peak experiences of love or of anguish, for example, the unity between the person's experience and his self-presence cannot be fully mediated by a concept. For example, one is never convinced that the limited ideas expressed by statements like, "I love you" or "I am afraid" have fully conveyed or encompassed the experience one is having. This does not mean that there is not a moment of reflection which belongs to one's original experiential knowledge. To the contrary, language, reflection, communicability, are all aspects of one's original self-possession. What is important, according to Rahner, is that prior to the constitution of scientifically objective concept, an idea as such, is "an inescapable unity in difference between one's original self-possession and reflection."[43]

By contrast, both classical modernism and the theological rationalism devised to combat this modernism resort to reductionisms to overcome the tension between idea and reality. In the former, "the concept or reflection is something *absolutely* secondary in relation to the original self-possession of existence in self-consciousness and freedom, so that reflection could also be dispensed with." In this model, faith is a more or less subjective state which cannot attain nor does it require any objective correlate as its ground and term. In the latter, on the other hand, "a reality is present for man in spiritual and free self-possession only through the objectifying concept, and this becomes genuinely and fully real in scientific knowledge." In this model, the free and subjective aspect of faith is subordinated to an abstract conception of faith's term which compels assent.[44] In both, the basic error is the same: The failure to see that even the most abstract concept has its genesis in experience and conversely that, even in its most primitive form, an experience cannot be had, is not *my* experience, without reflection.

There is a dynamic tension between one's original knowledge and any concept which would mediate it. This tension may be looked at from two points of view. On the one hand, "the original self-presence of the subject in the actual realizaton of his existence strives to translate itself more and more and more into the conceptual, into the objectified, into language." As human beings, we strive to tell others what we are suffering or experiencing. On the other hand, "one who has been formed by a common language, and educated and indoctrinated from without, experiences clearly perhaps only very slowly what he has been talking about for a long time."[45] Hence, the attempt to conceptualize more and more precisely what we have lived and the attempt to show how our concepts are merely the expression of a more primitive experience are equally important and complementary tasks. The reality and the idea of Christianity are, therefore, both irreducible and inextricably related to each other. An approach to the intellectual justification of Christianity which does not take this into account will never succeed.

The Transcendental Analysis of Cognition Revisited

Like Maréchal before him, Rahner adopts Kant's starting point in order to proceed beyond him. Ultimately, his purpose is to show that the intellectual justification for faith in the contemporary situation can only be achieved through reflection upon transcendental experience. He begins by providing a thumb nail sketch of the same basic epistemology which, in his *Spirit in the World,* he had elaborated by way of a painstaking interpretation of Question 84, Article 7 of the *Summa.*

In traditional defenses of epistemological realism, something like a "copy" or "mirror" paradigm is employed to describe how it is that one may know for oneself that which is other than oneself. In all such models, that which is known is thought to be something coming from outside (the "original"), which presents itself according to its own law, thus informing a receptive faculty of knowledge (the "mirror" which registers an image or copy). Such a paradigm, says Rahner, is misleading, since knowledge has a far more complex structure—not to mention all of the difficulties which are entailed in the comparison of an immaterial idea in the mind with a material thing outside the mind. Hence a more careful analysis of the knowing act is required.[46]

Every time a subject posits an act of knowledge, not only is some object known but also known is the subject's knowing. When I say that *I know* that this thing at which I am working is a computer, implicit in such a statement is another, namely, that *I know that I know* that it is a computer. (This is the case whether or not, in a subsequent act of knowledge, I reflect on my own self-presence in my knowledge.)[47] Put differently, it would be self-contradictory to claim to possess knowledge of something and, at the same time, to claim that it is not I who possess this knowledge. This consciousness of my own knowing or self-presence is unthematic. "It is something which goes on, so to speak, behind the back of the knower, who is looking away from himself and at the object."[48] In fact, the moment I thematize this co-known self-presence, thereby making of this subject and its knowing the object of a new act of knowledge, the same thing happens all over again. There is simply no escaping the fact that a subject's presence to itself, its knowing, is implicated in every knowing act—even when the object of that knowing act is knowledge itself.

The fact that in knowledge, not only is something known, but the subject's knowing is always co-known, would merely be a curious triviality were it not for the fact this self-presence of the subject is "the luminous realm . . . within which the individual object upon which attention is focused in a particular primary act of knowledge can become manifest."[49] If we were to visualize the knowing act as a bi-polar relationship between a knowing subject and a known object, what we are saying here would amount to this: The object itself could not appear were it not for a subject conscious of itself and of its act of knowing and, conversely, the subject cannot know itself except in its constitution of a known object.

In knowledge, not only is the subject's knowing and self-presence co-known along with the object, it is also co-determinative: " . . . the structure of the subject itself is an *a priori*, that is, it forms an antecedent law governing what and how something can become manifest to the knowing subject.[50] At first glance this may look like undiluted Kantian idealism, where the forms of sensible intuition, the categories of understanding, and the ideas of reason are said to direct the pursuit and achievement of a scientific knowledge which has no trajectory to things as they are but only to things as they are experienced by us. Rahner, however, is careful to distinguish his position from Kantian agnosticism about the *Ding an sich*. Following Maréchal's analogy of the lock and key, Rahner observes: "A keyhole forms an *a priori* law governing what key fits in, but it thereby discloses something about the key itself."[51] Rahner has no quibble with realism, if to be realistic is to say that we can attain knowledge of things as they really are. Where the more naïve and simplistic defenses of realism fail is in their neglect of the decisive contribution which the subject makes to knowledge. When the Thomistic principle about things being known according to the mode of the knower is applied, it becomes evident that our knowledge of things, excellent as it may be, is still limited and, in an ultimate sense, provisional.

Now the question arises: What is the nature of this subject which is known in its self-presence and act of knowing? Granted: The self-presence to which Rahner refers or the *reditio completa* is always mediated for human knowers by the experience of sense objects in time and space (since the intellect knows nothing without turning to the phantasm). Still, says Rahner, "this subject is fundamentally and by its nature pure openness for absolutely everything, for being as such."[52] Employing the logical technique of retorsion which we saw in Maréchal, Rahner argues that this openness for *Sein überhaupt* is actually confirmed by its denial:

> The denial of such an unlimited openness of the spirit to absolutely everything implicitly posits and affirms such an openness. For a subject which knows itself to be finite, and in its knowledge is not just unknowing with regard to the limited nature of the possibility of its objects, has already transcended its finiteness. It has differentiated itself as finite from a subjectively and unthematically given horizon of possible objects that is of infinite breadth.[53]

The absolute openness which characterizes the knowing subject indicates the presence in the subject of a pre-apprehension (*Vorgriff*) of being as such or God. Only against a pre-conceptual horizon which is completely unlimited can limit—which is the essence of conceptualization—be known. Even if one should suspect for a moment that the subject is intrinsically limited and not pure openness for being as such, he would thereby have posited himself as the subject of such an unlimited *Vorgriff*, "because even the suspicion of such an intrinsic limitation of the subject posits this pre-apprehension itself as going beyond the suspicion."[54] This pre-apprehension points to the distinctive element in the human person, namely, his transcendentality.[55] It does not surprise us to find, therefore, that Rahner's attempt to justify faith intellectually proceeds by way of an appeal to transcendental experience.

Transcendental Experience

Transcendental experience, according to Rahner, is "the subjective unthematic, necessary and unfailing consciousness of the knowing subject that is co-present in every spiritual act of knowledge, and the subject's openness to the unlimited expanse of all possible reality."[56] One cannot hope to show that it is possible to be a believer with intellectual honesty without pointing to this primitive level of experience, for only where there is unlimited openness can an unlimited object of knowledge (of course, God can only be talked about as an "object" of knowledge in an analogous sense) make its appearance. In Rahner's delineation of the elements of transcendental experience, a contemplative aspect again assumes prominence. *Indeed, the appeal to transcendental experience is essentially a directive to consider contemplatively man's contemplative capacity.*

The experience in question is termed "transcendental." Here *transcendental* has a dual force. As it had in Kant's critical philosophy, the term in Rahner's thought points to "the necessary and inalienable structure of the knowing subject itself,"[57] the *a priori* structure of the mind according to which the world is known by a concrete individual subject. *Transcendental*, in this sense, has to do with the conditions of possibility for knowledge.

Unlike Kant, however, Rahner accords to the term *transcendental* a second meaning which he would claim is inseparable from the first. The experience in question "consists precisely in the transcendence beyond a particular group of possible objects or of categories."[58] In other words, pre-eminent among the various conditions of possibility for knowledge is the capacity to reach beyond the field of finite particulars to that infinite horizon in which all of them make their appearance. Given the the description of contemplation provided in Part II of the present project, one could say that it is through contemplation that a person becomes aware of and capable of thematizing this aptitude for *Sein überhaupt*. For, in contemplation, one adjusts one's intellectual orientation from the myriad finite particulars, concepts, and systems which normally command attention to that inner dynamism whereby all knowledge is attained.

It is important to recognize that transcendental experience is not a merely cognitive or intellectual phenomenon, but has to do with the totality of human being, will as well as intellect, freedom as well as knowledge. The same character of transcendentality belongs to them [will and intellect], so that basically one can ask about the source and the destiny of the subject as a knowing being and as a free being together."[59] Here again we see an affinity with the notion of contemplation which we developed out of our earlier sources. The modification of intentionality whereby the inner dynamism of the human spirit comes into view is by definition free. In other words, though the the human spirit is always reaching out for being as such, absolute and unlimited, one may always choose to make this dynamism the object of one's reflection or to ignore it. Moreover, the myriad finite particulars, concepts, and systems which are transcended in the contemplative attitude are "gone beyond" not merely as objects of thought, but as objectives of moral choice. In other words, implicit in every free choice is some end or objective; contemplatively one is able to recognize one's immediate and proximate ends or objectives as limited precisely insofar as one recognizes them against the horizon of the one end or objective which is good and desirable without condition or qualification.

Precisely because transcendental experience is itself the prime condition of possibility for objective knowledge, it can only be spoken of indirectly. In other words, it can never be objectively represented in itself, but only by an abstract concept of it, which itself requires a trans-conceptual reaching beyond. It is not, thereby, less real than an object which may be represented in itself; but it is certainly *sui generis*. This fact, combined with the fact that transcendental experience involves freedom, makes it possible—even likely—that it will be overlooked. Unlike an object which is outside of us and which we "bump up against," this experience is always taking place and lacks the novel attraction of those contingent objects of experience which come and go.[60] One cannot know the world with its pluralism of limited and finite things except against the horizon of that which is, pure and simple; yet the horizon itself may be easily missed. It is as if there were a melody playing in the background which would go unnoticed unless it either stopped suddenly or one freely chose to advert to its presence and effect.

Holy Mystery: The Term of Human Transcendence
As we have already hinted, the inner dynamism of the human spirit which makes a person capable of contemplation and itself comes into view only in the contemplative attitude is not without term or direction. It is has a trajectory toward *Sein überhaupt*. In *Spirit in the World*, where the context is an analysis of Thomas' metaphysics of cognition, this term of human transcendence is talked about as "Absolute Being." In *Foundations*, Rahner talks about it as "Holy Mystery." In transcendental experience, "he whom we call 'God' enounters man in silence, encounters him as the absolute and the

incomprehensible, as the term of his transcendence which cannot really be incorporated into any system of coordinates."[61]

To say that the term of human transcendence is *mystery* is not to say that a being who is in principle comprehensible remains for the moment incomprehensible because of human fraility or failure. It means, rather, that the term of human transcendence is by definition the one whose being cannot be fully encompassed by human knowledge nor attained by human action, but only known through experience.

> The original knowledge of God is not the kind of knowledge in which one grasps an object which happens to present itself directly or indirectly from outside. It has rather the character of a transcendental experience. Insofar as this subjective, non-objective luminosity of the subject in its transcendence is always oriented towards the holy mystery, the knowledge of God is always present unthematically and without name, and not just when we begin to speak of it.[62]

To this extent, one may say that there is an element of self-evidence in an experiential knowledge of God.[63] This is not a self-evidence to be contrasted but rather to be identified with mystery. "All clear understanding is grounded in the darkness of God . . . What is made intelligible is grounded ultimately in the one thing that is self-evident, in mystery."[64] Just as on an objective and conceptual level we found an inventory of the field of knowledge leading to a kind of agnosticism, a recognition of the conditioned and provisional quality of all knowledge; so too on a transcendental level do we find that the very possibility of knowing any finite particular depends on a pre-conceptual affirmation or grasp of that which is without boundary or limit, that which is incomprehensible.

Here again a contemplative dimension evidences itself in the Rahnerian conception of rationality, for it is precisely in contemplation that openness to infinite possibility takes place, i.e. through a recognition of the utter poverty of all that is ordinarily included under the title of knowledge and the limits of every good that can be achieved or acquired. Contemplation, as we saw, entails as a prime condition of its possibility a preconceptual affirmation of that which is more than or beyond the world of space and time. In short, when Rahner talks about mystery as the term of transcendental experience, he is implicitly saying that the experience of mystery cannot be had except by one who is living or thinking contemplatively, except by one who freely and deliberately accords sustained attention not merely to the objects of knowledge and action but also to that which makes possible these objects and the human dynamism by which they are attained.

But Rahner writes not simply of mystery, but of *holy* mystery. At first, this kind of speech might seem to transgress the proper boundaries of a philosophical reflection. To attribute holiness to the mystery which human being is and toward which a human being is directed appears to settle "the God question" prematurely. In truth, however, it is posssible to attribute holiness to the mystery which is the term of human transcendence without being limited to the content of any particular revelation. In this context, holiness describes the human disposition toward the mystery: That for which the human spirit is perpetually reaching out is experienced as *valuable, attractive*, or *worthy*. Mystery is not just a neutral and inert horizon for all objective knowledge; it is the supremely desirable end of all human striving, whether through action or thought (though whether a particular person recognizes it as such at a particular moment is quite another question). This is why, for Rahner, it may be said that authentic knowledge is seen as fulfilled and perfected only through love. Only when the infinite and ineffable horizon of being is sought for its own sake, not merely for the sake of a more limited good, can one be said to have attained knowledge in the fullest sense of the term.[65] In concrete terms: I cannot know fully what I do not love, for only the freedom given to another to be what it is (which is the essence of love) makes it possible for that other to present itself in all its complex beauty. Conversely, when I deny another its freedom to be itself, through mastery and control, that other cannot be expected to appear as it is. And all of this is true, *mutatis mutandis,* whether that which is to be known is a material thing, another human subject, or Holy Mystery.

Here too a contemplative element figures prominently in the description of the term of transcendental experience, for how is the love described above to be realized except through the asceticism of contemplation? Only if one balances a voracious appetite for knowledge with a sober estimate of one's own limits, only if one engages in self-criticism as well as in the proud announcement of the findings of one's research, only if one can filter out one's own preconceptions and biases enough to allow the aspects of experience which might otherwise escape us to make their appearance—only if one exercises one's freedom to think and act in a disciplined way, are the possible objects of our knowledge and action given the freedom to be and to be precisely as they are.

Contemplation: The Difference between Rationality and Rationalism

It is perhaps this aspect of transcendental experience—the contemplative posture of active receptivity, if you will—which most clearly distinguishes rationality from rationalism and Rahner from many modern thinkers both within and outside the Catholic intellectual community.

It is the hallmark of all transcendental Thomism to adopt Kant's starting point in order to proceed beyond him. That starting point is the concrete situation of the individual human subject, particularly the contents of consciousness and the life of the mind. In the Rahnerian analysis of human cognition there is much which looks Kantian: The emphasis on the *a priori* element in knowledge, for example, as well as the acknowledgement of the human mind's dependence on sensible experience. Their conclusions, however, are radically different—different as rationality is from rationalism.

In Part I of the present study, we summarized the Enlightenment conception of rationality in terms of the allegorical description of reason in its scientific employment which Kant provided in his *Critique of Pure Reason.*

> This domain is an island, enclosed by nature itself within unalterable limits. It is the land of truth . . . surrounded by a wide and stormy ocean, the native home of iillusion, where many a fog bank and many a swiftly melting iceberg give the deceptive appearance of farther shores, deluding the adventurous seafarer ever anew with empty hopes and engaging him in enterprises which he can never abandon and yet is unable to carry to completion.[66]

For Kant, to be rational is to remain on the island, whose limits are space and time and whose laws are unchanging. The reasonable person is neither taken in through an uncritical acceptance of the appearances of things material nor misled by the illusory promise of the ideas which the mind itself has generated to give its laws their systematic quality—ideas of God, of the Soul, or of the World. The reasonable person is the abstract, ahistorical subject of the transcendental philosophy.

Even though Kantian philosophy itself no longer dominates the epistemological debate, and the way in which he tried to deduce the *a priori* structure of mind from the natural science and mathematics of his day is widely judged today as inadequate, Kant's basic attitude toward rationality seems still to prevail. The empirical sciences are still looked upon to provide criteria for rationality, and that which does not readily submit to the currently established conventions of the natural or mathematical sciences is looked upon with suspicion. In an essay on "Natural Science and Reasonable Faith," Rahner notes that there prevails today a certain positivism, " . . . that annoyance with metaphysics, that exclusive confinement to what can be demonstrated by direct experiment, which is liable to produce the arrogance of persons who can present their conclusions as beyond dispute, a mentality which does not have much patience with theology."[67]

Rahner's analysis of human cognition—presented only schematically in the Introduction to *Foundations*—also concludes with an allegorical description of reason. Both its superficial similarity to and profound difference from Kant's description are striking:

> For the person who has touched his own spiritual depths, what is more familiar, thematically or unthematically, and what is more self-evident than the silent question which goes beyond everything which has already been mastered and controlled, than the unanswered question accepted in humble love, which alone brings wisdom? In the ultimate depths of his being man knows nothing more surely than that his knowledge, that is what is called knowledge in everyday parlance, is only a small island in a vast sea that has not been travelled. It is a floating island, and it might be more familiar to us than the sea, but ultimately it is borne by the sea and only because it is can we be borne by it. Hence the existentiell question for the knower is this: Which does he love more, the small island of his so-called knowledge or the sea of infinite mystery? Is the little light with which he illuminates this island—we call it science and scholarship—to be an eternal light which will shine forever for him? That would surely be hell.[68]

For Rahner, to be rational is to acknowledge that the limits of all those finite particulars found on the island, as well as of the island itself, are only known in relation to the unlimited depth and breadth of the sea. While the reasonable person will not be taken in through an uncritical acceptance of the appearances of things in space and time, neither will the reasonable person think it possible to escape the contingency of appearances in space and time through appeal to some abstract ahistorical principle. Rather, the reasonable person will recognize as the principal condition of possibility for any spatio-temporal experience whatsoever a pre-apprehension of being as such, which is the only possible ground and *telos* of the unlimited moral and intellectual dynamism of the human spirit. In short, the rational person does not confine himself to the island, because there one is condemned to banality, hopelessly cut off from the origin and goal of one's striving. The rational person ventures out into the deep (which is what happens in faith) or, at the very least, acknowledges that there is something about the deep which is significant and even necessary for human existence on the island (which is what happens in contemplation). Rahner himself seems to have confirmed such a description of his conception of rationality when Meinhold Krauss asked Rahner whether his theology has "its own special brand of rationality." Rahner's response: "I would say that in theology as well as anywhere else one cannot think enough, think intensively enough, courageously enough, and precisely enough. And if you want to call this 'rational,' then I completely agree that my theology is rational. "[69]

The very raising of a question about human existence as a totality—which is what one does when one asks if it is possible to be a Christian today with intellectual honesty—the very raising of such a question reveals a contemplative dimension in rationality which is concealed by any kind of rationalism. By constrast, the philosophical rationalist will consider such a question to be unanswerable in principle, for one element of the question lies at least partially beyond the spatio-temporal framework within which alone one may claim to attain knowledge. At the same time, the theological rationalist will find himself capable of answering without too much effort or exertion, for it will be thought adequate simply to show how coherent are the central ideas of Christianity and how its core idea—the existence of God—may be supported by the traditional proofs.

Different as these rationalistic responses are, they are both decidedly non-contemplative; that is, their overriding concern is the array of finite particulars and the concepts and systems through which these are objectified and systematized, rather than the transcendental experience in which all objective knowledge is rooted. They are at once too optimistic and too pessimistic about the power of mind: In the case of philosophical rationalism, thinking that one has no need to reach beyond spatio-temporal boundaries to make sense of human existence and, at the same time, claiming that the human mind has no capacity for the infinite; in the case of theological rationalism, thinking that the incomprehensible God can be made comprehensible through formulas and, at the same time, fearing that grounding the justification of faith in transcendental experience will lead ultimately to atheism.

Rahner's position provides an alternative both to classical modernism and to the theological rationalism devised to combat it. By reaching beyond the cleavage between the real and the ideal to that unity of self-possession and reflection which marks human experience on its most primitive and original level, Rahner brings to light the genesis of all conceptual knowledge in experience and the necessity of objectifying reflection for the attainment of knowledge.

On this more original level, the level of transcendental experience, the co-known and co-determinative presence of the subject to itself which is implicated in every knowing act also comes to light. No human knowledge occurs apart from this unthematic and unfailing consciousness which the human subject has of itself and its openness to everything that is. The appeal by Rahner to transcendental experience amounts to a call to consider contemplatively one's own contemplative capacity. With this procedure, Rahner hopes to show that it is, in fact, intellectually honest to profess belief in that which utterly transcends and makes possible all action and knowledge in the spatio-temporal world.

Rahner refers to this utterly transcendent reality as holy mystery. It is *mystery* in the sense that the only adequate term for the unrestricted dynamism of the human spirit could be that which, by its own nature, eludes capture by human conceptions. But because this mystery is experienced, not as an inert horizon, but as having a particular value—worthy, attractive, compelling—it is also described as *holy*. Holy mystery comes into view only when the human penchant for mastery and control is balanced by the self-discipline and self-criticism of contemplation.

IX

Contemplative Anthropology:
To be Human is to be in Question

In the first chapter of *Foundations*, Rahner begins his reflection on transcendental experience by attempting to answer the question, "What kind of a hearer does Christianity anticipate, so that its real and ultimate message can even be heard?"[1]   Although he never says it in so many words, Rahner indicates that to be a "hearer of the message" is, at least in part, to be capable of contemplation.   Put differently: The contemplative capacity is an implicit but essential component of Rahner's philosophical anthropology.

Philosophy and Theology
The question "What kind of hearer does Christianity anticipate . . . ?" seems to suggest the possibility of providing a completely "natural" or "untheological" response, in order to prove that one can find outside of faith ample intellectual justification for that which is within faith. However, it is precisely this which a justification on the first level of reflection excludes. Quite to the contrary, the presuppositions about man which legitimize a description of him as a "hearer of the message" are nowhere available separate and ready-made, but are inextricably intertwined with the message:

> When the reality of man is understood correctly, there exists an inescapable circle between his horizons of understanding and what is said, heard, and understood. Ultimately, the two mutually presuppose each other. Consequently, intertwined in this specific way, Christianity assumes that these presuppositions which it makes are inescapably and necessarily present in the ultimate depths of human

existence, even when this existence is interpreted differently in its reflexive self-interpretation, and that at the same time the Christian message itself creates these presuppositions by its call.[2]

This mutually-conditioning relationship between hearer and message implies a parallel linkage of philosophy and theology.

Obviously, if one's goal is to show that one may be a believer today with intellectual honesty, one will need to show that one's presuppositions about the nature of the human person are accessible in principle to every theoretical reflection and self-interpretation of human existence. But this is quite different from saying that these presuppositions may bear absolutely no connection with the message or the reality of Christianity itself. The interpenetration of a philosophical and theological anthropology is necessitated both from the side of philosophy and from that of theology.

Philosophically, it would be difficult to sustain the position that there could be a systematic reflection on and interpretation of human existence that entirely prescinded from the reality of Christianity. The inescapably historical quality of all experience and thought makes this clear:

> Even the most basic, self-grounded and most transcendental philosophy of human existence is always achieved only within historical experience. Indeed, it is itself a moment in human history, and hence we can never philosophize as though man has not had that experience which is the experience of Christianity.[3]

At the very least, the philosophical anthropologist will have to take into consideration that there have been and are in fact people who claim to have heard a word addressed to them by God in time and space and that such people have individually and corporately figured in the philosopher's own historical existence. Indeed, the very moment one raises a question about the possibility of hearing the message of Christianity, one has assumed the task of working out, not only a good notion of personhood, but also an accurate understanding of the Christian experience. "A philosophy that is absolutely free of theology is not even possible in our historical situation."[4] Philosophy's autonomy, then, consists not in an *a priori* exclusion of all questions which may pertain to God or to the human experience of God, but only "in the fact that it reflects upon its historical origins and asks whether it sees itself as still bound to the origins in history and in grace as something valid, and whether this self-experience of man can still be experienced today as something valid and binding."[5]

Theologically, it would be equally difficult to argue that there could a systematic reflection on the idea and reality of Christianity which was free of philosophical presuppositions about the nature of the person. These presuppositions, argues Rahner, "themselves belong to the content of a revealed theology which announces Christianity to man so that this essential being of his, which is inescapable and is always historically oriented, does not remain hidden from him."[6] For theology to proceed without reference to man's self-interpretation as mediated by other sciences, and by philosophy in particular, would be for theology to betray its essential nature which is, at least in part, to show that its message necessarily has something to do with humanity, that its message addresses the human person wherever he or she may be existentially and historically. Properly understood, a philosophical anthropology, far from undermining theology's autonomy, actually "enables the message of grace to be accepted in a really philosophical and reasonable way, and . . . gives an account of it in a humanly responsible way."[7] Only if Christianity were a sort of determinism and faith emanated from divine necessity rather than from human freedom could Christian theology absolve itself of the task of philosophical anthropology.

Rahner is unyielding in this anthropological emphasis. In his "Ignatius Speaks to a Jesuit of Today," for example, Rahner puts on the lips of his spiritual mentor an insistence that there is no by-passing man in the search for God. Rahner's Ignatius is critical of those who attempt to turn Christianity into a purely abstract idea and look condescendingly upon the question of the Jesus of history which occupied the author of the *Exercises*.[8] Jesuit humanism lies at the very origin of contemporary systematic theological anthropology, says Rahner, and such humanism cannot be jettisoned without detriment to the fulfillment of theology's objectives today. If the Church is "to be the Church for the whole world and all cultures, and not just European Christianity as an export to the rest of the world," an anthropology which is fundamentally optimistic about "natural" man is necessary. Grace cannot be treated as a commodity which has no original connection to humanity and is granted entirely from without, but must be shown as God's self-communication receivable only by the kind of being who already bears an essential relationship to the same God. Faith cannot be depicted simply as intellectual adherence to a set of abstract propositions whose connection to one's concrete situation is indiscernable, but must be seen as an act in both freedom and knowledge whereby one entrusts oneself to the God who is always already involved in one's existence whether or not one adverts to that involvement.[9]

In the attempt to answer the question, "What kind of a hearer does Christianity anticipate, so that its real and ultimate message can even be heard?", it becomes clear that an anthropology is required which is not afraid to do its work on the frontier land which joins and distinguishes theology and philosophy.

Personhood and Transcendence

Among the claims that Christianity makes are that it is possible to have a personal relationship to God, that there is a genuinely dialogical history of salvation, that every human person has responsibility for his/her life and existence before God, that God has "verbalized" himself in Jesus, and that a human response to God's Word is possible through prayer. If any or all of these claims are to be made intelligible in the contemporary setting—with its suspicions about the metaphysical, its narrowly empirical mentality, and its consciousness of the extraordinary pluralism of religious experience—a coherent and accessible notion of person and subject is required.[10]

What is being sought in the development of such a notion is less the definition of one object in the world among many others—as if conceptualizing the human person were as simple an affair as conceptualizing one's experience of a rock or tree. The terms *person* and *subject* point less to a thing than to the dynamism of basic experience; and this fact determines the approach to be taken in a philosophical/theological anthropology:

> By the very nature of the subject matter, such concepts point to man's more original and basic experience of his subjectivity and personhood. They point to a basic experience which indeed does not simply take place in an absolutely wordless and unreflexive experience, but neither is it something which can be expressed in words and indoctrinated from without.[11]

Inner Self Disclosed through Consciousness of Outer Determinations

To a great extent, that to which we refer by the concepts of person and subject is determined. Individually and socially, we experience ourselves, at least in part, as products of that which is not ourselves. Our choices are limited by our social and historical situation. Our knowledge is confined by the boundaries of our senses and by our cultivated intellectual capacity. And so, the empirical sciences rightly set out to explain or derive humanity in terms of the myriad factors which determine us, and all anthropologies (whether biological, genetic, or sociological) understandably prove to be partial and perspectival.[12]

But philosophical/theological anthropologies differ from these other interpretations of man in at least one important respect: It is not that they are not also partial and perspectival. It is rather that they recognize, in the midst of the many empirical origins into which man seems to dissolve, that man nonetheless experiences himself as person and as subject, i.e., as a self over against the myriad factors without and within which affect him. Paradoxically, man experiences himself as person and subject precisely when he becomes conscious of himself as determined:

> This element, namely, that man also knows about his radical origins in these causes, is not explained by these origins. When he analyzes and reconstructs himself, it is not yet explained by this process that he does analysis and reconstruction himself and knows about it.[13]

It is through this very consciousness of self which comes to the fore in all knowledge that man shows himself to himself as more than the sum of his factors. I could not even entertain the possibility of being wholly determined if I did not possess an "I" which, of its own accord, could entertain such a possibility. Even if I were to posit that I am determined in such a way as to need to posit self-possession, it would still be I myself doing the positing.[14] "For a finite system of individual, distinguishable elements cannot have the kind of relationship to itself which man has to himself in the experience of his multiple conditioning and reducibility."[15] In other words, among finite beings, only man is capable of standing outside himself and positing himself in relation to that which is other than himself. Only man is capable of being in question. Only man is capable of asking questions about himself and about the totality of his existence. This questioning and the openness to the unlimited horizon of

Being which it expresses and engenders reveal the nature of the human person or subject as transcendent:

> [Man] can place everything in question. In his openness to everything and anything, whatever can come to expression can be at least a question for him. In the fact that he affirms the possibility of a merely finite horizon of questioning, this possibility is already surpassed, and man shows himself to be a being with an infinite horizon. In the fact that he experiences his finiteness radically, he reaches beyond this finiteness and experiences himself as a transcendent being, as spirit. The infinite horizon of human questioning is experienced as an horizon which recedes further and further the more answers man can discover.[16]

Questioning, Transcendence, and the Contemplative Capacity

Here we can begin to see how a contemplative element figures prominently, albeit implicitly, in Rahner's definition of the human subject. Man is understood to be "always still on the way." Whether in knowledge or in action, every goal, every step, every accomplishment is always partial and provisional. Every answer provides the basis for a new question; every free act sets the stage for another, and yet another, in a process which ends only in death. Man is a mystery to and for himself.[17] What is this mysteriousness but the recognition of the utter poverty of all that is ordinarily included under the title of knowledge and the limits of every good that he can achieve or acquire? What is the horizon against which the limitedness and relativity of all of man's strivings can be seen but that infinite possibility to which one becomes open in contemplation? To say that man is the being who can put himself into question, the being who is a mystery for himself, is to say that man is by nature contemplative—though whether or not one will exercise this contemplative capacity is by no means certain.

In fact, there are three ways at least that a concrete individual person may try to evade the mysteriousness of his own existence. Rahner's observations on this point provide the basis for a sort of typology of non-contemplative persons. One may be non-contemplative through naïveté, scepticism, or despair.

The first of these types, the *naïve* non-contemplative, seems to reflect the prevailing spirit of Western culture.

They live at a distance from themselves in that concrete part of their lives and of the world around them which can be manipulated and controlled. They have enough to do there, and it is very interesting and important. And if they ever reflect at all on anything which goes beyond all this, they can always say that it is more sensible not to break one's head over it.[18]

The second of these types, the *sceptical* or *agnostic* non-contemplative, is closed to the mysteriousness of his own existence, not because he has not reflected beyond the concrete part of his own life and world, but because the rationalistically unsatisfying results of his reflection cause him to determine that there is nothing to be gained by further questioning:

An evasion of [mystery] . . . . can also take place along with the resolve to accept categorical existence and its tasks, recognizing and accepting the fact that everything is encompassed by an ultimate question. This question is perhaps left as a question. One believes that it can be postponed in silence and in a perhaps sensible scepticism.[19]

The third of these types, the *desperate* or *absurd* non-contemplative, is not closed to the mysteriousness of his existence, but chooses rather to interpret that mysteriousness as meaninglessness:

One goes about his business, he reads, he gets angry, he does his work, he does research, he achieves something, he earns money. And in a final, perhaps unadmitted despair he says to himself that the whole as a whole makes no sense and that one does well to suppress the question about the meaning of it all and to reject it as an unanswerable and hence meaningless question.[20]

What is important to bear in mind in all of these cases of mystery-evasion or non-contemplative attitude, none of them in itself constitutes a disproof of man's contemplative capacity. In fact, this three-fold *via negativa*, as it were, provides at the same time a positive indication of that in which the human contemplative potential consists. In the first case, the intellectual dynamism which is the condition of possibility for and would come into focus through contemplation remains operative even though it is never made the naïve person's theme. In the second case, the agnostic's determination that the question of man's existence cannot be answered constitutes an implicit admission that, in the final analysis, the question cannot be evaded. In the third case, the absurdist's claim that there is no meaning behind or beyond the mysteriousness of human existence presupposes some prior notion of transcendent meaning as a basis for evaluation—an unlimited horizon (meaning-full-ness) against which to judge the limited case (meaning-less-ness). In short, man is by nature contemplative; that is, he questions and is a question to himself. He can only choose not to actualize this potential.

The Term of Transcendence Revisited: No Thing but not Nothing
If, as Rahner insists, there can be no adequate notion of the *hearer* of the message which is not informed by an adequate notion of the *message* which is heard, and vice versa; then, in a discussion of man as a transcendent being, a parallel requirement emerges: There can be no adequate notion of human transcendence which is not informed by an adequate notion of that unto which the human spirit transcends. Though Rahner does not go into a complete exposition on the nature and content of Christianity's message at this point (since the better part of the book is given over to this), he does begin in this first chapter to reveal something more about the term of human transcendence which, in his Introduction, we met only as an epistemological exigency.

Here is what is at stake: Several times and in several ways, Rahner has argued that all human knowledge and conscious activity is borne by a *Vorgriff*, an unthematic but ever-present knowledge of the infinity of reality.[21] Is it possible to be more precise about this "infinity of reality"? Is it at least possible to show that the term of human transcence is not nothing at all or merely some Kantian idea of reason or principle of synthetic unity?

Seeming to set himself against the position of Heidegger (or at least against Heidegger's position as he understood it), Rahner excludes the possibility that the term of human transcendence could be absolute nothingness. If it is the case that a pre-apprehension is the very ground of the openness which is exhibited by man's need to question, it is impossible that pure and absolute nothingness could be the term of this pre-apprehension. If the term of the grounding *Vorgriff* is itself a void, then the ground is ungrounded and no ground at all.[22] If the term of human transcendence is that which draws and moves and sets in motion the totality of a person's existence; it is difficult to see how absolute nothingness could do this.[23]

If, however, the term of the *Vorgriff* is not nothing, is it therefore some thing? Seeming to set himself against the position of Kant, Rahner includes the possibility that the movement of human transcendence is simply "the subject creating its own unlimited space as though it had absolute power over being."[24] (Recall that for Rahner, a human being attains knowledge of things through a limiting judgment made possible by a pre-apprehension of that which is absolutely unlimited.) If the term of this pre-apprehension were just another limited achievement of the mind (an idea or concept), knowledge of that fact would require still another transcending pre-apprehension, and so, *ad infinitum.*

> A finite system as such can experience itself as finite only if in its origins it has its own existence by the fact that, as this conscious subject, it comes from something else which is not itself and which is not just an individual system, but is the original unity which anticipates and is the fullness of every conceivable system and of every individual and distinct subject.[25]

Perhaps it can be said with some accuracy, then, that the absolute term of human transcendence, though it is not *nothing*, is certainly *no thing*—that is, neither a finite object in the world nor limited idea of the mind. Rather, it is being in an absolute sense, known surely but indirectly through the *Vorgriff,* the human reaching out beyond finite things to attain finite things which is the infinite horizon of being making itself manifest in time and space.[26]

In other words, the term of human transcendence—the "object" of contemplation, if you will—is being pure and simple. Therefore, it can never be fully encompassed by human thought or grasped by human action even though it is always present in experience. And therein lies the challenge for a justification of faith in the contemporary situation:

> Such an original experience of transcendence is something different from philosophical discussion about it, and precisely because it can usually be present only through the mediation of the categorical

objectivity of man or of the world around him, this transcendental experience can easily be overlooked.[27]

It seems quite certain then (and we will set out to demonstrate this in the following chapter) that only a person who has actualized that contemplative potential which is an essential aspect of human subjectivity will be able to satisfy himself that it is indeed possible to be a believer with intellectual honesty."[?]

Freedom and Responsibility in History and Society

If the human person is defined by a real but open and undetermined transcendence, then the human person must also be characterized by freedom.[28] We need to explore what freedom means in the context of a definition of the human subject which includes contemplation as an essential component and how that freedom is expressed historically and socially.

Freedom: Irreducible Ground of Human Experience

Freedom is not a novel theme within the context of a Christian anthropology, but Rahner is careful to distinguish his own interpretation of freedom from the standard description of traditional scholasticism:

> The traditional scholastic psychology . . . wants to discover freedom
> directly as an individual, concrete datum within the realm of human
> transcendentality and personhood, and this is indeed a good intention,
> but it is doing something which basically contradicts the essence of
> freedom.[29]

It is Rahner's view that this scholastic psychology has rendered the concept of freedom supremely vulnerable to empirical critique. Empirical psychologies, which of necessity do their work by causally connecting one phenomenon with another, can never discover any freedom. In fact, however, freedom itself is not discoverable at the level of phenomena but, like the transcendence to which it related, is an irreducible ground for the multiple phenomena which can be treated by an empirical psychology.[30]

Freedom is not just one more fact about the human condition, but is the signature of human transcendence within the sphere of action. Hence, just as in the sphere of human cognition, one needs to move beyond the myriad concrete objects of one's categorical knowledge to that unlimited dynamism whereby all knowledge is achieved in order to understand how knowledge is at all possible; so too does one need to move beyond the myriad limited acts of one's categorical life in order to understand what freedom is and that I am free.

> "I" always experience myself as the subject who is given over to himself. It is in this experience that something like real subjectivity and self-responsibility, and this not only in knowledge but also in action, is present as an *a priori*, transcendental experience of my freedom. It is only through this that I know that I am free and responsible for myself, even when I have doubt about it, raise questions about, and cannot discover it as an individual datum of my categorical experience in time and space.[31]

As person, I experience myself as having a self, i.e. as capable of distinguishing my own "I" from and relating my "I" to other selves and other non-transcendent beings in a limitless variety of ways. This capacity to distinguish and relate oneself to the world, actualized by the inexorable drive of the human spirit toward the fullness of being, is expressed through human judgment by means of concepts and logical systems. But it is also expressed through human activity by means of choices and decisions affecting the substance and shape of one's own historical existence. My knowledge, mediated through a combination of already-given and freely-formed conceptual frameworks, informs and directs my moral interests and choices. But, at the same time, my moral interests and choices, expressed through a combination of responses to given circumstances and freely-undertaken projects direct my cognitive processes and determine the scope and breadth of my objective knowing. Hence, transcendence and freedom are not two completely different parts of the human person; rather, they are one and the same human existence looked at from two points of view. And this point is especially significant when one recalls that, in Maréchalian Thomism, contemplation emerges as a theme at precisely the point where intellect and will, thought and action, are experienced in their interdependence and common origin.

Clearly, then, freedom is not discoverable as an individual datum of my categorical experience in time and space. This is not to say that it is entirely hidden or inaccessible; paradoxically, it is only through categorical experience in history and materiality, that one can know oneself as free.[32] To say that freedom is not discoverable as an individual datum of categorical experience is to say that, like human subjectivity and personhood, freedom and its concomitant responsibility "are experienced when a subject as such experiences himself and hence precisely not when he is objectified in a subsequent scientific reflection."[33] The difficulty is that, though transcendental experience is prior (both logically and chronologically) and is not an object in the usual sense of the term, it is never known except after the fact and as objectified.

Freedom, then, is not a neutral power possessed by a person as something different from the self:

It is rather a fundamental characteristic of a personal existent who experiences himself in what he has already done and is still to do in time as self-possession, as one who is responsible and has to give and account, and this includes the moment when a subjective and personal response to the infinite and the incomprehensible confronts this existent in his transcendence, and is either accepted or rejected.[34]

As in his argument for the openness of the human subject to *Sein überhaupt*, Rahner again employs the technique of retorsion to confirm the reality of freedom. Whatever position a person decides to take on freedom—whether one accepts or rejects it, despairs in it or reserves judgment on it—one has in fact exercised one's freedom in doing so. "So even when a person would abandon himself into the hands of the empirical anthropologies, he still remains in his own hands."[35]

This way of working out the issue of freedom obviously has implications beyond the realm of a philosophical anthropology narrowly construed. Here in *Foundations*, for example, Rahner is attempting to provide an introduction to the idea of Christianity, an idea which has as a prominent aspect the possibility of salvation. Whether or not it can be shown, for example, that one may believe in the possibility of salvation without doing violence to one's rational nature depends in large part on the way in which one works out the issue of freedom. If one should attempt to proceed from something other than an original experiential starting point—e.g. by treating freedom as one phenomena among many others which compose a man—"salvation can only appear very

strange and sound like mythology."[36]   Salvific liberation from the limits
imposed by materiality and the inclination to treat what is limited as if it were
unlimited (the essence of idolatry or sin) will appear to be wholly extrinsic—if
not completely contrary—to human nature, unless freedom in the sense
described here is included in the definition of the human person from the
outset.

With an appreciation of freedom as constitutive of the totality of man's
existence as self-possessed and self-transcending, one will not describe
salvation as a future situation which befalls one unexpectedly as if from without
on the basis of a moral judgment. Rather, as Rahner puts it, salvation can be
seen as "the final and definitive validity of a person's true self-understanding
and true self-realization in freedom before God."[37]   In other words, salvation
occurs when one freely chooses not to be delivered entirely over to the finite
objects of one's possible knowledge and action but accepts his own self as it is,
finite transcendence—i.e. a being open to unlimited being, but having its own
being and ultimate fulfillment not from itself or from any other limited being,
but from that being which can only be known in the end as Holy Mystery.
Obviously, an orthodox Christian account of salvation will have to elaborate
this categorically in terms of salvation history, the unique place of Jesus Christ,
the importance of the Church, and so on. In the final analysis, however, none
of this changes the basic point being made here: If the salvation which
Christianity promises in fact occurs, it is only in the deepest origins and roots
of a particular person's being, what Rahner call's a person's "transcendental
essence."[38]

Freedom: Experienced only in History and Society
In working out a conception of the free human subject, one could easily be
misled by this emphasis on the transcendental into overlooking or
misinterpreting the place of the world and history much as Enlightenment
rationalists had. One could develop a conception of human subjectivity, for
example, which depicts man's being in the world and in history as aspects of
man which are had alongside of or in addition to his free personhood. To the
contrary,   Rahner insists that worldliness and historicity, i.e. categorical
experience, are "aspects of the free subjectivity of a person as such,"[39] which is
to say the man's subjectivity and free personal self-interpretation take place
precisely in and through the world and time. In this way we can see that what

Rahner has to say in *Foundations* remains wholly continuous with a philosophy he worked out some forty years earlier when he described man as *Geist in Welt*. In a way unprecedented among his fellow Thomists, he emphasized Thomas' own insistence on the necessity for knowledge of a *conversio ad phantasmata* and showed how, if man were to be a *Hörer des Wortes*, that word could only be heard and accepted or rejected in time and history.

There is no need to review comprehensively Rahner's arguments for the inextricable connection between human spirituality or transcendence and worldliness.[40] It will suffice here simply to note that, in *Foundations*, man's spatio-temporal existence is more or less assumed, and the emphasis is put on the consequences of this in terms of historicity,

> that characteristic and fundamental determination of man by which he is placed in time precisely as a free subject, and through which a unique world is at his disposal, a world which he must create and suffer in freedom and for which in both instances he must take responsibility.[41]

A short excursus on the historicity of human freedom and transcendence is in order, then, to make it clear that the contemplative aspect of human existence which is implicit in all talk of freedom and transcendence is not an a-temporal principle of a disembodied and isolated subjectivity. As already noted in our Introduction, the etymological affinity of the word *contemplation* with the Latin *tempus* strongly suggests that the reality of contemplation consists, at least in part, in taking time with or in doing something over or about or with regard to one's time.

Historicity and Eternity. Human freedom is worked out in time. In fact, Rahner defines time in terms of human freedom: " . . . for me, time is ultimately the possibility to decide definitively about oneself in freedom. Time is a sort of open space that makes something like historical freedom possible."[42] Time is that open space in which human freedom creates history. History is not merely a succession of events. History consists in the moments of a person's, a community's, or the world's existence seen in their original unity and interrelatedness as emanating from one and the same freedom and moving toward one and the same infinite and unfathomable goal. With Heidegger, Rahner understood man to be a *Sein zum Tode;* but against Heidegger, Rahner did not treat death as an inevitable step which man makes into the abyss of nothingness which thereby brings about the movement and dynamism of a human existence without definite term or end. Rahner saw death as the inevitable step which man takes into the abyss of being, the incomprehensible mystery of God which certainly is no thing, but is infinitely far from being nothing at all. Freedom pertains to the fact that man may dispose of himself toward this inevitable goal willingly or unwillingly; trustingly or untrustingly.

For every person, time ultimately gives way to eternity through death. In a man's disposition toward death (which is not something determined only in the last instant of a person's life but is freely chosen and expressed through a personal history which bears the final moment), a man makes a definitive statement about the meaning of his life as whole. That is, the significance of everything a person has come to know and everything he has done receives its final and irrevocable determination through one's death. If death is rejected as ultimately void of all possibility—an empty and tragic moment to be held off at all costs—then it is the limited achievements of one's life which are accorded ultimate value, and eternity consists in an irreversible distancing of oneself from that which grounded and implicitly drew forth one's existence in time. If, on the other hand, death is faced with courage and hope, as the moment above all others whereby the true nature of one's existence as finite transcendence is revealed in the crucible of separation from the world as one has known it, then the achievements of one's life are seen in their proper place_ limited goods which have, in the end, given only a hint of the incomprehensible goodness to be met in God the origin and goal of a person's existence.

A notion like that of eternity is problematic in the contemporary setting, and Rahner realized this. If one has elected to confine one's attempts at understanding to the spatio-temporal sphere of empirical science, there will be no place for the concept of that which is definitionally beyond space and time. But even if the pervasive contemporary mentality about metaphysics were different, the truth of the matter is that the death through which eternity comes to be and is experienced cannot be anticipated by us. Even if one should commit suicide, one would have only determined the moment of one's passage into eternity (presuming the suicide was a free act); one would not have thereby obtained foreknowledge of death itself and the eternity into which it opens.[43] And so, if there is to be any talk of eternity in a philosophical anthropology—and there must be if man is affirmed to be free and transcendent—such talk will necessarily fall infinitely short of the reality it seeks to communicate.

Rahner proposes a sort of *via negativa* for understanding eternity. Eternity can be best understood by excluding the element of sequence and succession (i.e. the usual ways of construing time) from the notion of the real, the permanent, the definitive. If we proceed in this way, we can detect several evidences of eternity in time, cases of permanency without succession in our ordinary experience.[44] Plainest experience teaches, for example, that one and the same reality is capable of persisting while sustaining an alternation of qualities, phenomena, and occurrences.[45] There is also our experience of our own mental life in which past, present, and future are somehow combined in a unity.[46] Most relevant to the present discussion, there are our free personal decisions whereby action is posited definitively, not allowed to disappear into a void of nothingness.

> [T]here are free decisions in man, involving the person's total self-disposal, for which he bears an ultimate, inescapable responsibility . . . which he cannot shift off to anyone or anything else, neither by a psychology seeking to break down the ultimate character of man as subject nor by social sciences seeking to reduce man to a pure effect of social conditions. . . . ultimate personal decisions, at least when they involve a life in its totality, are irrevocable, they are truly eternity coming to be in time . . . here time really creates eternity, and eternity is experienced in time."[47]

And so, if the whole of human experience is allowed to speak for itself, it becomes clear that something which is in time—whether a living organism, one's own mental life, or a free decision—may be permanent without thereby being reducible to a mere succession of moments or states. In this light, eternity may be understood, neither as time ascending inexorably into the void, nor as a never-ceasing succession of moments.[48] Rather, eternity may be understood as the finality of the present life of freedom, the definitiveness of that moral and free act of our life in which we made ourselves the persons we wanted finally to be.[49]

In Rahner's philosophical anthropology, then, transcendental and categorical experience, far from being separate and opposed, are actually one and the same human existence looked at from two points of view. Their original unity is most clear in reflection upon death, where the free but finite acts which one has made in time are given definitive meaning by insertion into the infinite being of the one toward which one has been reaching one's whole life long.

Society and Personhood. Finally, a word is in order about the social significance of freedom in Rahner's thought. Because man's historical existence also includes shared life and communication with other subjects, "the unity of the history of all mankind and the unity of a salvation history is from the outset a transcendental characteristic of the personal history of every individual; and vice versa, because we are dealing with the history of many subjects."[50] Put differently: The freedom which is constitutive of human existence is not only historical it is also socially-significant. Human history is created through the free choices a human being makes about the disposition of himself and his world. Other free subjects, and not just a host of determined and determining objects, necessarily enter into this history forged by our freedom. Hence, Rahner's description of freedom should not be confused with any sort of false individualism.

At the same time, however, Rahner does not give an elaborate account of intersubjectivity or of the social dimension of the human person. This does not appear to have been a casual omission, but rather an expression of his conviction that, ultimately, one stands alone in that death which gives definitive meaning to one's life. In the final analysis, one cannot push responsibility for the totality and direction of one's life onto anyone else. Rahner's Ignatius may provide a clue as to Rahner's own thoughts on the question of the individual in society:

Perhaps my religious individualism, which has been described by you as 'modern' begins to take on new meaning when the individual is threated with decline and extinction in an organized mass in the post modern era. I have nothing against it . . . if you seek to discover today in the religious sphere as earlier in the humanistic, a communal feeling, a living group, a basic fraternal community and feel yourself at home there. But be wary and sensible. The individual can never lose himself fully in the community. Solitariness before God, security in his silent, immediate presence is man's sole possession.[51]

And so, though other free subjects enter into a person's life of freedom in a distinctive and undeniable way, one cannot be reduced to one's social existence any more than one can be reduced to the totality of individual determining factors which make up one's history.

Contemplative Anthropology

What kind of hearer does Christianity anticipate? Having begun to explore the boundaries of philosophy and theology to which such a question brings us, we have discovered that the hearer of the message is a person and subject characterized by a freedom which is worked out in history and society.

The hearer of the message is a person and subject. In contrast with the kind of science which reduces man to one or several of his empirical origins, philosophical/theological anthropology reflects on man's experience of having or being a self over against the myriad factors which determine him. However a human being may be affected, whether from without or from within, by his wondering and questioning man is always capable of transcending each and all of those determinants, thereby confronting the mysteriousness of his own existence. Revealed in this transcendence is the movement of the human spirit toward Being pure and simple or Holy Mystery. This capacity to confront mystery—what I have called man's "contemplative potential"—is an integral component of a complete description of the human person. It is so integral, in fact, that its presence is confirmed even when the mysteriousnesss of existence is evaded or denied.

Because the hearer, as person, is characterized by a transcendence which is open and undetermined, we also acknowledge that the hearer is free. We have seen that the freedom of which Rahner writes is more than one neutral power among many; it is rather the very condition of possibility for a person to take a stand about that infinite goal toward which he finds himself oriented in his transcendence. At the same time, this freedom is not absolute. One's freedom is always conditioned by limits which life in a spatio-temporal world imposes as well as by the fact that human freedom is always and only worked out in history and society.[52] More importantly, one's freedom is conditioned by that fact that man is not simply at the disposal of other things and other subjects, but also at the disposal of Being itself—Being which grounds and draws forth the speculative/practical dynamism of the human spirit, Being in the sense of that mystery which is constantly revealing and, at the same time, concealing itself:

> [Man's] transcendentality is . . . a relationship which does not establish itself by its own power, but is experienced as something which was established by and is at the disposal of another, and which is grounded in the abyss of ineffable mystery.[53]

If the ground of man's transcendentality and freedom is mystery, then man cannot help but experience himself as not-fully-determined, as on-the-way, as incapable of being fully encompassed, as being in question.[54] To say that to be human is to be contemplative is another way of saying that the hearer of the message is one who is *in question*. But, as we shall see in the following chapter, contemplation also refers to the fact that man experiences himself *as questioned*; i.e. as being at the disposal of another, as required by his existence to deal with his freedom in some particular way and to take a stand with regard to the mysteriousness of his own existence. If, in this chapter, we have seen contemplation characterizing Rahner's anthropology, we shall see in the following chapter, that it is also presupposed within the Rahnerian model of revelation. Contemplation is the only modality in which the human person may experience himself as addressed in such a way by others, his world, and ultimately by God, as to require a response. That is why it may be said that the freedom discovered in Rahner's anthropology entails *respons*ibility, i.e. the responsibility to listen in history for a word addressed to man by God and then to decide how to dispose oneself with regard to that word.

X

A Contemplative Model of Revelation: To be Human is to be Questioned

Contemplation does not only characterize Rahner's method and constitute an essential part of his definition of the human person; in his thought, it is actually the prime condition of possibility for revelation. Only a description of rationality which includes a contemplative aspect will leave open the possibility of God speaking to man in history. We have already seen that a distinctive aspect of man's nature is to be *in question*; but man is also *questioned*, i.e. addressed by God's Word in history, a Word for which man must listen and to which he must respond—even if negatively.

Whereas the first chapter of *Foundations* asks, "What kind of hearer does the message of Christianity anticipate?" the second chapter shifts the focus to that absolute mystery which is the origin and goal of human transcendence. But these are not two thoroughly unrelated tasks. *Foundations'* second chapter attempts to bring to explicit reflection the transcendental experience which distinguishes the human subject. "If man really is a subject, that is, a transcendent, responsible and free being who as subject is both entrusted into his own hands and always in the hands of what is beyond his control, then basically this has already said that man is a being oriented toward God."[1] Rahner's Ignatius says that a human experience of the divine really means, "not the indoctrination of something not previously present . . . but a more explicit awakening of and to the self, and the free acceptance of man's state of mind which is always a given factor, usually locked and repressed, but inevitable."[2]

In an explicit reflection on transcendental experience, says Rahner, one ought not take for granted the existence of the word "God" or presume that its meaning is self-evident. The very fact that there is such a word—a word whose existence is perpetuated even by the atheist who makes a point of its exclusion—is itself significant.[3] Although the eradication of the word is not inconceivable, such a development would not constitute an argument against the existence of what the word represents but would, instead, signal the end of man as such. Inasmuch as it is through the word "God" that one is brought into contact or relation with the single whole of reality and human existence, the elimination of the word "God" would mean that man had regressed to the level of a clever animal: Sounding a little like Heidegger who once wrote of the mystery of *Dasein* sinking into forgottenness,[4] Rahner describes a hypothetical world in which the lexicon has been purged of the God word: "Man would have forgotten the totality and its ground, and at the same time, if we can put it this way, would have forgotten that he had forgotten ."[5]

Hence, as we begin this more explicit reflection on transcendental experience, we are inescapably confronted, at the very least, with the word "God." This word does not enter our experience or existence for the first time by our thinking about it; it is rather a word which is given to us, which we hear and receive. "It comes to us in the history of language in which we are caught, whether we want to be or not, which poses questions to us as individuals without itself being at our disposal."[6] How a person ultimately answers the question or questions posed by the existence of this word can only be determined by each individual in freedom. But that man is in fact the addressee of such a question and that he must respond (even if it is to say "I will give no response")—these are difficult to refute.

The Possibility of Attaining a Knowledge of God
Reflection on Transcendental Experience

Since to describe man as addressed by God implies some initial affirmation of God's existence, Rahner considers the possibility of attaining a natural knowledge of God through reflection upon transcendental experience. Rahner insists that the reflection which he has recommended constitutes neither an *a priori* nor an *a posteriori* proof of God's existence. It is certainly not a purely *a priori* proof, for "man's transcendental experience of his free subjectivity takes place only in his encounter with the world and especially other people . . . every transcendental experience is mediated by a categorical encounter with a concrete reality in our world."[7] Nor is it an entirely *a posteriori* proof, as if knowledge of God were the reception of some particular datum by a neutral faculty. God is not discovered directly or indirectly among the realities which present themselves to us objectively, nor can God simply be indoctrinated from without as an object of knowledge.[8]

The reflection on transcendental experience (which is really Rahner's version of a "proof") seeks simply to bring to light or make explicit that existence of God which is implicitly affirmed in all knowledge and free human activity:

> We must get used to taking account of the fact that when we think and when we exercise freedom we are always dealing with more and always have to do with more than that which we are talking *about* in our words and concepts, and that *with which* we are occupied here and now as the concrete object of our activity. [9]

The intelligibility of all explicit and thematic knowledge of God depends on its being seen in its connection to this implicit and unthematic experience. It would seem, from a Rahnerian viewpoint, at any rate, that a metaphysics or theology which does not do this, which instead treats the knowledge of God as it treats the knowledge of objects in the world, must be considered rationalistic rather than rational.[10]

The question of the difference between the knowledge of God and the knowledge of individual realities in the world merits closer attention. While, as we have seen, individual realities become comprehensible and manipulable for us through differentiation from other individual things, God is not accessible to the human mind in the same way, since God is himself the unlimited horizon in the light of which differentiation or conceptualization takes place.[11] Hence, though one inevitably conceptualizes with regard to God, the concept named by the word "God" must be seen as differing fundamentally from the concepts we have of other realities:

> The concept "God" is not a grasp of God by which a person masters the mystery, but is letting oneself be grasped by the mystery which is present and yet ever distant. This mystery remains a mystery even though it reveals itself to man and thus continually grounds the possibility of man being a subject.[12]

One prime implication of this "mystery-not-mastery" approach to the knowledge of God is that a metaphysics, if it to be true to its task of reflecting on what is in its unity and totality, cannot absolutize the concepts with which it does its work.

This is particularly true if such a metaphysics is to be called upon to show that one can be a believer with intellectual honesty. "[All] metaphysical ontology about God must return again and again to its source, must return to the transcendental experience of our orientation towards the absolute mystery and to the existentiell practice of accepting this orientation freely."[13] In short, a metaphysics which aims to show that it is possible for man to hear a word spoken by God will have to be a contemplative metaphysics, since it is only with an appreciation of the human capacity to freely reorient one's cognitive and moral attention from individuals and individual goods to that ground and goal which they require to be what they are, that it can make any sense to say that man has been addressed by God.

Here as in our earlier review of Rahner's epistemology, we face the important question: Does this transcendental emphasis, this rejection of the attempt to gain mastery over the mystery of God, amount to a kind of subjectivism—a subjectivism which is not only philosophically inadequate but is also inconsistent with the predominant current in Catholic apologetics? One might argue, for example, that if the ground of our knowledge of God is in subjective experience, we are only able to say something about what God is *for us,* and not able to say anything about what God is *in himself*—leaving us with a kind of Kantian agnosticism about the existence of God. Rahner responds that, if one has understood what is meant by "the absolutely unlimited transcendentality of the human spirit," a radical distinction between the "for us" and "in himself" is not legitimate. Given the situation in which human existence finds itself, oriented toward the mystery in knowledge, but not capable of encompassing it, "the concept in its original ground and the reality itself to which this concept refers move beyond us and enter the unknown together."[14]

In the light of all this, the three modes of knowing God which were delineated by traditional Catholic theology—natural knowledge, knowledge through the revealed Word, knowledge through God's salvific activity in history—are not rejected here but rather are seen in their original experiential unity.[15] Hence, to say that God's existence can be known through natural reason unaided by faith is not to posit that man in some hypothetical state of "pure nature" could reason to the existence of a God which previously had nothing to do with his existence. It is rather to say that there is something about the nature of the human person—accessible in an analysis of human cognition and free action—which disposes him from the start to affirm God. Likewise, to say that God's existence may be known through revelation unsupported by subtle metaphysical reflection is not to suggest that faith is a kind of miracle which absolves the believer from thought and the responsible use of freedom. It is rather to say that one way of coming to know God—perhaps the normative way in a "Christian culture"—is through the historically constituted witness of the Church in its Scripture and Tradition of their interpretation.

But even if the way of faith does not require one to explore all the complex metaphysical and epistemological problems which concern the philosopher of religion, the believer cannot avoid the necessity of showing to himself that this outer word of revelation speaks directly and precisely to his or her inner experience.[16] The free and responsible person of faith can easily enough avoid being a philosopher in the narrow sense of the term; but he cannot avoid being contemplative, in the sense of assuming a posture which is open to the infinite.

> By its very nature, subjectivity is always a transcendence which listens, which does not control, which is overwhelmed by mystery and opened up by mystery. In the midst of its absolute infinity, transcendence experiences itself as empty, as merely formal, as necessarily mediated to itself by finiteness, and hence as a finite infinity. . . . if it does not want to mistake itself for an absolute subject and divinize itself, it recognizes itself as a transcendence which has been bestowed upon it, which is grounded in mystery, and is not at its own disposal.[17]

In Rahner's thought, the proper relationship of reason and revelation, knowledge and faith, is worked out in terms of their original unity which can only be experienced contemplatively. Of course, the human person always enjoys complete freedom to advert or not to advert to this original, unthematic, unreflexive, experience. Just as it is possible to evade one's subjectivity and freedom—through naïvté, scepticism, or desperation—so too can one hide from himself his transcendental orientation towards the absolute mystery referred to by the name "God."[18] But such an evasion would not constitute a disproof of God's existence and still less a disproof of man's contemplative capacity. As Heidegger wrote with regard to the forgottenness of the mystery of *Dasein*: "The forgottenness bestows on the apparent disappearance of what is forgotten a peculiar presence . . . Even in insistent existence the mystery holds sway, but as the forgotten and hence 'inessential' essence of truth."[19] The very possibility of mystery-evasion itself simply confirms the fundamental freedom with which man approaches his existence.

The *Telos* of Human Transcendence

Up to this point we have been trying to say something about the possibility of attaining a knowledge of God and have seen that, whether this knowledge is worked out in terms of natural reason or revelation or salvation history, it finds its ground in a more primitive transcendental experience of which one becomes aware through contemplation. What remains undetermined, however, is the precise way of talking about the *telos* of this transcendence. In other words, of what or whom does transcendental experience yield some knowledge ? How might we best describe where it is that human transcendence is directed, what it is that it encounters, and what is the source by which it is openned up?[20] We began with the unavoidable word "God," but is that name really adequate or helpful in the contemporary situation?

To be adequate or helpful, a name which is given to the *telos* of human transcendence must be capable of mediating the experience for an individual. According to this criterion, even a thousand names would not suffice, inasmuch as that the diverse situations of every individual could not possibly be anticipated. Even relatively broad and open-ended terms like "Absolute Being" (which Rahner himself seems to have favored in his earlier works) are problematic in that they suggest to our philosophical contemporaries an "empty and subsequent abstraction from the multiple experience of the individual realities which encounter us directly."[21] While Rahner rejects such an interpretation of "Absolute Being," he chooses to circumvent the difficulties brought about by this expresssion by speaking instead in terms of "Holy Mystery." We have already seen Rahner use this expression in the Introduction to *Foundations*; in the second chapter, he is more explicit about the rationale for its use.

There are at least two reasons why Rahner chooses to speak of the *telos* of human transcendence as "mystery" rather than as "God." For one thing, the employment of a less familiar expression prevents some of the misunderstanding engendered by the use of a term which carries with it so much conceptual baggage.[22]   Secondly, however, and perhaps more importantly, the word "mystery" speaks precisely to the ultimate unnamability of the *Woraufin der Transzendenz*. If, as we have seen, this *telos* of human transcendence is the unlimited horizon which makes possible all affirmation of limit, all defining, distinguishing, and all naming; then this *Woraufin* cannot itself have a name. To describe the *telos* of human transcendence as "mystery" is to say that finite transcendence has as its term that which is itself indefinable.[23]

As for the description of the mystery as "holy": Rahner's explanation of this is based on a constellation of points which we have seen again and again; namely, that freedom and transcendence are intimately related, that will and intellect subsist in the human person in an original unity, that true knowledge is fulfilled in love. Human transcendence is the possibilizing condition not only for knowledge, but also for moral action. One who is not a subject, capable of reaching out toward everything in general and at the same time capable of returning to oneself through thought, would not be capable of free activity. One who is not by his nature oriented toward an ineffable goal or ever-receding horizon would have no purpose for the kind of action in which human beings find themselves, above all love. To refer to the mysterious *Woraufin der Transzendenz* as "holy" is to say that freedom and love as well as knowledge—if they are properly understood—require us to posit that the human person is in the first instance dynamically oriented toward an infinite ground and goal, whether or not he or she chooses to advert to it.[24]

The Incomprehensibility of God

The notion of God as "Holy Mystery" is best understood in relation to Thomas' teaching on the incomprehensibility of God. In a 1974 lecture at Chicago, Rahner tried to make this doctrine accessible to an audience of scholars from a wide range of philosophical backgrounds. In doing so, however, he showed that Thomas' position could not be understood in a merely philosophical way. Thomas' basic teaching may be expressed as follows:

> [G]od is incomprehensible to every finite, created intellect and is so always and under any circumstances, hence even in the immediate vision of God, hence even for angels and men who have reached fulfillment and for the created soul of the God-Man, so that gradation of blessedness in individual souls is conceivable.[25]

This teaching, says Rahner, can only be understood in direct confrontation with Thomas' teaching on the immediate vision of God, and hence may not be viewed as a teaching "which would remain per se within the horizon of a self-evident philosophical truth."[26] Once more we can see Rahner's unwillingness to treat the question of the knowledge of God as if it could be given any intelligibility apart from concrete Christian existence.

Having given this caveat, Rahner indicates from the outset what he takes to be correct and incorrect interpretations of God's incomprehensibility. To say that God is incomprehensible is not to say that, when all is said and done, there is something about God which unfortunately remains unknown. Rather, to say that God is incomprehensible and remains so even in the beatific vision is to say that the excessus (or transcendence) of the intellect has as its origin and telos, not a finite object which could be encompassed by a finite intellect, but God—absolute, infinite, unfathomable. The difference between knowledge of God in the present life and knowledge of God in the beatific vision is not the difference between incomprehensibility and comprehensibility; it is rather the difference between that which is mediated and that which is immediate.[27]

The Doctrine of Incomprehensibility in Context. Rahner begins by explaining what the doctrine of incomprehensibility means in its own historical context. He argues that a proper understanding of the incomprehensibility teaching hinges on the resolution of a two-fold theological/philosophical problematic. First there is the relationship between divine being (where *esse* and *essentia* are one and the same) and finite beings (where esse and *essentia* are distinct, and the essence of a thing determines the degree of its participation in being). The epistemological claims that God is always going to be incomprehensible to the finite intellect, and that this incomprehensibility represents a positive content (not just an unfortunate reminder of what we do not know)—these claims can only make sense in the context of an ontology of the relationship between being pure and simple and individual beings. "This relationship itself means a positive finiteness and not the creation of a finite existent which vis-a-vis infinite being is stifled in its finiteness, since it would always be surpassed and made superfluous by the infinity of God himself and would thus be basically intolerable."[28]

The radical height of the ontological relationship between God and creature (which is that to which beatific vision refers) does not mean that God and creature are merged or made identical. Nor does it mean that the creature, at a certain point, becomes capable of encompassing God as an object of thought. It means rather that the creature has attained a direct and unmediated experience of that being by which it has its being. As we saw in Rousselot, this vision (which angels are said already to enjoy) constitutes a sort of Thomist critique of knowledge. That is, this is the goal toward which all human knowledge strives but falls short in its present condition.

The second part of the theological/philosophical problematic has to do with the relationship between the self-communication of God in grace and glory which makes possible immediate vision of God and the gratuitous light of glory which is required for immediate vision to actually be given. As we have already seen Rahner argue numerous times and in various ways, all human knowledge (and not just the immediate knowledge of God) has as the prime condition of its possibility the excessus of the human intellect which can be detected in its transcending pre-apprehension of Absolute Being, in its *Vorgriff*:

> If the affirmative synthesis in the thought of man always and inevitably relates a "what" to a "something" in unresolvable difference, then in the point of relation of the predicating statement, *esse* itself is always simultaneously affirmed as not comprehended, and therefore the incomprehensibility of God is operatively present. Despite every possible insight into the predicated "what," all of man's knowledge is rooted in an incomprehensibility which is the likeness of the incomprehensibility of God and in which even now God always appears as the nameless One."[29]

And so, the natural condition of possibility for a discursive knowledge of finite things also constitutes the condition of possibility for an intuitive knowledge of God, and it is one and the same *excessus* present and operative in both an act of human knowledge and in an act of human faith. In knowledge, this *excessus* is "a transcendental peculiarity" present unthematically in every act of knowing, the infinite horizon in the light of which finite things may be seen. In faith, a person freely accepts his essence, which is gratuitously ordered to the incomprehensibility of God, "and gives himself over to this incomprehensibility without condition as to his true happiness."[30] While it beyond the scope of the present project to examine this claim in greater detail, there is enough here to show once more that contemplation, the only rational intentionality in which one can experience incomprehensibility, stands on the threshold which joins and distinguishes faith and knowledge, revelation and reason, theology and philosophy.

Incomprehensibility in Modern Consciousness. In the second half of the lecture on incomprehensibility, Rahner renders a translation of Thomas' teaching in terms of the anthropocentric turn in modern consciousness. It is significant for an argument in favor of the continuity of Rahner's position with the Catholic intellectual tradition which preceded him that Rahner places Thomas at the origin of the so-called "transcendental turn." And so, "we shall ask first about the experienced incomprehensibility of man in order to find in precisely this way an approach to the incomprehensibility of God."[31]

Elaborating a theme which we have already seen in the Introduction to *Foundations*, Rahner reflects on the radical pluralism and temporality of all knowledge to argue that it is man's nature to be a question for which there is no answer (or, as I have put it, to be in question). Our experiences recede into an unrecoverable past, the myriad discoveries of the anthropological sciences provide no deductive certainty about the shape of the future.[32] Sober reflection on the individual system or systems according to which we order our lives and society brings to light the extent to which our way of making sense of the world is a function of "unreflexive *a prioris*, prejudices, and so on . . . "[33] One strives for "objectivity," but no one has the perspective of the omniscient observer. "What does one really know about oneself, if one has had the experience that one's own experiences are always limited, always 'arranged' by one's own freedom, which one cannot get hold of in knowledge?"[34] The human person has questions and is a question to himself. "Experience gives answers, but no answer which makes transparent, 'intelligible,' and manipulable what is being asked about, namely, man as one and as a whole."[35] Just as on an epistemological level, the agnosticism born of a reflex awareness of inescapable pluralism and temporality in the field of knowledge was viewed as evidence of the mysteriousness of human existence, so too on the level of a philosophical anthropology open to revelation: The inexorability of human questioning, which is man's incomprehensibility to himself, may be read as evidence of human transcendentality, which is man's given orientation to the incomprehensible God:

> [Metaphysical anthropology] must conceive of [man] as the essence with an unlimited transcendentality, as the spiritual subject which always transcends in questions every individual (finite) object (and only for this reason is spirit), as the existent that can nowhere come to a final rest. But this infinite breadth of possible knowledge, insights, and experiences never reaches a complete fulfillment of itself and by its own means. The space—the storehouse into which experience, life, knowledge, happiness, pain, and so on are brought—is infinite and thus always remains half empty (that is a much too optimistic estimate). Since we reach beyond every finite object, but always grasp immediately only such finite objects, we shall never be finished in a limited time. Every end is only a beginnning.[36]

Now it is important to note that Rahner is not saying that the description of the human situation which he has provided prevails in contemporary consciousness; but simply that, if the contemporary anthropocentric emphasis is pursued to its logical conclusions, something like this picture of man in question and as questioned, incomprehensible to himself and responsible to an incomprehensible God toward which he is dynamically oriented, emerges.

Rahner is well aware that one might object that a philosophy of unfulfilled transcendentality is little more than an uninteresting fantasy. His now-familiar response? "This unfulfilled transcendentality remains even if it is suppressed. It is at work behind countless phenomena of individual and collective life."[37] Some examples of this: That boredom in which every concrete thing gets swallowed up in indistinction, that "agitated agressiveness against the present which appears as intolerably imperfect," the various psychic techniques "for fleeing from a world which seems to be too narrow," the "attempt to enhance or intensify the limited pleasure or the limited meaning into a refined pleasure or into an ideology . . . that the finiteness of all these intensified realities is no longer experience."[38] Whether or not we want to make unfulfilled human transcendentality thematic for ourselves, it is always and everywhere operative.

Another objection which might be leveled against the Rahnerian insistence on transcendentality would be to say that one should refrain from speech about that which may not be spoken of clearly or, put in more existential terms, that the present moment is sufficient and beautiful, and we should not want to see beyond it.[39] Rahner's sober and sobering response to this objection: This "beautiful moment" is filled with the emptiness of death! Alluding to his own Heidegger-inspired analysis of human existence as *Sein zum Tode*, he elaborates:

> Our acquisition of knowledge in the mode of existence that we can experience is a temporal process. Our time is limited and ends with a death which is always very near. In such limited time only a limited knowledge is to be won by a temporal process of knowledge. We notice it very clearly: The progress of knowledge allows us to experience ever more inexorably the infinity of the horizon of our questions and its permanent incompleteness. The pride of the spirit in nowhere having to come to a final end is also the pain (ever more clearly felt) of never finally arriving.[40]

Just as for Socrates wisdom consisted in an awareness of one's ignorance, and for Aristotle philosophy began in wonder, for Rahner understanding in its fullest and most fundamental sense consists in the understanding that one does not understand. This is nothing other than the immediate experience of the incomprehensible one, of Holy Mystery.[41]

Responses in the Face of Mystery

From a reflection on transcendental experience, then, one may attain knowledge of God as "Holy Mystery." We have attempted to clarify the meaning of this Rahnerian expression in terms of the incomprehensibility of God—a doctrine which he increasingly came to believe belonged at the very center of Catholic intellectual life.[42] Rahner found the incomprehensibility of God to be as unavoidable and irrefutable as our incomprehensibility to ourselves. We are not only a question to ourselves, but are the recipients of a question posed by the existence of the one who can only be described as unfathomable, unnamable, and ineffable: How ought I to respond in the presence of Absolute Mystery?

Here, as in the context of the agnosticism (discussed in Chapter VIII) and the mysteriousness of human existence (discussed in Chapter IX), four basic options at least lie open to the human person: One may ignore, reject, despair, or surrender in the face of the incomprehensibility of God. These four options mark points along the spectrum which runs from least to most contemplative.

One may certainly choose to *ignore* the incomprehensibility of one's existence and of its ground. This would be an instance of a nearly complete non-contemplative attitude. This is what Rahner seems to be talking about when speaks of "bourgeouis normality . . . which restricts itself to the normal and the attainable, and which denies the holy utopia of absolute hope as foolishness." One who lives in this way condemns himself to "everlasting narrowness."[43]

One may *reject* the incomprehensibility of one's existence and its ground either through a resolute skepticism which refuses to take a stand on anything metaphysical or through a dogmatism which attempts to confine God and human existence within strict and unalterable conceptual limits. Here, a certain degree of contemplative thought and living may be present. In the case of the skeptic, for example, one may have accorded enough sustained reflection to the dynamism of human knowledge and action to be circumspect about the real extent of human achievement; but in choosing a skeptical alternative which excludes the possibility of affirming God, one has short-circuited the contemplative dynamism by terminating in one's own skeptical system. Rahner argues that this type of skepticism is something completely different from the "true skepticism" of the Christian:

> For if he really believes in the incomprehensibility of God, he is convinced that no individual truth is really true except in the process which necessarily belongs to its true essence, the process in which the truth becomes a question which remains unanswered because it is asking about God and his incomprehensibility.[44]

Likewise, in the case of the dogmatist, even the religious dogmatist, one may have accorded enough reflection to the human situation and to the data of revelation to affirm the existence of God. But in attempting to confine God too narrowly within one's own unchanging concepts or system, one might bring a halt to contemplation and effectively cease allowing God to be God. In a 1965 interview, Rahner notes an important distinction between two kinds of contemplation: "Subtle contemplation is not necessarily loving contemplation; the ancient debates on the primacy of the intellect and the primacy of the will seem to me to be foolish and obsolete. In the last analysis, we cannot truly know God unless we know him as the one who speaks the Word and breathes love, the Holy Spirit. Likewise, we cannot be known except through this mutual compenetration of love and knowledge. Both demand each other."[45] Hence, even the person who professes to have accepted the Absolute Mystery in whose presence he finds himself and describes himself as a contemplative of sorts, may effectively be rejecting the Mystery and living non-contemplatively through a lack of love; i.e. an unwillingness to give the other the freedom to be as it is.

One may *despair* in the face of God's incomprehensibility. In such a case, it is likely that one has exercised his or her contemplative capacity. Indeed, the overwhelming ineffability and unfathomability of the mystery of human existence would not be evident except to one who has modified his attitude enough to let the radical pluralism and contingency of human existence to show itself from out of the field of individual things and experiences. In a sense, the situation of the one who despairs in the presence of Absolute Mystery—this case is to be distinguished from the case of the one who has naïvely ignored it or rationalistically rejected it—is remarkably close to the situation of the one who surrenders to it. Hence, this third type is probably best understood through comparison to the fourth.

To *surrender* oneself to God in his incomprehensibility is to let God be God through worshipful love and to move with the natural dynamism of one's spirit in the only direction which is completely worthy of it. Man is an unanswerable question for himself, and contemplatively one comes to realize that this inexorable questionability is an evidence of man's origin and terminus in the infinite. To the extent that one gives oneself over to his real nature, one finds meaning, happiness, fulfillment.[46] What is involved in this surrender to God's incomprehensibility is captured well by Rahner's Ignatius:

> When I say that it is as possible to encounter God in your age as in
> mine, I mean God really and truly, the God of incomprehensibility, the
> ineffable mystery, the darkness which only becomes eternal light for
> the man who allows himself to be swallowed up by it unconditionally.

But it is precisely this God, he and none other, whom I personally experienced as the God who comes down to us, who comes close to us, the God in whose incomprehensible fire we are not, in fact, burnt away but become ourselves and of eternal value. [47]

In *Foundations* Rahner alternately describes this surrender as letting oneself fall into the incomprehensible,[48] the fulfillment of knowledge through love,[49] and the attainment of true and lasting happiness.[50] And still, having come to the point of contemplatively recognizing the utter mysteriousness of one's own existence and that of God, one might conceivably choose instead to refuse to fall into the incomprehensible, to avoid the risk involved in love and continue to seek knowledge through complete mastery over one's existence, and thus to condemn oneself to final and eternal frustration of one's deepest longings. It is in this sense that the option of despair may be distinguished from the option of surrender.

In a *Schriften* essay on the problem of meaning, Rahner seems to be describing something like this despairing response to the presence of Absolute Mystery when he describes an agnostic repudiation of meaning an any ultimate sense, "a total and definitive meaning of existence cannot be found. Life ultimately fades away into a void; the question of and the demand to a definitive, all-embracing meaning of existence are meaningless from the very outset."[51] What separates this attitude from that of surrender is not its agnosticism, for we have already seen that one cannot reflect on the human situation with respect to knowledge without arriving at certain level of agnosticism. What distinguishes the despairing thinker from the one capable of surrendering to the mystery in love is the decision made with regard to this unavoidable agnosticism. The contemplative attitude becomes faith when "the admission that with all one's individual knowledge one has still become lost and confused in the darkness of unknowing . . . is accepted in humble serenity as the ultimate wisdom of life . . . "[52] The contemplative attitude becomes despair when this same admission is viewed as evidence of one's ultimate destruction, an absurd afront to what one takes himself to be. In a sense, the problem with the alternative of despair—and of its less-contemplative relatives, dogmatism and skepticism—is not that it is too radical, but that it is not radical enough. A truly radical agnosticism is a *doctrina ignorantia*—a learned ignorance which "really admits the mystery that accepts and overwhelms us."[53]

The Self-Communication of God
The Inseparability of the Transcendental and the Categorical

We have seen that it is possible to attain a knowledge of God through reflection upon transcendental experience. We have seen that God is not known as one among many objects of conceptual knowledge but is encountered as the incomprehensible ground and goal of all human knowledge and free activity. God is the Holy Mystery in whose presence the human person finds himself and to which the human person must respond in some way. Only to this extent and in this way can it be said that God's existence may be "proved."

In a sense, there is only one proof of the existence of God: the effort to show explicitly and thematically that "all knowledge, even in the form of a doubt or a question or even a refusal to raise the metaphysical question, takes place against the background of an affirmation of the holy mystery or of absolute being, as the horizon of the asymptotic term and of the questioning ground of the act of knoweldge and its object."[54] The many "proofs" of God's existence—whether cosmological, teleological, kinetic, axiological, deontological, noetic, or moral—these many proofs simply seek to work out this one fundamental proof from a wide range of departure points in categorical experience.[55] This is as it should be, for the objective in all this reflection is for the individual subject to make it clear to himself that it is possible to be a believer with intellectual honesty—that, given his or her individual experience looked at as a totality, it is possible to explicitly affirm God's existence in a manner that does no violence to the life of the mind or to human freedom. Given this objective, "the individual person must reflect precisely upon whatever is the clearest experience for him."[56] Hence, there may be an unlimited number of ways, proceeding from myriad categorical starting points, of working out the basic transcendental proof of God's existence.

Paradoxically, then, if an introduction to the idea of Christianity is to proceed by way of reflection on transcendental experience, it may only do so in context of the categorical—the world of time and space. The intellect knows nothing without turning to the phantasms. The human being knows nothing of God without turning to the world. The prime condition of possibility for hearing a word spoken by God is contemplation, but the arena and immediate object of that contemplation is the world and one's life in it.

Assuredly, there are certain extremes to be avoided in this "turning to the world." Rahner is careful to avoid either dualism (whereby God is placed next to the non-divine as two things alongside each other) or pantheism (which sees no difference between God and the world, between the categorical and the transcendental).[57]Problematic as pantheism is, however, Rahner saw a certain truth preserved in it, namely, its "sensitivity to . . . the fact that God is the absolute reality, the original ground and the ultimate term of transcendence."[58] He implies that in the contemporary situation, dualism is the more persistent and immediate tendency:

> [T]hat God really does not exist who operates and functions as an individual existent alongside other existents, and who would thus, as it were, be a member of the larger household of all reality. Anyone in search of such a God is searching for a false God. Both atheism and a more naïve form of theism labor under the same false notion of God, only the former denies it while the latter believes that it can make sense out of it.[59]

The fact that the transcendent is humanly experienced and expressed categorically entails that human speech about God is going to differ in some important ways from human speech about finite realities. Since the thematization of transcendental experience requires the use of categorical concepts which are contraries within the realm of the categorical, language about God cannot help but be dialectical. For example, we may say that God is "the innermost reality by which a finite subject and the categorical reality which confronts him are borne from within."

At the same time, we may also say that "God holds sway in absolute and untouchable self-possession and that his reality is not simply the function of being the horizon for our existence."[60] Both statements are true and irreducible to each other, and there is simply no way of escaping the discursiveness involved in the description of this intuitively-experienced reality. The experience of God winds up being treated as another individual object of knowledge, even though it is not. Of necessity, then, discourse about God is analogical, and, as it turns out, univocal and equivocal discourse are deficient modes of the analogical grasp of that original relationship in which we are related to the *telos* of our transcendence—not vice versa!

Analogical Existence, Analogical Discourse

Rahner notes that there is in analogy a tension between the categorical origin of a given reflexive statement and its attaining that towards which the statement points. I may say, for example, that God is omniscient. The categorical origin of that statement is my own experience of knowledge which, by definition, falls infinitely short of any kind of knowledge which the infinite horizon of my knowledge may possess. This tension between what I bring to discourse about God from my experience and what God is in himself "is not produced by us at a logically subsequent midpoint between a univocal 'yes' and an equivocal 'no.' It is rather a tension which we ourselves as spiritual subjects originally are in our self-realization and which we can designate by the traditional term 'analogy.'"[61] Hence it is not the case that in an analogical statement the original understanding of the content of the statement comes from something which does not have much to do with God. To the contrary:

> [T]ranscendence . . . this reaching beyond toward the unlimited horizon of the whole movement of our spirit, is precisely the condition of possibility, the horizon, and the basis and ground by means of which we compare individual objects of experience with one another and classify them . . . it follows from the nature of transcendental experience that the analogous statement signifies what is most basic and original in our knowledge.[62]

Analogical predication, therefore, is simply the thematization of analogical existing, which is the tension between our inescapably categorical departure point (we are "in the world") and our transcendent orientation (we are "spirit"). Analogy is not an inexact and subsequent mid-point between clear (univocal) concepts and concepts with two or more meanings (equivocal), as its positivistic detractors would have it.[63] Rather, analogy points to the very condition of possibility for any conceptualization whatsoever--be it univocal or equivocal—to take place:

> We ourselves . . . exist analogously in and through our being grounded in this holy mystery which always surpasses us. But it always constitutes us by surpassing us and by pointing us towards the

concrete, individual, categorical realities which confront us within the realm of our experience. Conversely, then, these realities are the mediation of and the point of departure for our knowledge of God.[64]

It is for this reason that I am arguing, not simply that a word from God may be heard only by one who is in a contemplative posture, but that this contemplative posture is unavoidably situated in and directed toward the world of space and time. That is, God's word is addressed to and heard by human beings always and only in history. Our analogical existence and our analogical knowledge of God may be elaborated in terms of three themes.

God as person. An integral component of the "idea of Christianity" is the notion of personal God; that is, of a God who may be related to by persons as a person. Within the context of Rahner's approach, it is self-evident both that personhood may be legitimately attributed to God and that this attribution is analogous.

We saw in our analysis of the kind of hearer that the message of Christianity anticipates that the human being is aptly described as person and subject. Man experiences himself as such when he experiences himself as a self over against the myriad factors without and within him which affect him. It is the human being as person and subject who, not only knows that which is other than himself, but also knows that he knows. What kind of being could be the ground of such a being but that which possesses within itself this same personhood, this same self-presence? Hence God must also be, albeit in his own unique way, personal.[65]

And yet, if the *telos* of human transcendence is what it must be to make possible human knowledge and free activity—i.e. if the *Woraufin* of the *Vorgriff* is really an infinite and unlimited horizon—then it is also self-evident that an individual, finite, and limited personhood is not attributable to God. And so, Christianity can and must speak of God as person, but it must guard against two equally problematic emphases: Either the idolatry of "the formal emptiness and empty formality of the transcendental concept of person" (which is really making God an impersonal person)[66] or the too narrow confinement of God within the parameters of a particular conception of personhood, whether one's own or that of a specific philosophical or theological system. We must "allow God to be person in the way in which he in fact wants to encounter us and has encountered us in our own individual histories, in the depths of our conscience, and in the whole history of the human race.[67]

God as creator. Another integral component of the "idea of Christianity" is the notion of the human being as a creature related to a creator. Here again we are necessarily involved in the language of categorical experience to talk about a transcendental reality.

In a primitive notion of creatureliness, the human being as creature would be conceived of as related to Creator as an effect is related to its cause—much the way a work of sculpture can be described as a creation of its artist, though the block of marble and the artist bear no original relationship. In a primitive notion of creatureliness, the human being as creature would be conceived of as related to his creator primarily in a chronological sense: "Who made me? God made me." But neither of these notions of creatureliness are adequate with relation to God.[68]

On the contrary, the relationship between God and man is *sui generis*, for it is not just a causal or functional relationship between two things, but the relationship between a personal being and its personal ground—a relation which is mediated to us only in transcendental experience as such.[69] And, though the creation of man is the creation of an existent who is extended in time, man's existence does not enter into time but is the very ground of time. There is no temporal succession without an "I" to succeed itself.[70]

Man's creatureliness is analogous language for the radical difference between God and man and for man's radical dependence upon God. Many times and in many ways, we have seen that every intellectual and spiritual enounter which a person has with the realities of the world takes place against "the ontologically silent horizon" of the absolute and incomprehensibly real. If this horizon were just another object of knowledge, it could not also be knowledge's ground, and would require still another and another, ad infinitum. God is radically different from all finite realities in the world, including man.[71] At the same time, the human being is radically dependent on God, but not in a sense that necessitates God—the way a master is dependent upon his servant. Here again the relation of creature and creator is seen in its uniqueness. Whereas in the world of finite things, one thing might be dependent on another without everything having to be dependent on that same other, there is nothing in the world which is not radically dependent upon God. Whereas in the world of finite things, one thing might be dependent on another by way of natural necessity to which both "creature" and "creator" are subject, it is God himself who establishes a relationship with creatures in complete freedom. In short, the causality at work in the creature/Creator relationship is a radically transcendent causality.[72]

Creatureliness then like personhood is a transcendental experience which, paradoxically, can only be had and expressed categorically. "A person experiences his creatureliness and encounters God in it . . . in himself and in the world as known by him and as freely administered in the unlimited openness of his own spirit."[73] There is in this experience that analogical tension between its origin in space and time and the infinite term toward which it inclines. To remain in the truth, one must be willing to live with this dialectical tension. Indeed, false understandings of creatureliness result precisely from the effort to neatly resolve this analogical tension. Either one "understands himself as only an empty appearance through which the divinity acts out its own eternal drama, runs away from his responsibility and his freedom" or else "understands the truth and the genuine reality which we are in such a way that they no longer truly come from God but have their meaning independently of him."[74] The contemplative attitude that would enable one to hear a word spoken by God is that which is neither wholly delivered over to the world nor that which seeks to take flight from it. The contemplative attitude, which we are arguing is a prime possibilizing condition for revelation, both turns to the world and looks beyond it to find its God.

God in the world. According to Rahner, if God were discoverable in the world, then he would be by implication another appearing object—may be even a magnificent one—but not the ineffable and incomprehensible presupposition, ground, abyss by which a human being has knowledge and freedom and toward which a human being is inclined as toward his own fulfillment. At the same time, however, it is also integral to the "idea of Christianity" which *Foundations* seeks to make intelligible, that there are phenomena existing within our experience which are "definite and exclusive objectifications and manifestations of God."[75] The *aporia* is this: In the contemporary setting, a transcendental starting point is required to talk at all about God; yet, this same starting point would appear to be inconsistent with an historical religion. How can these two competing exigencies of Christianity today be reconciled?

There are two alternatives for a religion which starts out from transcendental experience. One, which Rahner characterizes as "devotion to the world" seems to be a kind of natural religion, or what Kant would have called "religion within the limits of reason." In this alternative, "religion is respect vis-a-vis the categorical structures of the world insofar as all of these together have a transcendental orientation towards their primoridal ground, and in this kind of 'religion,' God really plays only an indirect role."[76] The other alternative, which Rahner characterizes in terms of the "true self-communication of God" is a supernatural religion, which preserves the dynamic tension between immanence and transcendence. The religion leaves open "the possibility of an immediacy to God in which, without ceasing to be really himself by being made a categorical object, he no longer appears merely as the ever-distant condition of possibility for a subject's activity in the world, but actually gives himself . . . in such a way that this self-communication can be received."[77]

The Possibility of an Individual and Abidingly-valid Self-communication

Obviously, in the context of a philosophical discussion, we can not make it our business to work out all of the specific ways in which this actual self-communication is accomplished. However, we do have a responsibility to address briefly the question of its possibility. Actually, there are two questions to be considered here: Is it possible for an individual existent in its categorical individuality and limitations to mediate God? If so, could such mediation be considered historically, abidingly valid for all of humanity?

An individual categorical mediation of God. To answer the first question, Rahner talks about God's direct self-communication in terms of a "mediated immediacy." In other words, the immediacy of God to some finite subject does not entail the disappearance of all that is creaturely and non-divine in the subject. To the contrary, through God's mediated immediacy, the finite subject "reaches its fulfillment and hence its fullest autonomy as subject. This autonomy is at once the presupposition and the consequence of this absolute immediacy to God and from God."[78] For such a theory to make sense, i.e. for us to secure the possibility of an individual existent mediating God to a finite subject, we need a proper notion of secondary causality. In other words, God cannot be depicted as one cause alongside many others, not even a "super-cause." God must be understood as the very ground of the entire network of causal chains.

> If . . . there is nevertheless to be an immediacy of God to us, if we are to find him in his own self here where we are in our categorical world of time and space, then this immediacy both in itself and in its categorical, historical objectification must be embedded in this world to begin with. . . . A special "intervention" of God, therefore, can only be understood as the historical concreteness of the transcendental self-communication of God which is already intrinsic to the concrete world.[79]

Here again it becomes evident that the transcendental and categorical are not opposed, but are intimately related as condition of possibility to that which it makes possible. The various categorical objectifications of God's self-communication are indeed valid and valuable, but they have their validity and value only within a transcendental experience of God, i.e. "only insofar as they really and truly exist within this subjective context, and therefore they can also be recognized in the special character which belongs to them only in this context."[80]

The phenomenon of worship is a case in point. Without going into Rahner's theology of worship in detail, it is still possible to see how this transcendental founding for God's categorical self-communication works. In a *Schriften* essay on worship, Rahner constrasts two models of grace with respect to their possible implications for liturgical life. One model of grace emphasizes God's intervention in the world at a definite point in space and time on the assumption that grace is an unmerited gift of God only if it becomes present in a secular and sinful world in which it is mostly denied. The other model of grace emphasizes, not a salvation of successive spatio-temporal interventions by God, but a history of free human response to habitual grace. In this model, which Rahner clearly prefers, sacraments are seen as "outbursts" rather than "incursions" of God.[81] Here again, we can see Rahner's rejection of a conception of the world as possibly in a state of "pure nature" over against a state of "pure grace."

> From the outset, God is lovingly seeking in freedom to bestow himself and, because he so wills in freedom, because he wills grace, he must create a 'nature' to which he can impart himself as free love. Nature is, because grace has to be. From the outset, as ground of nature,

grace is the innermost centre of this nature. Consequently, nature is never actually purely and simply secular; it is always nature graciously endowed with God himself.[82]

And so, the Church's worship—that aggregate of individual categorical actions and things whereby God is said to really communicate himself—has its primordial basis in "the liturgy of the world" (the history of God's self-communication and man's response) and that about the nature of the human person which would be required to make this liturgy possible.[83] Anyone who cannot identify any evidence in his or her own experience of God's "mediated immediacy" will not be able to see the Church's liturgy as anything but a "strange ritualism."[84] On this assumption, it could still be said that the worship of the Church possesses as certain objective validity—God is in fact communicating himself at this time and in this place—without foreclosing on the question of whether or not God's address has in fact been heard or accepted under these specific circumstances.

If it is possible for God to communicate himself at all, and an existential philosophical anthropology confirms that it is, it will only be in history and will only be discernable to one who is contemplatively available, i.e. to one who has pursued sustained reflection (whether implicitly or explicitly) on transcendental experience. But in none of this description of God's self-communication is freedom compromised. God's freedom to self-communicate is subject only to those ontological structures founded in the very nature of God's own being. Likewise, the human freedom to ignore, reject, despair, or surrender in the face of Absolute Mystery is also unaffected by possbility of God's mediated immediacy, for that freedom is itself a primordial sign a God's immanence in human existence.

An abidingly valid historical revelation. Having laid out what it is that would be need to secure the possibility of an individual existent in its categorical individuality and limitations mediating God, we are left with a final question: Could such a mediation be considered historically, abidingly valid for all of humanity? After all, the "idea of Christianity" includes as an integral part—indeed its central claim—an affirmation of Jesus as the definitive revelation of God in human history. Here, as in the case of the first question, we can only hope to provide some indication as to whether or not it would be intellectually honest to maintain such a position.

Rahner makes a great deal of the temporal and historical conditioning of all human activity. For him this even constitutes a prime evidence of the existence of that which is absolute and necessary; i.e. God as incomprehensible and mysterious horizon for knowledge and freedom. But Rahner discerns in human existence and experience some real limitations to temporal and historical conditioning. It is just such a limitation he is identifying when, for example, he rejects the argument that human existence is a dynamism without term, a kinesis reaching into the void of nothingness. In an essay on Christianity's absolute claims, Rahner identifies three more concrete evidences of the limits of temporal conditioning.

First, there are concepts, the permanent validity of which can be recognized without locating them outside of history. The principle of non-contradiction, for example, "cannot be conceived as existing only in finite time, because the conception of a mere temporally limited validity of the principle of contradiction nullifies itself inasmuch as the statement denying the principle of contradiction has meaning only in its implicit affirmation of this principle.[85] Secondly, there are statements of straightforward historical fact later refutation of which cannot be seriously considered.[86]   Thirdly, there are certain statements that cannot be thought of as one day being destined to pass out of existence, because a future refutation would annul the meaningfulness of the present moral existence of human beings. If I were to say, for example, that the future includes an abrogation of the moral demand of fidelity, of necessity I will have already ushered in the period its nonvalidity.[87] These three instances of the limits of historical and temporal conditioning do not themselves constitute a proof that Jesus is the historically binding and final revelation of God in history; but they do show that such a claim is not wholly discontinuous with human experience.

To say that something or someone in history could be absolutely binding one would have to presuppose the existence of God, the irreversability of a history which cannot cast off its past, and the nature of freedom as more than a chain of arbitrary succession but the very capacity of a human being to posit something with irrevocable finality.[88] We have treated all of these presuppositions in one form or another. If God is to address man, it will take place only in the world of time and space, in history. A reflection on transcendental experience—and the description of man, God, and the world which may be provided on the basis of this reflection—make it at least clear that an abidingly valid historical revelation may not be excluded *a priori*.

Contemplation: A Condition of Possibility for Revelation

To secure the possibility of revelation rationally, one must show that a person can be addressed by God without contradicting what is thought to be essential either to the human or the divine. In this chapter, we have seen that this claim carries with it two further implications: First, that revelation cannot occur, nor can it be made intelligible as a concept, except for one who is in a contemplative posture, and second, that the contemplative posture in which God may be known and heard consists not in a flight from the world but precisely in according sustained attention to one's spatio-temporal existence in all of its dimensions.

We have seen Rahner move beyond the traditional preoccupation with providing proofs for the existence of God to a reflection on transcendental experience (contemplative consideration of man's contemplative capacity) which brings to light the existence of God which is implicitly affirmed in all knowledge and free human activity. Only with an appreciation of the human capacity to reorient freely one's cognitive and moral attention from individuals and individual goods to that ground and goal which they require to be what they are, can it make any sense to say that man has been addressed by God.

The knowledge of God achieved through reflection on transcendental experience is marked above all by incomprehensibility. Here, contemplation marks the boundary not only between the person who can make sense of the revelation concept and the one who cannot, but also between the person who actually experiences revelation and the one who does not. In the face of the incomprehensibility of his own existence and of that holy mystery which insinuates itself into every aspect of human experience, a person faces a range of choices from least to most contemplative—from ignorance and scepticism to despair or surrender. Though one may certainly be contemplative without explicitly professing faith in the God of revealed religion, one may not be a believer, freely and responsibly engaged in a relationship with God, without being first and simultaneously contemplative, maximally open to the mystery which characterizes and impels human existence.

In light of all this, Rahner looks to the traditional proofs, not as if to a way of deductively guaranteeing God's existence, but as evidence that the contemplation by which one becomes open to God's word is inescapably conditioned by and exercised in the world of space and time. The one and only "proof" for God's existence, required for revelation to make sense and to be received, consists in the effort to show that all knowledge takes place against the backdrop of an affirmation of holy mystery as the *telos* of human transcendence. But that effort can be undertaken from a host of categorical staring points: reflection on the cosmos, on causality, on the moral life, etc. So while contemplation is clearly a prime condition of possibility for hearing a word spoken by God, the arena and immediate object of that contemplation will always be the world and one's life in it.

The tension between the transcendental goal and categorical starting point for this type of contemplation is experienced and expressed through analogy: God is person, creator, in the world. To the extent that one contemplatively preserves the dynamic tension between immmanence and transcendence out of which analogous language arises, one will not be misled into crude and superficial anthropomorphisms which can never constitute a suitable object for faith, but will remain open and available to the only reality worthy of complete trust, the only one capable of filling the breadth of human pre-apprehension and satisfying the human desire for the good. Only a contemplative in the broad sense can be a believer in the strict sense: One who, through the myriad decisions of life and death surrenders himself to mystery—holy, absolute, nameless, and unfathomable.

Conclusion

The major premise of the argument of this book has been that one cannot hope to relate reason and revelation accurately and adequately without having first worked out a conception of rationality. And so, I have attempted to distill from the thought of Karl Rahner his particular view of human reason, in the conviction that his distinctive place at a crucial historical and cultural juncture rendered him uniquely qualified to address the new problem of rationality without losing living contact with that history which is the soil in which the new problem has its roots.

The argument of this book has been executed in three movements. In the first part, I sketched out the problem both historically and in contemporary form, and I showed how the very loss of consensus on rationality is what characterizes the current state of the question. I argued that, in the face of a range of competing options—from objectivism to relativism—Karl Rahner, with his emphasis on the dynamism of the human person as a questioner, offers a more promising alternative. His early thought, worked out most comprehensively in *Spirit and the World* and *Hearers of the Word*, exhibits a constellation of characteristics which may be aptly described as contemplative.

In the second part, with the aim of determining whether and to what extent this contemplative aspect of rationality gets expressed in Rahner's mature thought, I proposed the hermeneutics of retrieval as a way of bringing out the implicit but significant contemplative component with greater clarity. Reaching back in order to move forward, I considered three important contributions to the evolution of Rahner's conceptual horizon and discovered that contemplation figures prominently in each. A definition of contemplation developed out of a consideration of the Thomas of Rousselot and Maréchal, the Ignatius of the *Exercises*, and the early Heidegger provided a new lens through which to read Rahner's late major work *Foundations of Christian Faith*.

And so, in the third part, I have executed the retrieval prepared for by Part II and have found contemplation characterizing Rahner's philosophical method, entering essentially into his philosophical anthropology, and figuring significantly in his model of revelation. Instead of attempting to unite subsequently and artificially two wholly unrelated principles, Rahner detects an already-present organic unitiy binding the aspirations of reason and the light of revelation. It his his attentiveness to the contemplative dimension which enables him to do so.

But does Rahner's approach represent a viable language and thought structure for dealing with the reaon/revelation problematic specifically in its contemporary form? In order to answer this question, I will outline five basic principles for a contemplative conception of rationality and address the most substantitve objections which can be raised against each of them. Then I will propose three possible contemporary applications of Rahner's contemplative model.

Theses and Critiques
First Thesis: Mystery Oriented toward Mystery

A contemplative conception of rationality takes as its starting point the dynamism of the human person as a questioner and is elaborated through an epistemology which understands knowing and being, human spirituality and materiality, intellect and will, all in terms of their original unity and interdependence. The centerpiece of this epistemology is the Vorgriff, *the unthematic, pre-conceptual, affirmation of Absolute Being which accompanies every knowing act as its principal possibilizing condition. Sustained reflection upon this pre-apprehension reveals the fundamental nature of the human person to be mystery oriented toward mystery.*

On the face of it, a conception of rationality which takes the knowing subject as its point of departure appears doomed to the same fate as much of the philosophy inspired by Descartes' *cogito*. The objection might go something like this: Begin in the mind, and you will never get out of the mind. Specifically: Can we really show that the Absolute Being affirmed in the *Vorgriff* is anything other than an idea of the mind, that it is something which actually transcends reason and experience?[1]

In fact, Absolute Being or (as Rahner later preferred to call it) Holy Mystery is not an idea or concept at all, but the very condition of possibility for conceptualization. The function of the *Vorgriff* in contemplative epistemology is not to delineate the range of sensible intuition; nor is it even to unify categories for understanding. *Vorgriff* is a way of talking about the quality of human intellect which makes objectification possible. One cannot set oneself as a self over against a limited other unless one, at the same time, is reaching for and grasps unthematically the full possibility of all that is. Indeed, if what was pre-grasped were simply an idea, still another transcending pre-apprehension would be required to provide the unlimited horizon against which this limited idea could be known, and so on *ad infinitum*. In every judgment, what is affirmed is a certain in-itself—something which is recognizable as distinct from the being of the knower. But the condition of possibility for such recognition can only be a familiarity with in-itselfness as such, Absolute Being, that which transcends worldly reality and, at the same time, accounts for its being and being known.

But, another objector will ask, does this not make the contemplative appeal to transcendental experience a kind of apriorism or intuitionism, placing it in outright contradiction to the Thomism with which it purports to be in continuity and short-changing the objectivity of divine revelation?[2]

First of all, it must be admitted that the development of this contemplative conception in juxtaposition to the preponderance of rationalistic approaches and their preoccupation with the empirical and *a posteriori* may have produced a somewhat lopsided emphasis on the *a priori*. In an effort to "rescue" reason from the vicissitudes of subjectivity, philosophical positivism and theological dogmatism have tended to focus on the extramental almost to the exclusion of the life of the mind. It is precisely attention to the *a priori* side of Thomas' thought—e.g. the innate grasp of first principles which every person has and the operation of agent intellect—which is required to forge a conception of rationality which can get beyond the the irresolvable conflict between objectivism and relativism.

This emphasis on the *a priori* should not be confused with apriorism. Although the *a posteriori* element (the categorical side of the transcendental-categorical dialectic) receives decidedly more attention in his later writings than in the earlier, even in *Spirit in the World*, Rahner is emphatic that the innate spiritual light (i.e. agent intellect) is only visible to the mind as reflected in *a posteriori* experience.[3]   The dynamism of the human person in the direction of the utterly transcendent is only co-known with as the condition of possibility for the intellectual apprehension of what is sensibly given—much the way the headlights of a car are visible to the driver of the vehicle only by reflection in a highway billboard.[4]   The God affirmed in the *Vorgriff* is not, therefore, a first order object of knowledge but is copresent as the ultimate term of every act of human transcendence—making possible but never circumscribed by any and every knowing act.

Second Thesis: Truth in Time and Eternity

A contemplative conception of rationality, because it acknowledges the genesis of all knowledge in sensible experience, understands truth to be related to human historicity—i.e., to one's free existence in the world of space and time. At the same time, because the relentless dynamism of the human mind always takes place in the face of death and gives indication of a pre-apprehension of that which is true pure and simple, without condition or qualification, it may also be said that truth is related to eternity. Therefore, while there is no entirely abstract standard of rational justification to which one may have legitimate recourse, neither may one conclude that truth is exclusively a function of an individual subject's experience in time. Still, to the extent that an object of knowledge may always be addressed by new human questions and questioners under a limitless number of conditions, the human mind's grasp of an object is always incomplete and provisional. This is particularly the case when one takes as the object of his knowledge a spiritual reality, e.g. one's own finite transcendence or the Holy Mystery, the pre-apprehension of which accompanies every knowing act.

Metaphysically and epistemologically, two different trains of thought seem to be travelling the contemplative route: One emphasizes ontological becoming and subjectivity; the other reaches out for stable being and objectivity. Critics of Rahner have expressed misgivings about the possible collision of these two powerful forces in varying ways. Dewart, for example, argued that Rahner, Lonergan, and other transcendental thinkers tried to keep alive an objectivist metaphysics complete with Absolute Being, at the same time employing a transcendental method which by definition is entitled to begin with nothing but the being of consciousness.[5]   Sheehan, in his recent work on Rahner's epistemology talks about Rahner having used Heidegger to extort an existential transcendental turn out of Aquinas and having used Aquinas to extort an affirmation of God out of Heidegger.[6]   Are there two contrary forces in a contemplative conception of truth which are in principle unrelatable, even dialectically?

First of all, as for "extorting" any modification of opinion from any thinker: This clearly could not have been Rahner's aim, nor is it mine.   If Rahner's own personal reflections as chronicled by his interviews make anything clear, it is that his allegiance to any thinker or system was subordinated to his principal concern, which was the furtherance of Christianity's self-understanding in the contemporary world.   If Thomas or Heidegger or anyone else has stimulated his thinking or ours, so be it; but in a contemplative conception of rationality, philosophical orthodoxy possesses no intrinsic value.   All the same, if one could prove that there are elements of this conception of truth which are in open conflict and incapable of being reconciled on some higher level, the objection would have to be taken seriously.

As it happens, the metaphysics and epistemology proposed here are neither as delivered over to the vicissitudes of history as they may first appear to a strict Thomist nor as objectivist as they may seem to a Heideggerian.   It is true, of course, that the term of human transcendence was described by the early Rahner as Absolute Being.   It is also true that there is a more than a superficial resemblance between this and Thomistic *esse*.   But it would be a mistake to interpret this Absolute Being as a Supreme Essence which grounds all other essences,[7] a kind of philosophical *Deus ex machina* which arbitrarily brings to a halt all human striving for the truth.   Absolute Being has, as we have seen, both a formal and transcategorical universality.   This means that, though there is nothing in the world which can be or be known apart from it, it utterly outstrips everything that is, including the human capacity to know.   It is, after all, mystery; and as such it never itself become the object of our thought, but always accompanies the objects of our thought as a sort of ultimate critique.

But, a Heideggerian may reply, does not the contemplative dynamism of knowledge come to a halt the moment that, in its openness to historical revelation, it chooses to identify Holy Mystery with the God of Christianity?   Would not Christianity, to qualify for the title of a contemplative religion, have to relinquish its claims to normativity and abiding validity? If so, adds the orthodox Christian theologian, would the transcendent God encountered in reflection upon transcendental experience not turn out to be the prisoner of a history forged by human freedom? And don't we wind up in that same relativist *cul de sac* we were trying to avoid in the first place?

As the thesis above emphasizes: Contemplatively, truth always has something to do with both time and eternity. As an achievement of free and limited human beings in time, the pursut of truth will have to take history—including that which pertains to Jesus and the Church—seriously. As an achievement of persons living always in the face of death, the pursuit of truth always points in the direction of something having eternal significance. In the fifth thesis, I emphasize that incomprehensibility is an essential mark of this eternal truth contemplatively beheld. Hence, while there is no *a priori* reason why the Christ event could not impose real limits on the temporal and historical conditioning of truth, it would have to be admitted that even this Christ event lies at least partially concealed behind a veil of mystery.

Third Thesis: Mystery Addressed by Mystery

A contemplative conception of rationality not only affirms the reality of an infinite term of human transcendence—i.e. Absolute Being, Holy Mystery, God—in positing a Vorgriff, *it also opens up the possibility of Holy Mystery addressing the human person in the mysteriousness of his own historical existence. This free self-communication, revelation properly speaking, is already affirmed as a definitive historical reality within the context of an orthodox Christianity. But such an affirmation presupposes that there have been, are, and will be concrete individuals who, in some here-and-now, have actually received and responded to this address. This could be the case only if human beings had a contemplative capacity; i.e. the ability freely to modify their intellectual and moral intentionality from the myriad finite particulars, concepts, and systems which are the preoccupation of mundane existence to the inner dynamism of the human spirit and its infinite term by which all things come to be and to be known. Revelation in a broad sense, one's awareness of one's own transcendence and its term, is the condition of possibility for*

revelation in the strict sense, the reception of a definite word spoken
by God.

I have indicated that the genius of the contemplative approach to reason and revelation has something to do with discovering through reflection upon transcendental experience a primitive and original unity out of which reason and revelation may only subsequently be distinguished. Historically, we saw how remote are the chances of a successful synthesis between reason and revelation when rationality is conceived of entirely apart from a notion of being or God. Likewise, with regard to the mysterious human dynamism toward Holy Mystery: In a contemplative anthropology, human mystery and divine mystery are always already (*immer schon*) proportioned to one another. It is only through an unwise use of freedom—one's own or someone else's—that a person can evade or be blinded to this mystery.

Here is the problem which this description of the human situation creates (and I am paraphrasing Peter Eicher on this point): If the whole content of God's Word is always already transcendentally given, then what purpose is served by the historical or categorical? Tradition becomes a function of religious subjectivity, and the effort at historical, critical work can *a priori* bring to light nothing more than the self-revelation of God in which all human persons *immer schon* take part.[8]

First of all, it is important to bear in mind Rahner's purpose in the works which elaborate what I am calling his contemplative approach. Above all, he is attempting to show that, even in the face of the staggering pluralism which characterizes the contemporary sphere of knowledge and the unsettling agnosticism which that pluralism has engendered, it is still possible to be a believer with intellectual honesty. Such a purpose would not justify a reduction of the historical side of Christianity to the status of a mere objectification of the yearnings of religious subjectivity. But if it could be shown that history in fact plays a more essential role in a contemplative conception, then the over-emphasis of the transcendental side will at least be understandable.

As a matter of fact, the historical/categorical does enter more fundamentally into the Rahner equation than Eicher seems to allow, and it is precisely a contemplative interpretation of Rahner which makes this evident. The fact, for example, that the accordance of sustained attention to the dynamism of the human spirit uncovers a natural openness to Holy Mystery does not mean *ipso facto* that the bestowal of Holy Mystery is any less gratuitous or that the mystery is any less mysterious. There is nothing in the contemplative model *per se* which conflicts with a doctrine of creation; hence, there is no reason why God could not structure the human person with a view to his actual self-gift.[9]

Moreover, as we have seen at several points throughout the book, the dialectical method employed here, while undeniably a cousin to the Hegelian system, has even more vital connections with the dialectics of the ancient Greeks, the Medieval *disputatio*, and Christian mysticism.[10]   Historical particularities—the reality of Jesus and Christianity chief among them—do not simply provide an inert basis on which the transcendental movement of the human spirit may come to light. If it is true that the soul in a sense becomes all things, that the mind knows nothing without turning to the phantasms, then the content of historical revelation is anything but superfluous.   Using the headlight/highway sign metaphor: It may well be that the light of the agent intellect becomes visible to the knower in any *a posteriori* encounter, but what is written on that sign in which the headlights of the human spirit are reflected is decisive. Should that sign be lettered with only the limited goods which a world separated from the Christ-event may offer, the light will be reflected back only dimly, providing little if any direction. If, however, that sign should be lettered with the one Word in which a human being can recognize his or her true destiny and fulfillment, the light reflected back will point the way home for a restless spirit.

When I say, therefore, that revelation in fact takes place for one who is in a contemplative posture, in no way do I mean to suggest the self-sufficiency of the human spirit or the superfluity of historical revelation (revelation in the strict sense). To the contrary, only a contemplation reflexively situated in the world—a world which has been transformed by the Christ-event—can serve as a propaedeutic for faith properly speaking.

Fourth Thesis: Loci of Revelatory Action
In a contemplative conception of rationality, revelation in both the broad and strict sense can occur only in the world and in history. Hence, the imagination, human relationship and community, and worship, as well as the Scripture of the Church and the Tradition of their interpretation are all possible loci of revelatory action.   The

analogical character of all these experiences is indicative, not of a deficient level of knowledge, but of the human aspiration for the highest form of knowledge possible: an unmediated vision of and presence to that which alone can fulfill the dynamism of the human spirit.

We have seen that, in a contemplative model of rationality, freedom and responsibility are always experienced in their historical and social dimensions. Hence the word addressed to man by God will always be spoken and given its response in history and community. But for all the importance which this model purports to attribute to history, it may be complained that it is lacking exegetical sophistication. And, despite the nod given to the way in which other subjects enter into my historical life, intersubjectivity does not appear to be integral to the contemplative conception. Indeed, it appears highly individualistic.

As for the historical problem,[11] it must be admitted that our contemplative conception of rationality depends heavily on a version of Thomistic epistemology which is not informed by a particularly careful appraisal of the meaning of Thomistic doctrines in their own distinctive historical context. Rahner does not conceal this fact, nor should we. A parallel problem emerges in the theological Rahner: Even in the latter parts of *Foundations* which we have not considered, historical details and hermeneutic fine points are subordinated to the one over-riding concern, namely the demonstration of the possibility of being a Christian today without offense to one's rational nature.

Although one might have hoped that the epistemology and fundamental theology in which the contemplative conception of rationality is based were enriched by a more thorough historical-critical propaedeutic, there is nothing in principle to prevent one from undertaking this as a beneficial or maybe even necessary complementary task. Still, as O'Donovan has noted in his own review of *Foundations*, it may have been concern about "the consequences of free-floating research into the circumstances and intent of texts, etc." which persuaded Rahner not to apply himself to historical research with the same verve he displays in transcendental analysis.[12] The fact is that one problem which looms large in the sciences in general and in theology and philosophy in particular is the practice of scholarship for its own sake, the kind of display of intellectual virtuosity which seems to subordinate truth to technique. At the heart of a contemplative conception of rationality is the claim that one's fundamental speculative and practical intentionality—that to which one is open and the reason why—is prior to and determinative of the tools and techniques one will use for one's research. In the present case, the lack of attention to the work of historical critical analysis is counterbalanced by a more penetrating analysis of the conditions for its possibility and its ultimate purpose.

With regard to the question of the social or inter-subjective aspect of contemplation, it is best perhaps to let a "friendly" critic articulate this *aporia*. Rahner's student, J. B. Metz, has argued that the transcendental method of his teacher was determined in part by its need to counteract the neo-scholasticism which preceded it and to come to terms with the Kantian and post-Kantian philosophies which were thought to pose the greatest intellectual threat to Catholicism. Consequently, Rahner's own thought was characterized more by a concern for the life of individual consciousness than for social or political realities. It was driven more by the speculative interests which Metz believes were and are the preoccupation of bourgeois Western society and less by the practical interests which appear to have been the pre-eminent concern of Jesus and the early Church.[13]

It must be candidly admitted that, at least insofar as it has been elaborated here, the contemplative conception of rationality and revelation does not treat the social dimension of the human person as much more than a corollary to its anthropology. We have said that other free subjects and not just a host of determined and determining objects necessarily enter into the personal history forged by each individual in freedom; but we have not shown what is distinctive about the contribution, nor have we even entertained the possibility that ontological significance be attributed to relationships themselves and not just to the related individuals. Is it not possible or even likely that, when it comes to intersubjectivity, the whole is indeed greater than the sum of its parts? Is it not possible or even likely that there exists a shared contemplation which is more than a mere rhapsody of my thoughts and your thoughts, but a unitary experience in which two persons or even a whole community share together? Here is where lived faith and theology have perhaps ventured beyond professional philosophy in the adequacy of their anthropologies. For the practicing Christian, nothing is more evident than that the community—in its daily life, its worship, and its hierarchical constitution—is a privleged place for hearing the address of Holy Mystery. And yet, Rahner's caveat bears repeating:

"Solitariness before God, security in his silent, immediate presence is man's sole possession."[14]

As for the absence of a concern for praxis in the contemplative approach: While the conception worked out here could not be described as praxis-based (as contrasted, for example, with the epistemology proposed by Clodovis Boff[15]), there can be little question about the integral part which praxis plays. Every ancestor in the contemplative family tree gives praxis pride of place: From the Thomism of Rousselot and Maréchal which has contemplation emerge as an explicit concern precisely where intellect and will are experienced in their interdependence and common origin, to the mysticism of Ignatius with its emphasis on the making of a practical decision, to Heidegger whose very conception of truth locates its essence in freedom. There is nothing inherent about this contemplation which justifies its characterization as either bourgeois or merely speculative.

At the same time, it should be acknowledged that my own decision to focus on the Introduction and first two chapters of *Foundations*, while defensible and even necessary given the scope of the project, may give a somewhat lopsided impression of Rahner's thinking. Depsite his insistence on the unity of intellect and will as well as on the transcendental irreducibility of freedom, from the early part of *Foundations*, one may still be led to think of Rahner's conception as narrowly intellectualist or individualistic and lacking penetrating insight into human persons, society, or history. Although a careful reading of these early chapters confirms that this is not the case, and though Rahner conceived of each chapter as a "*Gang*" or "way" rather than as an integral piece of a larger argument, some reference to others parts of the work—where sin and suffering, the person of Jesus and the reality of the Church are dealt with in some detail—may help to mitigate the impression of Rahner as what Rousselot might have called an "idolater of abstraction."

Fifth Thesis: Incomprehensibility

In a contemplative conception of rationality, revelation will always be accompanied by a "negative" element expressed as darkness, death, or silence. In the experience of agnosticism or wonder in the sphere of the sciences, in the frustration of one's highest moral inclinations, or in the inscrutability of human behavior both unimaginably generous and unconscionably cruel—in such experiences, the contemplative person recognizes the incomprehensibility of his existence considered as a whole and the incomprehensibility of the one in which this existence is grounded and toward which it is dynamically oriented. The way in which one exercises his or her freedom in the face of such experiences is indicative of the extent to which one is thinking and living contemplatively and, ultimately, of the extent to which one is living entirely within the paramenters of a natural knowledge or has surrendered himself to Holy Mystery through a supernatural faith. Surrender to the mystery is neither a sacrifice of intellect nor an eradication of incomprehensibility. Rather, it is a decision to pursue knowledge and to exercise one's freedom in constant mindfulness of the inexhaustibility of that in which one's existence is rooted and toward which it is directed as toward its own fulfillment.

From the beginning, we have identified a loss of consensus about the nature of rationality as a principal factor in the difficulty of relating a reconciling reason and revelation in the contemporary situation. The myriad attempts to discover or formulate a fixed and universal standard of rationality for use in the sciences as well as ethics have all met with only limited success, for rival standards are never in short supply. The result has been seemingly irresolvable chaos.

What I have argued here is that the mere quest for a rational standard, and even the apparent chaos which has resulted, are themselves pointers to a more viable way of talking about rationality—a way which takes as its starting point the dynamism of the human being as a questioner. However, to the reader of scientific or mathematical bent, a way of talking about rationality which, regardless of where it begins, ends in incomprehensibility will hardly seem an improvement over a clearer standard with at least some adherents or a multiplicity of standards in conflict.

There are two responses which the proponent of the contemplative conception of rationality may give. One is to carefully distinguish incomprehensibility from absurdity, in order to show that the contemplative option is at least viable as an alternative. The second response (which is more ambitious) is to show that this incomprehensibility-based approach can account for that which is excluded in more empirically-satisfying systems of thought.

First of all, the previous chapter's discussion of incomprehensibility provides an adequate vantage point from which to see that what we are talking about here is something quite different from—though not entirely unrelated to—the chaos of a hundred conflicting rational standards. For the contemplative person, that chaos is a sign of humanity's unfulfilled transcendence. It points not to a lamentable lack which one hopes will be remedied at some point in the future, when the one universal standard which puts an end to all questions is found. It points rather to the inexhaustible transcendence of God, which we can never hope to encompass, but to which we can only surrender in that complete act of trust which alone satisfies the dynamism of the human spirit. A doctrine of incomprehensibility need not deny the value of developing criteria of rationality; it only suggests that the application of such standards ought always to be accompanied by an awareness of their origins in the limited, concrete, historical lives of those who have forged them, lest they be absolutized and foreclose the human inquisitive dynamism.

However, even if the difference between mere speculative chaos and incomprehensibility be granted, does not a conception of rationality without an empirically verifiable bottom line lack the kind of rigor and certitude after which the contemporary mind seeks—a quasi-mathematical certitude in which everything adds up? Early in his career, Rahner remarked, "[Mathematical truths] are accepted by all merely because, belonging as they do to the most peripheral of human activity, that of space and number, they are never able to contradict the deliberate understanding of being through the method of free love."[16] Later, in *Foundations*, he defended the "pre-scientific" character of his first level of reflection as inevitable in view of the peculiar nature of its object, nothing less than "the totality of one's existence in the world."[17]

If one has chosen to preoccupy himself only with those aspects of the human situation which pertain to space, number, and so on, more precise standards of rationality are clearly in order. But it would be underestimating the depth of contemporary man's searching to suggest that this is all that is of concern to him. Anyone who has been in love or disappointed in love, who has faced death or recovered from illness, who has been hounded by questions of life's meaning or confronted by a bewildering ethical dilemma knows experientially that no single standard of rationality is wholly adequate—that, in the end, there is mystery, which one may choose to enter trustingly or else evade at all costs.

The beauty of a conception of rationality which is not afraid to take time with incomprehensibility is paradoxically that it most comprehensively accounts for the range of human experience. Indeed, this is precisely where the complaint made by von Balthasar and others that Rahner's theology has no place for the cross[18] meets its response:

> A properly understood philosophy of transcendentality is one in which the human person is precisely the subject who opens onto an incomprehensibility that cannot be systematized. Let his be said against German idealism, and I don't know if it is not ultimately the same thing in Heidegger and *mutatis mutandis* in Husserl as well, and so on. . . . it is death, real death naturally, not speculation about it in a lecture hall, that is the only real fulfillment of this fundamental structure of the human person.[19]

Three Applications of the Contemplative Model
The Relationship of Philosophy and Theology

The first and most obvious area in which the implications of a contemplative conception of rationality may be felt is in the relationship of theology to philosophy and to the host of other non-theological sciences through which man reflects upon himself and his world. The contemporary challenge in this arena is two-fold: From the side of theology, it is a matter of situating Christianity within the intellectual horizon of people today without doing anything that might compromise the distinctiveness and definitiveness of the revelation which is said to have occured in Jesus. From the side of philosophy and other secular sciences, it is a matter of maintaining autonomy and freedom of inquiry as against any conceivable attempt to subsume all science under a single, comprehensive, and already-completed metaphysical system.

Any attempt to work out this relationship according to a completely predetermined framework unilaterally imposed by one or another discipline cannot succeed. A principal strength of the contemplative conception of rationality is its anthropological starting point. It begins with reflection upon the only experience which can be said with certainty to bind theology and the various forms of man's secular self-understanding: the human person as questioner. If there is to be any subsequent dialogue between sciences already established and developed, it can only be based upon a recognition of a prior unity. That unity is nothing other than the experience of personhood, human existence reflected upon as a dynamic and inexhaustible whole, rather than as a static sum of individual determinants.

When the human person is reflected upon in this way—and such is the business of a philosophical anthropology—differentiation and change can be seen as emanating necessarily from the relentless dynamism of human existence, not appearing only later as welcome or unwelcome phenomena (depending on one's point of view) of a materialistic, spiritualistic, or dualistic description of "human nature." Inasmuch as man finds himself constantly transcending himself through knowledge and freedom, never coming to rest, revealing an appetite for anything whatsoever that is, man affirms his own spirituality. At the same time, man has no knowledge which cannot be traced back, in the first instance, to sensible experience in the world of space and time. Man cannot exercise his freedom except as circumscribed within certain limits imposed by his materiality and historicity. Even the experience of God had in reflection upon the *Vorgriff* cannot be seen as an intellectual intuition but as a special kind of knowledge which is co-present with and gained through a spiritual/material, intellectual/sensible act of knowing. The human person exercises his self-transcending spirituality precisely in the world and in history; conversely, the human person is capable of freely and knowingly acting in the world and creating history only because he is spiritual. A twofold conception of humanity which resolutely refuses to be reduced either to monism or dualism, which can stay with the fruitful tension which joins and distinguishes man's spirituality and worldliness, implies a critique of both the secular sciences and theology as they are practiced today.

To every particular "school" of philosophy and to every empirical science (whether anthropological or natural), a contemplative conception of rationality constitutes a warning not to get carried away by its own achievements. It reminds the philosopher and the scientist of the inescapably historical origin and context of all her findings and elaborate systems, relativizing their value, though stopping short of sheer relativism. It reminds the secular researcher and scholar of the unavoidable limits of their enterprise—limits which are not the function of a lamentable and correctible failure to gather together all the necessary information, but which are the principal indication for the scientist that an infinite, unfathomable, indefinable, and unnamable "something more" is the condition of possibility for the forging of their finite concepts, systems, and theories about man and his world.

Philosophy practiced in the contemplative mode does not envision epistemological rigor and openness to mystery as mutually exclusive or radically opposed. They are, if anything, two sides of the same coin. The rationale for rigor—for precision in language and concern for logical form, for exhaustiveness in the analysis of data and subjection to contrary arguments—is precisely an awareness of the fact that there is and always remains more than what appears on the surface. Conversely, it is in part the comprehensiveness of a genuinely scientific procedure which makes possible the appearance—along with the concepts, laws, and systems which are the stock and trade of modern science—of that infinite and incomprehensible horizon in the light of which alone these could make any sense.

At the same time, the two-fold conception of the human person which is at the heart of a contemplative conception of rationality also constitutes an implicit critique of theology as it is sometimes practiced in the contemporary setting. It suggests, for example, that an approach to fundamental theology which is either purely deductive or purely inductive is essentially flawed. If one proceeds from the assumption that an original unity binds theology and philosophy, then it makes no sense to proceed either as if the basic tenets of Christianity could be made absolutely clear apart from any concrete historical experience, or as if Christianity were something to be discovered entirely outside a person, having nothing whatsoever to do with who and what a person is to begin with.

The contemplative conception of rationality and revelation suggests that an approach to dogmatic or systematic theology which does not proceed with an explicit awareness of God's incomprehensibility will likewise exhibit certain difficulties: It will tend to minimize the reality and/or the importance of genuine doctrinal development, contrary to the clear witness of history. It will insist on an absolute uniformity of method and language, despite the obvious pluralism with which persons have experienced and expressed a relationship to God. It will dismiss as unimportant or corrosive the interpretation of dogmas in their proper social and historical contexts, despite the fact that this may be the only way in which any sense could be made of a claim to binding validity. It will resort to arguments from ecclesiastical authority without elaborating a reasonable basis for doing so, creating in effect simply one more problematical doctrine. Finally, a non-contemplative dogmatic theology will reduce God to mere human concepts about him, even though a sober analysis of these concepts reveals how infinitely short they fall of expressing fully the God-reality.

Just as it is quite unlikely that a union of persons wholly convinced of their absolute self-sufficiency will evolve into a friendship, so too is it clear that the forging of a fruitful relationship between theology and philosophy, along with the natural and anthropological sciences, depends upon a mutual acknowledgement of limitations and interdependence. Each of the sciences requires a certain legitimate autonomy in order to succeed in its proper objectives; but each of the sciences, whether theological or secular, needs to acknowledge the partiality of its own perspective and to bring its own findings into contact and conversation with that of the others. This is the case, not simply because, in the course of their investigations, all of the sciences come upon certain boundaries, but also because the only horizon against which boundaries as such could be recognized is that of Absolute Mystery.

Roman Catholic Apologetics
The second area in which the implications of a contemplative conception of rationality and revelation may be felt is related to the first. Just as, in the academic arena, this distinctive approach to philosophical anthropology may be viewed as providing a basis for dialogue between theology and secular science; so too, in the pastoral arena, the contemplative model may be seen as providing a way for prospective believers to find for themselves a "reason for the hope" that Christianity intends to offer them. Deep within Christianity is a universalizing tendency; viz. Christianity understands itself as bearing an historical revelation which has abiding validity for persons living in any and every conceivable cultural, social, and historical milieu. If its universalizing tendency is to be fulfilled, Christianity must be able to show both to non-believers and to its own merely-nominal adherents that it has something to say specifically *to them*.

One overriding difficulty which the Roman Catholic community faces with regard to apologetics at the end of the twentieth century is that there remain remnants of that decidedly defensive posture which the Church, at the end of the previous century, assumed in response to the Enlightenment. Officially, the

Church has yet to incorporate fully an awareness of the depth of change which has taken place during the intervening years—particularly the way in which the classical Enlightenment emphasis on the experience of the subject has been radicalized through a intensified awareness of human historicity and cultural pluralism. The approach to apologetics which has prevailed until now—whereby a person is presented with a set of dogmas, shown their admirable clarity and "reasonableness" as well as their "objective" superiority to a host of contrary positions only superficially considered—such an approach no longer meets with great success. The contemporary man or woman is less concerned with the correspondence of Christianity's message to an abstract standard of reason and more concerned with its relationship to the totality of his or her own existence in the world.

Two features of the contemplative conception of rationality and revelation provide an orientation for a new apologetic. First of all, it resolutely avoids entitative language about God. It recognizes that, while a reflexive knowledge of and about God inevitably involves one in the use of limiting concepts, these concepts will always have to be embedded in a form of discourse which makes clear the fact that they conceal as well as reveal the truth of who and what God is. Admittedly, this involves one in the use of inelegant expressions, e.g. "the infinite term of finite transcendence co-present with every knowing act." But if God is not a particular, we will sometimes need to resort to a form of discourse which will, at first, strike the reader and hearer as strange.

The second feature of a contemplative conception of rationality and revelation which may point the way for a new apologetic is the fact that it locates "primitive revelation" (i.e. revelation from the Patriarchs to Jesus) in a broader history of revelation as a whole. If the human person is mystery oriented toward and addressed by mystery to begin with—and not just because of a direct or indirect exposure to the idea of Christianity—then God's self-communication has always already occurred in every person from the beginning of time. Whether and how revelation in this broader sense is brought to reflex consciousness and embraced is obviously important. But, for the contemporary apologete operating within a contemplative framework, this is not a matter of searching for reasons outside of a person's existence to justify a faith which is radically discontinuous with what that person is "by nature." To the contrary, a contemplative apologete will search precisely within the context of an individual's concrete experience to identify that original awareness of Holy Mystery which can then be reflected upon in terms of primitive revelation, the abidingly valid self-communication of God in Jesus, experienced and sustained in the community of the Church.

The apologetic significance of the contemplative model may, in turn, be elaborated in term of three specific questions of contemporary concern: inter-faith and inter-religious dialogue, the problem of atheism, and the mystagogy of those who are already members of the Church. For example, does it make sense in the present context to attempt a union of Christian Churches solely or even primarily through a concordance of dogmatic formulations? Or would it not also be important to create a climate in which Christians of various traditions can reflect upon and articulate for each other their own experience of God's historical self-communication worked out, not only in specific dogmatic formulations, but also in worship, common life, praxis, and prayer. Perhaps a degree of pluralism in doctrinal expression wider than previously assumed is possible.

With regard to atheism: Do the standard ways of framing the issue of atheism reflect an awareness that the form of atheism which dominates today is not the speculative or intellectualist atheism of the eighteenth and nineteenth century, but a more subtle and complex phenomenon which may be found both within and outside Christianity? Atheism today takes multiple forms—from the methodological atheism of the positive scientist, to the nearly-total indifference of the person preoccupied with all the details of categorical existence, to the trivializing of God in which the religious dogmatist is engaged. The apologete operating out of a contemplative model of rationality and revelation—with its anthropological starting point and courage to linger with rather than to eliminate all dialectical tensions—will not suppose that it is possible to overcome atheism merely through the construction of elaborate arguments which, while impressive, may actually have little to do with the root causes of the specific atheism in question.

Finally, with regard to the mystagogy of those already belonging to the Church: One of the outstanding features of religion in the West today is the growth of nominal or cultural Christianity. Men and women find it possible to identify themselves as "Christian" or "Catholic," may even participate occasionally in the ritual life of the Church, without really having been inwardly transformed, without having brought to consciousness and accepted in all its incomprehensibility an experience of God. Although it is impossible for an observer to say with certitude whether or not an acceptance has taken place in this or that particular case, there is ample evidence that there are numerous individuals in which this has not taken place—at least to any great extent. From the perspective of a contemplative apologetic, the challenge here is not primarily indoctrination; indeed, it is quite possible for someone to have mastered a host of dogmatic formulations without perceiving any significant connection between these and one's own concrete situation. The challenge is rather to create conditions favorable to a contemplative modification of intentionality. A person who has not accorded any sustained attention to the totality of his existence in the world, who has not discerned the mysteriousness of his own situation and the trajectory of the dynamism of his own spirit toward Holy Mystery (however he might describe that for himself) will not be in the position to recognize in the word of historical revelation anything more than an interesting and perhaps harmless phenomenon of one's own cultural background and existence. At best, religion will provide for the non-contemplative Christian validation of one's own life style and mores. At worst, it will be a mere ornament, an aesthetically-pleasing bauble adorning one's personal or social life. In either case, it will not have progressed to the level of faith as such.

Ethics in a Plural and Changing Culture
The third and final area in which I want to note the possible effects of a contemplative conception of rationality is the challenge of ethical discourse and dialogue in a world deeply aware of its temporality and cultural pluralism. Pluralism and change are not themselves new phenomena in the sphere of morally significant human conduct; but the ntensified awareness of these in a world made both smaller and more complex through advanced technology presents a uniquely contemporary challenge: On what basis may ethical discussion be had and ethical choices be made in the public arena, when the parties to that discussion bring with them radically different presuppositions about humanity, goodness, knowledge, truth, and so on? In a previous era, a relatively uniform culture, more or less separated from different cultures by geography or time, could be counted on to give birth to or support a relatively uniform ethic. Today, in the West at least, nearly everyone is aware that there are a host of ways of analyzing and deciding an ethical situation and that the

validity of one over another is not immediately and overwhelmingly clear and evident.

This new set of circumstances poses a particular challenge to Catholic Christianity which not only discerns in the person and message of Jesus concrete implications for human living, but also claims to be able to provide authoritative direction in the moral order. At one time, an appeal to natural law was thought to provide a "rational" foundation for the ethical principles at which Christians arrived by faith. Today, however, when no single conception of rationality can make an undisputed claim to validity and when the very idea of a person being constituted in a particular way "by nature" is itself placed in question, the standard natural law approach alone cannot be expected to provide the justification required to make Christianity's ethical demands intelligible in a pluralistic setting—let alone to provide a common basis for ethical discourse and dialogue.

There are two features of a contemplative conception of rationality which suggest the possibility of forward movement in this arena. First of all, there is the emphasis on the interpenetration of intellect and will, knowledge and freedom. This interpentration was not overlooked in the conception of rationality forged by Christianity's greatest natural law thinker Thomas Aquinas; but, for a host of reasons, it does not seem to have been brought out with sufficient clarity by many of his commentators. In a crude scholastic anthropology, will and intellect seem to be two entirely distinct and separable faculties which operate on each other in an extrinsic way. The intellect determines the good and the extent to which the facts of the particular moral situation correspond to the good. The will then implements (or fails to implement) the objective judgment rendered by the intellect. Ultimate goodness prevails when an unruly will is brought under the rule of reason.

In the contemplative model, by contrast, the relationship of will and intellect is seen in its complexity. Knowledge itself is acknowledged as involving freedom from the outset. Things and circumstances have a givenness about them which the subjective operations of an individual person cannot take away. But that which in fact comes to be known is also a function of free choice—exercised through the questions which are asked, which determine the degree to which one is opened up to what is really there. The choices which one makes on the basis of knowledge thus attained, in turn, affect one's disposition with respect to the acquisition of future knowledge, and so on until death. There is, in other words, a kind of circularity to the freedom/knowledge relationship which defies facile reduction. An acknowledgement of this fact constitutes a warning to the Christian ethician not to suppose that arguments which are perfectly "rational" to him from an "objective" viewpoint will necessarily be convincing to his partner in dialogue. Prior dispositional factors—a person's interests and ultimate values, his or her past experiences and current life situation—these are as going to be as important to the success of an ethical discussion as the structure of the competing arguments and the evidence brought to bear in favor of the conflicting positions.

The second feature of a contemplative conception of rationality which suggests the possibility of movement in the ethical arena is its emphasis on the inseparability of the transcendental and the categorical, the spiritual and the historical. As we have repeatedly noted, even where knowledge of God is concerned, there are no intellectual intuitions; God is experienced only as co-present with every spiritual/material act of a human being. Even when a person is thinking about God, he must rely on the images born of sensible experience in a spatio-temporal world. The same principal applies, mutatis mutandis in the ethical arena; viz. the moral meaning of a human act cannot be known except in reference to this particular act, with this particular objective, under these particular circumstances.

In traditional Catholic ethics, one may have felt confident in determining moral meaning according to "the nature of the act" and providing "exceptionless moral norms" whose truth, it was thought, could be made transparent even apart from the light of Gospel and the experience of historical religion. In the contemplative model, by contrast, it is recognized that the only acts that have moral meaning in the strict sense are those which belong to concrete human actors with freedom and knowledge; talk of "the nature of the act" is a subsequent abstraction which will always fail to capture fully the mysteriousness of the original human experience. In the contemplative model, the hope of determining exceptionless moral norms will be tempered by the realization that there is infinitely more about the reality of man and the reality of God which remains concealed than is revealed in any judgment—whether that judgment is speculative or practical. This does not mean that it will be impossible to formulate and to make clear for others certain principles for human conduct based upon an interpretation of human existence; but such principles, especially the more specific they become, will have to remain open in principle to further clarification and even revision.

Most importantly, in the contemplative model, it will not be supposed that one can prescind from the historical particulars out of which an ethical position has emerged and still be able to demonstrate convincingly its validity. The abortion issue is a case in point: The effort is sometimes made to show that the inviolability of innocent life is not a uniquely Catholic or even Christian position, but bespeaks a fundamental stance toward reality and human existence which, though it finds support in historical revelation, does not require the doctrine of a particular religious group for its justification. If Christianity wants to be true to its universalizing impulse and not become sectarian, the effort to demonstrate the reasonableness of this and other ethical positions can and must be made.

At the same time, however, it should also be acknowledged that orthodox Christianity *in fact* arrived at its opposition to abortion, for example, not simply through a reflection upon abstract moral principles. To the contrary, such moral principles are themselves the product of a reflection upon the concrete historical experience of the believing community. If the teaching authority of the Catholic Church were to lose sight of the way in which its position on human life is embodied in and borne by its particular tradition, the danger would exist that the connection of its position to the real life situations of concrete persons would be obscured and the teaching made to appear irrelevant. If, on the other hand, Christianity were to remain conscious of and reflective upon the way in which its extraordinary solicitude for the dignity of the human person has emerged from a particular conception of man—a conception of man as *imago Dei,* exemplified most fully in the figure of Jesus whose life and death reflected a valuing of persons which transcended the relative goods of utility, pleasure, and achievement—if Christianity were attentive to its own roots and inner dynamism, it would be in a better position to help others reflect on their own experience in such a way as to discover for themselves a sense of humanity's incalculable worth.

In short, then, in a world profoundly aware of its temporality and cultural pluralism, a contemplative conception of rationality provides a new basis for ethical discourse and dialogue. Cognizant of the interpenetration of freedom and knowledge in the dynamism of the human spirit, a contemplative model creates the space and clearing in which ethicians of various perspectives may come together and begin to listen to eachother—and not simply to each other's ethical theories but also, and perhaps more importantly, to the concrete historical, social, and cultural experiences out which these theories have emerged. Rather than reaching for the least common denominator of rational agreement artificially purged of all historical and metaphysical assumptions; the approach to ethical discussion proposed here invites participants to "come as they are," open to the possibility that they may find some common ground, if not in their conclusions, at least in their searching.

A Concluding Contemplative Postscript

It should be admitted frankly that this has been a largely sympathetic treatment of Rahner. As such, it is not only permeated with the power of his thought but also plagued by its pitfalls. It may be objected, for example, that Rahner is in the end too much the product of the metaphysics in which he was trained to be able to address adequately the philosophical concerns of the post-metaphysical period. By comparison with Heidegger, for instance, who attempted to move beyond his transcendental analysis of *Dasein* in an effort to recover a primal experience of Being itself, Rahner's explicitly philosophical thought remains basically transcendental in its emphasis. And so, a great deal of attention is given in this book to the idea of contemplation as a particular rational intentionality, while that unto which contemplation is ultimately directed, i.e. Mystery, does not receive the kind of attention which, as a pivotal ontological category, it perhaps deserves.

Let this be said in defense of Rahner: His particular scholarly interests did not permit him to follow the line of thought which Heidegger was only beginning to develop during the years that Rahner knew him. What Rahner would have done with the philosophical question of *Sein* had he followed the debate more closely is a moot question. As it is, because from 1936 onward Rahner gave his considerable talent and energy to the doing of theology, he cannot be faulted for having failed to address this problem.

However, let this also be said: The practitioner of retrieval would probably benefit from a careful combing of Rahner's late writing on Christology, ecumenism, or culture and science, for example, to see if there is not some evidence of post-metaphysical ontology. In any event, at some point in the future, even apart from a discussion of Rahner, it would be important to take up again the issue of the usefulness and necessity of mystery as a philosophical category. The vitality of a dynamic and truly contemplative conception of rationality requires this.

Notwithstanding these limitations, I am content that this project has at least brought to light a dimension of rationality which is either rejected or ignored in most contemporary discussions of the topic. To be human is to be rational, and to be rational is, at least in part, to be contemplative: To be in question and to be questioned, to hear the beckoning call of that silence which is the non-answer to our most ultimate question. This pregnant silence is the only indication we have—apart from historical revelation—of that supramundane, eternal, and infinite horizon which is always co-present in our knowledge of the world and motivates us to morally-meaningful action.

Contemplatively, the unity to be sought—between philosopher and theologian, between apologete and non-believer, between the adherents of conflicting ethical viewpoints—is not forged subsequently to our conceptual differences, but is discovered as present antecedently in reflection upon an experience that we all share. This experience is captured in the words of Novalis which Rahner quotes and adopts as his own in an early essay on Heidegger:

> We are men without a country, and it is restlessness itself, a dynamic restlessness which makes us have to philosophize. And this restlessness is our limitation, a limitation to us who are finitude itself. ... This is our indispensable disposition: not to let oneself be grasped is for oneself not to be able to grasp. How empty and vain, when faced with the ultimate questions, is all our speculative subtlety—a grasp we have tried and practiced—if it is not animated first of all by this being grasped which we undergo in our own depths.[20]

To let oneself be grasped: That is contemplation.

Endnotes

Abbreviations Used in Endnotes

EM   Martin Heidegger, *An Introduction to Metaphysics*, Ralph Manheim, trans., (NY: Doubleday [Anchor], 1961).

GG   Karl Rahner, *Foundations of Christian Faith*, William V. Dych, trans., New York: Seabury [Crossroad], 1978). *[Grundkurs des Glaubens: Einfürung in den Begriff des Christentums*, (Freiburg im Breisgau: Herder, 1976).]

GW   Karl Rahner, *Spirit in the World*, William Dych, trans., (New York: Herder and Herder, 1968). [*Geist in Welt*, (München: Kösel-Verlag, 1957).]

HW   Karl Rahner, *Hearers of the Word*, Michael Richards, trans., (New York: Herder and Herder, 1969). [*Hörer des Wortes*, (München: Kösel-Verlag, 1963).]

IST   Pierre Rousselot, *The Intellectualism of St. Thomas*, James E. O'Malony, trans., (New York: Sheed and Ward, 1935). [*L'Intellectualisme de saint Thomas*, (Paris: Beauchesne, 1924).]

KRD   *Karl Rahner in Dialogue: Conversations and Interviews*, Paul Imhof et al, eds., (NY: Crossroads, 1986). [This edition is based on the more complete, two volume German edition, *Karl Rahner im Gespräch*, Paul Imhof et al, eds., (Munich: Kösel Verlag, 1982, 1983).]

PDM   Joseph Maréchal, *A Maréchal Reader*, Joseph Donceel, ed. and trans., (New York: Herder and Herder, 1970). [The reader consists largely of excerpts from *Le point dé départ de la métaphysique, Cahier V*, (Paris: F. Alcan, 1926).]

SE   Ignatius of Loyola, *Spiritual Exercises*, Elizabeth Meier Tetlow, trans., (Lanham, MD: University Press of America, 1987). [All direct quotations of the exercises are from the Tetlow edition. Also consulted were Elder Mullan's 1914 translation and David Fleming's contemporary reading both contained in Fleming's *The Spiritual Exercises of St. Ignatius: A Literal Translation and A Contemporary Reading*, (St. Louis: Institute of Jesuit Resources, 1989).]

SPM   Joseph Maréchal, *Studies in the Psychology of the Mystics*, Algar Thorhold, trans., (London: Burns, Oates, and Washbourne, Ltd., 1927).

ST   Karl Rahner, *Theological Investigations*. [Publication data for specific volumes is provided in the notes. This collection of essays was originally published in German under the title *Schriften zur Theologie*.]

SZ   Martin Heidegger, *Being and Time,* J. MacQuarrie and Edw. Robinson, trans., (NY: Harper and Row, 1962).

Notes

Introduction

1   Alisdair MacIntyre, *Whose Justice? Which Rationality*, (Notre Dame: University of Notre Dame Press, 1988), pp. 2-3.

2   See Richard Bernstein, *Beyond Objectivism and Relativism: Science, hermeneutics, and praxis*, (Philadelphia: University of Pennsylvania Press, 1983), p. 2. From a rather different standpoint than MacIntyre, Bernstein also identifies the question of "the nature and scope of human rationality" as foundational in a host of contemporary philosophical debates and controversies and rich in practical implications.

3   *Webster's Ninth New Collegiate Dictionary*, (1987), s.v. "contemplate" and "temple."

4   John Dudley, *"La Contemplation Humaine Selon Aristotle,"* Revue *Philosophique de Louvain*, 80(August 1982), pp. 388-92. Francis Parker, "Contemplation in Aristotelian Ethics," contained in The *Georgetown Symposium on Ethics*, Rocco Porreco, ed., (Lanham, MD: University Press of America, 1984), pp. 208, 210 (n.13).

5   Plato, *Republic*, Alan Bloom, trans., (NY: Basic Books, 1968), 485b [marginal notation]. For a good overview on contemplation in Plato's

thought, see A.J. Festugière, *Contemplation et vie contemplative selon Platon*, (Paris: Vrin, 1936).

6   Ibid., 517b.

7   Ibid., 517d.

8   Ibid., 516a.

9   Ibid., 532b. See also *Philebus*, 57e.

10   Ibid., 533d.

11   Aristotle, *Nichomachean Ethics*, W.D. Ross, trans., contained in *The Basic Works of Aristotle*, Richard McKeon, ed., (NY: Random House, 1941), 1098a 15.

12   Ibid., 1177a 20.

13   Ibid., 1177a 29-1177b 4.

14   Ibid., 1178a.

15   Ibid., 1178b 27-31.

16   Jon Moline, "Contemplation and the Human Good," *Nous*, 47(March 1983), pp. 37-53; Moline defends the irony hypothesis. For other perspectives on this problem, also see Parker (above) and Richard Kraut, "The Peculiar Function of Human Beings," *Canadian Journal of Philosophy*, 9(September 1979), pp. 467-78.

17   Karl Rahner, *Hearers of the Word*, Michael Richards, trans., (New York: Herder and Herder, 1969), Preface by J.B. Metz, pp. 107. [*Hörer des Wortes*, (München: Kösel-Verlag, 1963), p. 132.] All direct quotations from *Hearers of the Word* are from the Richards translation. This work will henceforth be referred to as "HW", with the English page numbering given first and the German numbering second and in brackets.

Chapter I

1   1 Corinthians 1:18-25. [Biblical citations are from the *New American Bible Revised New Testament*, (Northport, NY and Grand Rapids, MI: Costello Publishing and William B Eerdmans Publishing, 1988).]

2   Acts 17:22-34.

3   1 Peter 3:15. Note that Aquinas cites this passage in support of his
     argument that the human intellect ought to inquire into divine
     realities; see Thomas Aquinas, *St. Thomas Aquinas: Faith, Reason,
     and Theology: Questions I-IV of His Commentary on the De Trinitate
     of Boethius*, Armand Maurer, ed., (Toronto: Pontifical Institute of
     Medieval Studies, 1987), Q. 2, A. 1, p. 36.

4   Clement of Alexandria, *Stromata*, contained in *Greek and Roman
     Philosophy after Aristotle*, Jason L. Saunders, ed., (NY: The Free
     Press, 1966), pp. 306-7, 321.

5   Ibid., pp. 305-6.

6   Ibid., p. 323.

7   Ibid., p. 316.

8   Ibid., pp. 312, 327.

9   Ibid., p. 312.

10   Ibid., p. 319.

11   Tertullian, *Prescription Against Heretics*, contained in Saunders (see
     note 4 above), p. 344.

12   Ibid.

13   Ibid.

14   Ibid., p. 357.

15   Ibid., p. 346.

16   Ibid., p. 349. Cf. Martin Heidegger, *Being and Time*, J. MacQuarrie
     and Edw. Robinson, trans., (NY: Harper and Row, 1962), p. 37.
     [Henceforth referred to as "SZ".] Against an ahistorical and acultural
     notion of access to Being, Heidegger sounds curiously like Tertullian
     when he writes, "We must rather choose such a way of access and such
     a kind of interpretation that this entity can show itself in itself and

from itself [*an ihm selbst von ihm selbst*]. The Rahnerian debt to a contemplative Heidegger is spelled out in Chapter VII.

17   John Wippel, "The Condemnations of 1270 and 1277 at Paris," *Journal of Medieval and Renaissance Studies*, 7(1977), pp. 173-4. See also Etienne Gilson, *Reason and Revelation in the Middle Ages*, (NY: Charles Scribner's Sons), for a somewhat different way of classifying the main currents of medieval thought with regard to faith and reason.

18   Augustine, *On the Gospel of Saint John*, XXIX, 6, contained in *Homilies on the Gospel of St. John*, H. Browne and J.H. Parker, trans., (Oxford: Library of the Fathers, 1948), Vol. I, p. 440.

19   Anselm of Canterbury also contributed to the Neo-Austinian tradition, as did Bonaventure, John Pecham, and Roger Bacon. See John Wippel, "The Possibility of a Christian Philosophy: A Thomistic Perspective," *Faith and Philosophy*, 1(July 1984), pp. 273-4.

20   Gilson, p. 5. Theologism, according to Gilson, describes a system of thought which views revelation "as a substitute for all other knowledge, including science, ethics, and metaphysics."

21   James Weisheipl, *Friar Thomas D'Aquino*, (DC: Catholic University of America Press, 1983), pp. 272 ff.

22   Thomas P. Bukowski, "Siger of Brabant vs. Thomas Aquinas on Theology," *The New Scholasticism*, LXI(Winter 1987), p. 30.

23   Gilson, p. 69. "Theologism would maintain that every part of revelation should be understood, while rationalism would uphold the view that no part of revelation could be understood."

24   Armand Maurer, "Introduction" to *Faith, Reason and Theology*. According to Maurer, this commentary was written early in Thomas' theological career. Still, a comparison with other texts indicates that Thomas' position remained consistent over time. Cf. Thomas Aquinas, *Summa Theologiae*, Part I, Q. 12, Part II-II, Qq. 1-2, contained in *Basic Writings of St. Thomas Aquinas*, Anton Pegis, ed., (NY: Random House, 1944).

25   A great deal of controversy surrounded the agent intellect in medieval thought. Aristotle's *De Anima* (see especially 430a10ff.) leaves ample

room for speculation about the precise nature of the agent intellect. Analogically, agent intellect may be understood as that principle of intellect by which the potentially intelligible is made actually so, much the way light is the principle of vision by which potential color is actually seen. Aquinas interpreted the agent or active intellect as that by which intelligible notions are actualized through abstraction. "By abstracting from matter and those material conditions which are the principles of individuation," the mind comes to know the specific nature of a thing. (See Thomas Aquinas, *Questions on the Soul*, James H. Robb, trans., [Milwaukee: Marquette University Press, 1984], Question 4, Response, pp. 78-9. Also see Aristotle, *On the Soul*, Hippocrates G. Apostle, trans., [Grinnell, Iowa: The Peripatetic Press, 1981], Commentary, p. 159.) Whether Thomas' interpretation of Aristotle on this point is correct is a moot point which cannot be discussed here. Let it suffice to note that, against theories of knowledge as innate or any form of illuminationism, Thomas holds that knowledge of the natural world and first principles is the achievement if an active mind using its intrinsic powers and not the purely passive reception of already-intelligible data from elsewhere.

26   Thomas Aquinas, *Commentary on the De Trinitate*, Armand Maurer, trans., Q. 1, A. 1, pp. 16-7.

27   Ibid.; see also Q. 1, A. 4, p. 31.

28   Ibid., Q. 1, A. 2, pp. 21-2; see also *Summa Theologiae*, I, Q. 12, A. 12, p. 109 in Pegis edition.

29   Thomas Aquinas, *Summa Theologiae*, I, Q. 2, A. 3, pp. 21 ff. in Pegis edition.

30   Thomas Aquinas, *Commentary on the De Trinitate*, Q. 1, A. 2, pp. 22-24.

31   Ibid., p. 22.

32   Ibid., Q. 2, A. 1., pp. 37-8. The very raising of a question about the permissibility of investigating divine realities presumes the importance of freedom; i.e. the knowledge of God is not a purely speculative affair. One is free to study or not to study; one is free to speak of God or to remain silent. Also note the contemplative link to Aristotle's *Nichomachean Ethics*; see p. 7 of the present work.

33   Ibid.

34   Ibid., p. 39; see also Q. 2, A. 2, pp. 42-4. Having thus established the propriety of investigation into divine realities, Thomas in the second article of the second question proceeds to establish the possibility of a science which does precisely that. This discussion focuses primarily on the analogy between the place of first principles in philosophy and the truths of faith in theology.

35   Ibid., Q. 2, A. 3, p. 48.

36   Ibid., p. 49.

37   Ibid., Q. 3, A. 1, p. 65.

38   Ibid., p. 66.

39   Ibid., pp. 66-7.

40   Ibid., p. 69.

41   Ibid., pp. 69-70.

42   Ibid., Q. 3, A.2, pp. 72-3.

43   Ibid., p. 73.

44   Gilson, pp. 84-85.

45   Wippel, "The Condemnations," pp. 179-86, 194-97.

46   Ibid., p. 200.

47   Gilson, pp. 86-7, 90. William of Ockham, the father of medieval nominalism, argued that only individuals enjoy real being and that the universal terms we predicate of things are mere names which we use as a matter of convenience and convention. Hence, without recourse to real essences and the affirmation of existence, the best natural reason can achieve is a certain set of dialectical probabilities. In other words, philosophy achieves knowledge, not of things as they are but of things as they probably are and of the terms and words which human beings use to describe them. According to this view, absolutely nothing about God can be proved through natural reason.

48   Ibid., pp. 89 ff. The "modern devotion" was a movement in popular spirituality which looked with suspicion on speculative theology, urging its adherents toward mystical union with rather than philosophical understanding of God. *The Imitation of Christ*, for example, encouraged a simple and uncritical faith and warned against the dangers of philosophical speculation.

49   See, for example, Paul Oskar Kristellar, *Renaissance Thought*, (NY: Harper Torchbooks, 1961).

50   See Kristellar, *Marsilio Ficino and his Work after Five Hundred Years*, (Leo S. Olschki Editore, 1987), p. 13: "The visible world is only a part of the universe itself which is a metaphysical hierarchy extending from God and the angels through the rational soul to the corporeal qualities and material bodies. God, and the intelligible world of ideas inherent in his mind, are the ultimate object of our knowledge and the goal of our will. In the universal hierarchy, the rational soul (which includes the human soul) occupies the center, connects all other parts of the universe with each other and thus constitutes the knot and bond of the universe."

51   Giovanni Pico della Mirandola, "On the Dignity of Man," Charles Glenn Wallis, trans., contained in *On the Dignity of Man and Other Works,* (Indianapolis, IN: Bobbs-Merrill, 1965), p. 5. See also Introduction by Paul J. W. Miller, p. xiv: "The most remarkable contribution he makes is his notion that the root of man's excellence and dignity lies in the fact that man is the maker of his own nature."

52   Galileo Galilei, *The Assayer,* contained in *Discoveries and Opinions of Galileo*, Stillman Drake, trans., (NY: Anchor Books, 1957), pp. 237-38.

53   See discussion of Bacon and the "new science" in Aldo Tassi's "Modernity as the Transformation of Truth into Meaning," *International Philosophical Quarterly*, XXIII(September 1982), pp. 185 ff.

54   René Descartes, *Meditations on First Philosophy* contained in *The Philosophical Writings of Descartes*, John Cottingham, trans., (Cambridge, England: Cambridge University Press, 1988), p.12.

55   Bernstein, pp. 17-8. Bernstein develops this point in terms of what he describes as the "Cartesian anxiety." Without a fixed and firm foundation for knowledge, some "Archimedean point," there is no way to "escape the forces of darkness that envelop us with madness, with intellectual and moral chaos." The contemporary crisis of rationality, i.e. the irresolvable conflict between objectivism and relativism, says Bernstein, is borne of this anxiety. We will see that Rahner also acknowledges the presence of the anxiety. He will read it as an abyss to be plumbed in faith rather than a void to be evaded through reason.

56   Immanuel Kant, *Prolegomena to Any Future Metaphysics,* James Ellington, trans., (Indianapolis, IN: Hackett, 1977), 256 [marginal notation].

57   Ibid., 255.

58   Ibid., 256.

59   Ibid., Part I, 280-94.

60   Ibid., Part II, 294-326.

61   Ibid., 287-92; see also Part III, 355-62.

62   Immanuel Kant, *Critique of Pure Reason,* Norman Kemp Smith, trans., (NY: St. Martin's Press, 1965), B295 [marginal notation].

63   G.W.F. Hegel, *Phenomenology of Spirit,* A.V. Miller, trans., (Oxford: Oxford University Press, 1977), p. 3, para. 5.

64   Ibid., see cc. 1-4. In Cc. 1-3, Hegel shows that consideration of consciousness alone is inadequate. In c. 4, he shows the importance of self-consciousness in the pursuit of truth through his famous allegory of the Master and Slave. As it turns out, however, the Enlightenment discovery of or emphasis on self-consciousness is the not the final moment in philosophy's history, but the prelude to that moment which Hegel believed he was announcing.

65   Ibid., see cc. V and VI. C. V shows that the reason is not apart from or above history but emerges precisely as a phenomenon in history. C. VI shows how reason (understood as system) emerges in the Enlightenment, making possible for the first time the doing of science in the fullest sense of the term.

66   Soren Kierkegaard, *Concluding Unscientific Postscript*, D. Swenson and W. Lowrie, trans., (Princeton: Princeton University Press, 1974), p. 78-9.

67   Ibid., pp. 99-100.

68   Ibid., p. 108.

69   Selections from *The Gay Science* contained in *The Portable Nietzsche*, Walter Kaufmann, trans., (NY: Viking Press, 1968), p. 95, sec. 125.

70   Sections from Thus Spoke Zarathustra contained in *The Portable Nietzsche* (see above citation), pp. 124-6; part 1, sec. 3.

71   Ibid., p. 307; part 3, sec. 2.

72   Ibid., p. 129; part 1, sec. 5.

73   MacIntyre, p. 6. A similar reading of the Enlightenment is given by Johannes Baptist Metz, though in the service of a very different project, the development of a practical fundamental theology.   The Enlightenment consisted, at least partially, in a crisis of metaphysical reason. Whereas, in much of medieval thought, reason was conceived of as independent of the individual subject and its practical aspects, in the Enlightenment, reason was thought of precisely as the creation of the subject and specifically in its relation to the practical and political order.   The problem with this conception of reason, however, was its degree of abstraction: Man, existence, person--these were all treated apart from the concrete human subject living in history and society. See *Faith in History and Society*, David Smith, trans., (New York: Seabury, 1980), pp.ix, 29, 33, 37, 42-5.

74   For a similiar delineation of the options see Larry Laudan, *Progress and its Problems*, (London:Routeledge and Kegan Paul, 1977), p. 3.

75   John Caputo, *Radical Hermeneutics: Repetition, Deconstruction, and the Hermeneutic Project*, (Bloomington, IN: Indiana U. Press, 1987), p. 223.   Simililarly, Bernstein describes objectivism as "the basic conviction that there is or must be some permanent, ahistorical matrix or framework to which we can ultimately appeal in determining the nature of rationality, knoweldge, truth, reality, goodness, or rightness." See *Beyond Objectivism and Relativism*, p. 8.

76   Ibid., p. 229.

77   MacIntyre, p. 5; see also p. 214

78   Caputo, *Radical Hermeneutics*, pp. 229 ff.

79   MacIntyre, pp. 394 ff.

80   Bernstein, p. 8.

81   MacIntyre, p. 397.

82   Bernstein, pp. 18-9.

83   Ibid., p. 24.

84   MacIntyre, p. 7.

85   Ibid., pp. 353-4.

86   Caputo, *Radical Hermeneutics*, p. 1.

87   Ibid.

88   Ibid., p. 209; see also p. 7.

89   Ibid., p. 211.

Chapter II
1   To a great extent I am relying on Gerald McCool and James Hennessey for their excellent historical/theological work on the era in question. See Gerald McCool, *Catholic Theology in the Nineteenth Century,* (New York: Seabury, 1977) and James Hennesey, "Leo XIII's Thomistic Revival: A Political and Philosophical Event," *The Journal of Religion,* 58(1978 Supplement).

2   McCool, *Catholic Theology*, p. 24.

3   Hennessey, pp. 186-7.

4   McCool, *Catholic Theology*, pp. 25-6.

5   Hennesey, p. 187.

6   Ibid., p. 188.

7   Gerald McCool, "Neo-Thomism and the Tradition of St. Thomas," *Thought*, 62(June 1987), p. 133.

8   Hennesey, p. 190; see also McCool's *Catholic Theology*, pp. 28 ff.

9   McCool, *Catholic Theology*, p. 17.

10   Ibid., p. 18.

11   Ibid.

12   Ibid., pp. 32 ff.

13   Ibid., p. 18.

14   Ibid., p. 19.

15   Ibid., pp. 2 ff.

16   Ibid., p. 9.

17   Ibid., p. 11.

18   Ibid., p. 21.

19   Ibid., p. 9.

20   Ibid., p. 221.

21   Vatican I, *Dei Filius,* contained in Henry Denzinger, *The Sources of Catholic Dogma,* Roy Defarrari, trans., (London, St. Louis: B. Herder Book Co, 1957; based on the 30th edition of *Enchiridion Symbolorum*), 1789 [paragraph notation], p. 445.

22   Ibid., 1790, p. 445.

23   Ibid., 1791, p. 445.

24   Ibid., 1795, pp. 446-7.

25   Ibid., 1785, pp. 443-4.

26   Ibid., 1796, p. 447.

27   Ibid., 1798-9, pp. 447-8.

28   Ibid., 1800, p. 448.

29   Hennesey, p. 189.

30   McCool, *Catholic Theology*, pp. 226-8.

31   Leo XIII, *Aeterni Patris*, contained in *One Hundred Years of Thomism: Aeterni Patris and Afterwards, A Symposium,* Victor B. Brezik, ed., (Houston, TX: Center for Thomistic Studies, 1981), p. 174.

32   Ibid., p. 191.

33   Ibid., p. 193.

34   Ibid., p. 174.

35   Ibid., p. 175.

36   Ibid.

37   Ibid., pp. 177-8.

38   Ibid., p. 178.

39   Ibid., p. 179.

40   Ibid., pp. 180-1.

41   Ibid., p. 186.

42   Ibid., p. 188.

43   Ibid., pp. 189 ff.

44   Ibid., p. 195.

45   Hennesey, p. 197; see also McCool, *Catholic Theology*, pp.2, 236.

46   McCool, *Catholic Theology*, p. 235; see also McCool's "Neo-Thomism," p. 141.

47   Hennesey, p. 190.

48   McCool, *Catholic Theology*, p. 235.

49   Joseph Owens, "The Future of Thomistic Metaphysics," contained in Brezik, p. 156.

50   McCool employs the diachronic approach; see *Catholic Theology*, pp. 242-5. Helen James John treats Thomistic pluralism thematically; see *The Thomist Spectrum*, (New York: Fordham University Press, 1966).

51   McCool, *Catholic Theology*, pp. 245-51.

52   John, pp. 32-49.

53   Ibid., pp. 139-49.

54   Ibid., pp. 87-107.

55   Ibid., p. x.

56   Ibid., pp. 257-60.

57   For a summary of biographical information see Robert Kress, *A Rahner Handbook*, (Atlanta: John Knox Press, 1982); pp. 2-18. For more detailed information on Rahner's life, see Herbert Vorgrimler, *Understanding Karl Rahner: An Introduction to His Life and Thought*, (New York: Crossroad, 1986).   His interviews contained in *Karl Rahner in Dialogue: Conversations and Interviews*, Paul Imhof et al, eds., (NY: Crossroad, 1984), also contain valuable biographical information. [Henceforth referred to as "KRD." This edition is based on the more complete two volume German edition, *Karl Rahner Im Gespräch*, Paul Imhof, et al, eds., (Munich: Kösel Verlag, 1982, 1983).

58   Even after having moved into theology, Rahner continued to be interested in properly philosophical issues.   See the following:

"Aquinas: The Nature of Truth," Andrew Tallon, trans., *Continuum* 21(1964); "The Concept of Existential Philosophy in Heidegger," Andrew Tallon, trans., *Philosophy Today* 13(1969); "The Logic of Concrete Individual Knowledge in Ignatius Loyola," contained in *The Dynamic Element in the Church*, (NY:Herder and Herder, 1964). A large number of Rahner's other essays, though theological in motivation, are strongly philosophical in character.

59   For an excellent English language bibliography of Rahner's work and of the secondary literature, see C.J. Pedley, "An English Bibliographical Aid to Karl Rahner," *Heythrop Journal* XXV(1984), 319-365. For a complete listing of Rahner's publications through 1969, consult *Biliographie Karl Rahner 1924-1969*, R. Bleistein and E. Klinger, eds., (Freiburg, 1974). For his publications between 1974 and 1979, consult *Wagnis Theologie*, H. Vorgrimler, ed., (Freiburg, 1979). For his publications between 1979 and 1984, consult *Glaube im Prozess*, E. Klinger and K. Wittstadt, eds., (Freiburg 1984).

60   Interview with Leo O'Donovan for America, March 10, 1979; KRD, 196-7.

61   Anne E. Carr, *The Theological Method of Karl Rahner*, (Missoula, MT: Scholars Press, 1977), p. 4.

62   Karl Rahner, *Spirit in the World*, William Dych, trans., (New York: Herder and Herder, 1968), Author's Introduction, p. 1. [*Geist in Welt*, (München: Kösel-Verlag, 1957). pp. 11-12.] Note: All direct quotations from *Spirit in the World* are from the Dych translation. This work will henceforth be referred to as "GW", with the English page numbering given first and the German numbering second and in brackets.

63   Leo O'Donovan, "A Final Harvest: Karl Rahner's Last Theological Writings," *Religious Studies Review*, 11(October 1985), p. 360.

64   Leo O'Donovan, "A Journey into Time: The Legacy of Karl Rahner's Last Years," *Theological Studies*, 46(1985), p. 644.

65   John P. Galvin, "Grace for a New Generation," *Commonweal*, 25(January 1985), p. 40.

66   Ibid.

67   Thomas Sheehan, *Karl Rahner: The Philosophical Foundations*, (Athens, OH: Ohio University Press, 1987) p. 317.

68   Andrew Tallon, "Getting to the Heart of the Matter: Spirit," *Louvain Studies*, 11(Spring 1969), p. 281.

69   Andrew Tallon, "Karl Rahner, Philosopher (1904-1984)," *Philosophy Today*, 28(Summer 1984), p. 104.

70   Ibid., p. 102.

71   Carr, p. 114. See also Clifford Stevens, "The Rahner Equation," *Listening*, 17(Autumn 1982), p. 239.

72   Carr, p. 56.

73   O'Donovan, "A Final Harvest," p. 361.

74   Joseph Donceel, "Transcendental Thomism," *Monist*, 58(1974), p. 70.

75   Ibid., p. 84. It should noted that there has been some question among "strict observance" Thomists as to whether or not the transcendentalism of Maréchal and his followers is really Thomism at all. Although it will be important to listen later to some of their criticisms which may have bearing on the present topic, it must be said at this point that the question as to whether or not this is bona fide Thomism is clearly secondary in importance to the question of whether it provides an adequate means of talking about human existence and knowledge in our own day.) For more on the debate between transcendental and strict Thomists, see Leslie Dewart, "On Transcendental Thomism," *Continuum*, 6(1968), 389-401 and "A Response to J. Donceel." Continuum, 7(1969), 453-462. See also Joseph Donceel, "A Thomistic Misapprehension?" *Thought*, 32(1957) 189-98 and "On Transcendental Thomism." *Continuum*, 7(1969), 164-68.

76   Carl J. Peter, "A Shift to the Human Subject in Roman Catholic Theology," *Communio*, 6(Spring 1979), p. 62.

77   Kenneth Baker, "Rahner: The Transcendental Method," *Continuum*, II(1964), p. 54.

78   Carr, p. 259.

79   Ibid., p. 56.

80   GW, 1 [12].

81   In these works, the Rahnerian reading of *conversio ad phantasma* which was worked out in his metaphysical anthropology is elaborated in the context of theology. Every such *conversio* is seen in its radical temporality, as a *conversio ad phantasma per tempus.* See O'Donovan, "A Journey," p. 637. See also, p. 629. Carr makes a similiar point on p. 57 of her *Theological Method of Karl Rahner.* See Chapter III of the present project for an explanation of *conversio* and its importance to Rahner.

82   Sheehan, p. 317; see also Carr, p. 266.

83   O'Donovan, "A Journey," p. 645.

84   Ibid.

85   Leo O'Donovan, "The Word of the Cross," *Chicago Studies*, 25(April 1986), p. 96.

Chapter III

1   GW, xlvii [9].

2   HW, see Preface by J.B. Metz, pp. vii ff. Inasmuch as Rahner has taken no exception to the revisions made to the second of edition, it will serve as the basis for what follows here.

3   GW, liii, [14-15]. Obviously, in the backgroud is Kant's claim that metaphysics properly practiced can never deal scientifically with that which lies beyond space and time, e.g. God. Like Maréchal before him, Rahner attempts to use Kant's own method to refute his argument.

4   GW, 66, [79-80].

5   GW, lii, [13-14].

6   GW, 22, [36-37].

7   Aristotle, *Metaphysics*, W.D. Ross, trans., contained in *Introduction to Aristotle,* Richard McKeon, ed., (NY: Random House, 1947), [982b], p. 247. "[I]t is owing to their wonder that men both now begin and at first began to philosophize; they wondered originally at the obvious difficulties, then advanced little by little and stated difficulties about the greater matters."

8   GW, 57, [71].

9   GW, 42, 58-63, [47, 72-78].

10   GW, 42, [56]; see also 36, [50].

11   GW, 68, [81].

12   GW, 75, [88].

13   GW, 69, [82].

14   GW, 77, [90].

15   GW, 45-6, [59-60].

16   GW, 81, [94].

17   GW, 119, [130-1].

18   GW, 118-20, [129-31].

19   GW, 120-3, [131-3].

20   GW, 123-6, [134-6].

21   GW, 126-9, [136-40].

22   GW, 133-4, [144-5].

23   GW, 135-6, [145-6].

24   GW, 140-1, [151-2].

25   GW, 142, [152-3].

26   GW, 142, [152-3].

27   GW, 142, [153].

28   GW, 143 ff., [153 ff.].

29   GW, 146, [156].

30   GW, 147, [157].

31   GW, 148, [158].

32   GW, 149-50, [159-60].

33   GW, 154, [164].

34   GW, 156, [166].

35   GW, 157-60, [167-70].

36   GW, 168, [178].

37   GW, 158-9, [168].

38   GW, 160, [170].

39   GW, 171, [180].

40   GW, 174, [173].

41   GW, 175, [184].

42   GW, 181, [190].

43   GW, 181, [190].

44   GW, 182, [191].

45   GW, 309, [311-12].

46   GW, 278, [282].

47   HW, 15, [29].

48   HW, 19-23, [33-6].

49   HW, 22, [37].

50   HW, 22, [37].

51   HW, 25, [40-1].

52   HW, 27, [43-4].

53   HW, 27, [43-4].

54   HW, 67, [87-8].

55   HW, 108, [133].

56   HW, 161, [200].

57   HW, 36-8, [53-4]; see also 65-6, [85-6].

58   HW, 31, [47].

59   HW, 32, [48].

60   HW, 72-3, [92-3].

61   HW, 93, [115-6].

62   HW, 89, [111].

63   HW, 100, 106, [123-4, 131-2].

64   HW, 107, [132].

65   HW, 132, [163-4].

66   HW, 134, [165-6].

67   HW, 160, [198-9].

Chapter IV

1   Churchill has opted for repetition as a translation of *Wiederholung* in his version of *Kant and the Problem of Metaphysics*, as have MacQuarrie and Robinson in their version of *Being and Time*. [*Kant and the Problem of Metaphysics*, James S. Churchill, trans., (Bloomington: Indiana University Press, 1962.]

2   William Richardson, *Heidegger: Through Phenomenology to Thought*, (The Hague: N. Nijhoff, 1962), p. 89, n. 181.

3   SZ, 427, translators' note 1.

4   John Caputo, *Radical Hermeneutics*, p. 36.

5   SZ, 276.

6   Ibid.

7   Ibid., p. 277.

8   Ibid., p. 428.

9   Ibid., p. 437.

10   Ibid., p. 438. For an interpretation of Heidegger on this point, see also Richardson, pp. 89-92.

11   Martin Heidegger, *An Introduction to Metaphysics*, Ralph Manheim, trans., (NY: Doubleday [Anchor], 1961), p. 32. Henceforth referred to as "EM."

12   Ibid., p. 150.

13   GW, William Dych, trans., (NY: Herder and Herder, 1968), Author's Introduction, p. lii.

14   Josef Pieper, *The Silence of St. Thomas*, John Murray and Daniel O'Connor, trans., (NY: Pantheon, 1957), p. 45

15   Ibid., p. 46.

16   John Caputo, *Heidegger and Aquinas: An Essay on Overcoming Metaphysics*, (NY: Fordham University Press, 1982), p. 247.

17   Jacques Derrida, *Of Grammatology*, Gayatrix Charkravorty Spivak, trans., (Baltimore: John Hopkins University Press, 1974), p. xlix.

18   Caputo, *Radical Hermeneutics*, p. 64.

19   See Richardson, p. 92, who interprets Heidegger on the communal character of retrieval.

20   Caputo, *Radical Hermeneutics*, p. 88.

21   Ibid., p. 39; see also p. 59.

22   Ibid., p. 61.

23   GW, pp. 142ff. See also HW, p. 33 where he contrasts his retrieval with a "mere repetition of St. Thomas."

24   In addition to KRD, also see *Karl Rahner, I Remember: An Autobiographical Interview*, (NY: Crossroad, 1985), [*Erinnerungen: Im Gespräch mit Meinhold Krauss*, (Freiburg im Breisgau: Herder, 1984)] and *Glaube in winterlicher Zeit: Gespräche mit Karl Rahner aus den letzten Lebensjahren*, Paul Imhof et al, eds., (Düsseldorf: Patmos Verlag, 1986).

25   With Leo O'Donovan, Munich, 1979, KRD, 191-2.

26   With Manfred Waldenmair-Lackenbach and Thomas Untersteiner, Innsbruck, 1982, KRD, 354.

27   With Patrick Granfield, Washington, D.C., 1965, KRD, 18.

28   Ibid., p. 12.

29   Ibid., p. 14.

30   Ibid.

31   With Albert Raffelt, Freiburg, 1974, KRD, 132.

32   With O'Donovan, 190.

33   With Peter Pawlowsky, Vienna, 1980, KRD, 255.

34   With O'Donovan, 191.

35   Ibid., pp. 195-6. See also interview with Siegfried von Kortzfleisch, Hanover, 1981, KRD, 292.

36   With Wolfgang Feneberg, Munich, 1978, KRD, 176.

37   Ibid., pp. 177-8; see also p. 175.

38   With O'Donovan, 190.

39   With Leonhard Reinisch, Munich, 1982, KRD, 337.

40   From Karl Rahner's contribution to the 1969 Festschrift for Heidegger, *Martin Heidgger im Gespräch*, Richard Wisser, ed., (Freiburg: Alber, 1970), pp. 48-49.

41   With Pawlowsky, 257.

42   With O'Donovan, 191; for more on his ambivalence about Heidegger's influence see interview with Joachim Schickel, Hamburg, 1981, KRD, 310.

43   With Schickel, 311.

44   With Pawlowsky, 257.

45   With Schickel, 311.

46   With Granfield, 13.

47   *I Remember*, p. 45.

48   With Pawlowsky, 257. See Sheehan, p. 5, for a list which Rahner kept of the courses he did with Heidegger.

Chapter V
1   Rousselot's scholarly career was cut short when, as a soldier of the French army, he was killed in battle. See James O'Malony, Introduction to Pierre Rousselot's *The Intellectualism of St. Thomas*, Jame E. O'Malony, trans., (New York: Sheed and Ward, 1935), pp. v-vi. [*L'Intellectualisme de saint Thomas*, (Paris: Beauchesne, 1924).

All direct quotations from *The Intellectualism of St. Thomas* are from the O'Malony translation. This work will henceforth be referred to as "IST" with the English page numbering given first and the French numbering second and in brackets.]

2   IST, 1, [III].

3   IST, 2, [IV-V].

4   IST, 4, [V-VI].

5   IST, 5-6, [VII-VIII].

6   IST, 8, [XI].

7   IST, 8, [XI].

8   IST, 10, [XIV].

9   IST, 9, [XIII-XIV].

10   IST, 11-12, [XV-XVI].

11   IST, 13, [XVI].

12   IST, 19-20, 28; [6, 15].

13   IST, 31, [19].

14   IST, 32, [20].

15   IST, 33, [21].

16   IST, 36, [24-5].

17   IST, 46, [37].

18   IST, 48, [38].

19   IST, 50, [40].

20   IST, 51-2, [41-3].

21   IST, 53, [44].

22   IST, 56ff., [47ff.].

23   IST, 57, [48].

24   IST, 55-60, [46-51].

25   IST, 66-7, [56-8].

26   IST, 69ff., [60ff.].

27   IST, 92-4, [85-7]. Perhaps it was for similar reasons that Heidegger resolutely refused to have the *Sein* whose meaning he sought equated with God.

28   IST, 110, [106].

29   IST, 133ff., [133ff.].

30   IST, 147ff., [149ff.].

31   IST, 149ff., [151ff.].

32   IST, 149, [151].

33   IST, 153ff., 159; [156ff., 162].

34   IST, 162, [166].

35   IST, 162, [166-7].

36   IST, 169, [173].

37   IST, 175, 181; [179, 186].

38   IST, 178-80, [183-4]; for more on faith see 186, [191-2].

39   IST, 183, [188].

40   IST, 192, [198-9].

41   IST, 201ff., [205ff.].

42   IST, 223, [229].

43   Joseph Maréchal, A Maréchal Reader, Joseph Donceel, ed. and trans. New York: Herder and Herder, 1970. [The reader consists largely of excerpts from *Le point dé départ de la métaphysique, Cahier V*, (Paris: F. Alcan, 1926). All direct quotations from *Le point départ* are from the Donceel translation. The work will henceforth be referred to as "PDM" with the page numbering from the Donceel reader given first and the original numbering second and in brackets.]

44   PDM, 69-70, [49-51].

45   PDM, 70, [51].

46   PDM, 71, 92; [51-2, 92].

47   PDM, 76, [58].

48   PDM, 79-81, [62-65].

49   PDM, 84-5, [68-9].

50   PDM, 86, [71]; see also 81, [65].

51   PDM, 114, [124-5].

52   PDM, 131, [205].

53   PDM, 143, [223].

54   For Maréchal's formulation of the problem the ontological status of the transcendentals see PDM, 146ff., [260ff.].

55   PDM, 161-2, [359-60].

56   PDM, 151, [313]; see also 164-5, [379-80].

57   PDM, 166ff., [396ff.].

58   PDM, 169, [402-3].

59   PDM, 193, [463].

273

60   PDM, 172-5, [412-24].

61   PDM, 198, [468].

62   PDM, 220ff., [531ff.].

63   From a letter quoted by Algar Thorold in his edition of Joseph Maréchal's *Studies in the Psychology of the Mystics*, Algar Thorhold, trans., (London: Burns, Oates, and Washbourne, Ltd., 1927), p. v. Translation of quotation is my own: "*Vous voyez, cher Monsieur, que je me suis intéressé à des sujets assez divers, trop divers même . . . il y a cependant une certaine unité dans cette diversité; vous me comprendrez d'un mot: la mystique m'a toujours attiré comme couronnemnet de la métaphysique et de la pyschologie; c'est d'en bas, comme philosophe et comme homme de science que j'ai voulu l'envisager et que je me suis efforcé de la comprendre, très modestement.*" *Studies* henceforth to be referred to as "SPM."

64   SPM, 6.

65   SPM, 5.

66   SPM, 204, n. 1.

67   SPM, 151.

68   SPM, 154.

69   SPM, 155.

70   SPM, 155-167.

71   SPM, 168.

72   SPM, 168.

73   SPM, 168-70.

74   SPM, 170.

75   SPM, 170-3.

76   SPM, 174-5.

77   SPM, 175.

78   SPM, 177.

79   SPM, 185.

80   SPM, 186-90.

81   SPM, 192.

82   SPM, 194.

83   SPM, 195.

84   SPM, 197-8.

85   SPM, 198.

Chapter VI

1   Because of the unique status of Ignatius among the sources being used in this project, I will make reference to works by two recognized authorities in the field of Ignatian studies: Harvey Egan, *Ignatius Loyola the Mystic*, (Wilmington, DE: Michael Glazier, 1987); Joseph de Guibert, *The Jesuits: Their Spiritual Doctrine and Practice*, W.J. Young, trans., (St. Louis: Institute of Jesuit Sources, 1972).

2   Translator's Preface to *The Spiritual Exercises*, Elizabeth Meier Tetlow, trans., (Lanham, MD: University Press of America, 1987), p. x. [All direct quotations of the exercises are from the Tetlow edition. Also consulted were Elder Mullan's 1914 translation and David Fleming's contemporary reading both contained in Fleming's *The Spiritual Exercises of St. Ignatius: A Literal Translation and A Contemporary Reading*, (St. Louis: Institute of Jesuit Resources, 1989). Henceforth, this work will be referred to as "SE" followed by the marginal number and page number from the Tetlow edition.

3   Egan, pp. 32-47.

4   Ibid., pp. 36-7, n. 6.

5   Ibid., pp. 48-66.

6   Ibid., p. 18.

7   Ibid., p. 21.

8   Ibid., p. 22.

9   Ibid., pp. 23-4.

10   Ibid., pp. 24-5, 43; see also de Guibert, pp. 44-5.

11   de Guibert, p. 45.

12   Ibid., p. 59.

13   Ibid., p. 55.

14   For a more extensive treatment of the history and composition of the exercises, see de Guibert, pp. 113-22.

15   SE, 1, p. 3.

16   de Guibert, pp. 168-9.

17   Ibid., pp. 137-8.

18   Egan, p. 98.

19   Ibid., pp. 98-9.

20   Ibid., pp. 99-103.

21   Ibid., p. 105.

22   SE, 190-261.

23   SE, 204ff., 220ff., 226, 230.

24   SE, 47, p. 23.

25   SE, 66-7, p. 29.

26   SE, 124, p. 45. See also 24-31, 74, 87; pp. 13-15, 32, 34.

27   SE, 2, p. 3.

28   SE, 54, p. 25.

29   SE, 114, p. 43.

30   SE, 205, p. 68; see also 17, p. 8.

31   SE, 14, p. 7.

32   SE, 365, p. 118.

33   Egan, pp. 174-5.

34   SE, 365, p. 117.

35   SE, 365-369, p. 118.

36   SE, 5, p. 4.

37   SE, 23, p. 11.

38   SE, 234, p. 79.

39   SE, 23, p. 11; see also 135, p. 48.

40   SE, 234, p. 79.

41   SE, 175-77, pp. 58-9.

42   SE, 1, p. 3.

43   Rahner, "The Logic of Concrete Individual Knowledge in Ignatius of
      Loyola," pp. 111-12.

44   Ibid., p. 109.

45   Ibid., p. 112.

46   Egan, p. 144, see also p. 142.

47   SE, 330, p. 109.

48   Rahner, p. 143; see also, pp. 94-5, n. 9.

49   Ibid., pp. 145-6.

50   Ibid.

Chapter VII
1   Since there are already several works devoted to the comparison of Rahner and Heidegger or the determination of the latter's influence on the former, I attempt neither of these tasks here. For a consideration of the affinities between the thought of Rahner and Heidegger one might profitably consult: Sheehan's work cited in Chapter II (n. 67); Jack Arthur Bonsor, *Rahner, Heidegger, and Truth: Karl Rahner's Notion of Christian Truth, the Influence of Heidegger*, (Lanham, MD: University Press of America, 1987); and Robert L. Hurd, "Heidegger and Aquinas: A Rahnerian Bridge," *Philosophy Today*, (Summer 1984), pp. 105-137. The scope of the present discussion of Heidegger's contribution to Rahner's conceptual framework is limited by our specific interest in the contemplative dimension of rationality.

2   EM, 168.

3   EM, 17.

4   EM, 24. See Edmund Husserl, *Cartesian Meditations*, Dorion Cairns, trans., (The Hague: Martinus Nijhoff, 1960), Second Meditation, para. 20, pp. 46-7 in Cairns edition.

5   EM, 71.

6   Martin Heidegger, "What is Metaphysics?" *Martin Heidegger: Basic Writings*, David Farrell Krell, ed., (NY: Harper and Row, 1977), p. 112, see also pp.96-7, 109.

7   EM, 10.

8   EM, 9.

9   EM, 9.

10   EM, 9.

11   SZ, Chapter IV, n. 1, pp. 24-5.

12   EM, 1.

13   EM, 2.

14   EM, 3.

15   EM, 3.

16   EM, 23.

17   EM, 23.

18   Heidegger, "What is Metaphysics?" p. 105.

19   Ibid., p. 108.

20   EM, 127.

21   SZ, 21.

22   SZ, 21.

23   SZ, 22-3. Recall that Rahner also made a point of underlining the transcategorical universality of Being. See C. III of the present project.

24   SZ, 23.

25   SZ, 23.

26   SZ, 26.

27   SZ, 27. It should be noted here that Heidegger employs different approaches in EM and SZ. Without speculating about a possible development in thought and emphasis from the earlier SZ to the later EM, it can at least be observed that these two approaches are neither identical nor mutually-exclusive. In the former, the approach is through an analysis of the structures of human existence, with special emphasis on temporality as the primordial ontological basis for *Dasein*. In the latter, the approach is primarily through etymology, With an emphasis on the way the development of language about

Being has tended to conceal the primitive experiential unity of Being and thinking which the ancient Greeks enjoyed. Heidegger's project in the 1935 course is not totally discontinuous with his earlier thinking. However, because Rahner shows no indications of having been significantly influenced by the later linguistic emphasis, we will pursue Heidegger's investigation into Being primarily through an overview of SZ's analytic of *Dasein*. Where pertinent, I will point to parallels and supporting material in EM.

28   EM, 3.

29   SZ, 32.

30   SZ, 32-3.

31   SZ, 34.

32   This is what Heidegger takes Parmenides to be getting at in the proem of his well-known work on being and not-being. "A truly sapient man is, therefore, not one who blindly pursues a truth, but only one who is always cognizant of all three paths. . . . Superior knowledge—and all knowledge is superiority—is given only to the man who has known the buoyant storm on the path of being, who has known the dread of the second path to the abyss of nothing, but who has taken upon himself the third way, the arduous path of appearance." EM, p. 96.

33   EM. 96.

34   Martin Heidegger, "On the Essence of Truth," *Martin Heidegger: Basic Writings,* David Farrell Krell, ed., (New York: Harper and Row, 1977), p. 132.

35   Ibid.

36   Ibid., p. 133; see also p. 135. Heidegger's exegesis of the Antigone of Sophocles simililarly accentuates the fundamental mysteriousness of Being in its relation to *Dasein*. See EM, 123-38.

37   SZ, 43.

38   EM, 33.

39   EM, 31.

40   EM, 170.

41   SZ, 27.

42   SZ, 27.

43   SZ, 29, 30-1; see also EM, 21, 102, 119.

44   A similar point is made etymologically in EM where Heidegger discusses the historical reduction of the meaning of *physis* from "revelatory appearing" to mere appearance (85ff., 149ff.) and of *logos* from "collecting collectness" to mere collection according to formal logical principles (106ff., 140 ff.). When properly understood, *physis* and *logos* are not two conflicting principals whose subsequent relation must be explained, but one and the same happening talked about from two different viewpoints.

45   SZ, 28.

46   SZ, 38.

47   SZ, 37.

48   SZ, 61.

49   SZ, 44.

50   EM, 6.

51   EM, 34.

52   SZ, 342-3; see also 344-8.

53   EM, 172.

Chapter VIII

1   In the selection of texts from the late Rahner corpus, no effort was made to be comprehensive; indeed, the last four volumes of the *Schriften* alone amount to over two thousand pages! Rather, two principles have guided our selection of texts for consideration: First, an effort has been made to select texts from among the various genre

in which Rahner worked out his thought. Much of the material considered consists of essays taken from the *Schriften zur Theologie, Theological Investigations.* [All references to the *Schriften* are indicated by the initials "ST" followed by the publication data specific to the volume in question. English edition data is given first followed by the German in brackets. The short essay on pastorally-motivated themes seems to have been Rahner's preferred mode of expression.] But an effort has also been made to consult his interviews, devotional works, lectures, and major works. The second principle of selection has been thematic. The fact of the matter is that Rahner nowhere treats directly the post-metaphysical crisis of rationality, and still less the contemplative dimension of rationality. Yet he does treat a host of themes which are closely related to these concerns of ours and, in fact, presuppose an established position on them. Hence, whatever its literary genre, each work which has been selected takes one or more of the following as its theme: faith, revelation, salvation history, knowledge of God, incomprehensibility, anthropology, natural science, dogma, worship, and so on.

2   Karl Rahner, *Foundations of Christian Faith*, William V. Dych, trans., (New York: Seabury [Crossroad], 1978), p. xii. [*Grundkurs des Glaubens: Einfürung in den Begriff des Christentums*, (Freiburg im Breisgau: Herder, 1976), p. 6.] Note: All direct quotations from *Foundations* are from the Dych translation. This work will henceforth be referred to as "GG," with the English page numbering given first and the German numbering second and in brackets.

3   GG, xiii, [7]. See also Vatican II, *Optatam Totius, The Documents of Vatican II*, Walter M. Abbott, ed., (NY: Guild Press, 1966), para. 14, p. 450.

4   HW, 176, [215].

5   Karl Rahner, "Foundations of Christian Faith," ST, Vol. 19, Edward Quinn, trans., (NY: Crossroad, 1987), pp. 4-5. ["Grunkurs des Glaubens," B. 14, (Zurich: Benziger, 1980), pp.49-50.]

6   GG, xi, [5].

7   Only the Introduction and first two chapters are treated here, not because the entire work does not constitute a justification for faith, but because after the second chapter the discussion begins ranging into more specifically theological issues which lie beyond the explicit scope

282

of the present project. Support for this selection may be found in Otto Hentz's review of *Foundations* in *Thought*, 53(1978), pp. 433-41.

8   For more on the notion of the human person as a questioner, see Chapter III (especially pp. 54 ff.) and Chapter VII (especially pp. 126 ff.).

9   GG, 1, [13].

10   GG, 2, [14].

11   GG, 2, [14].

12   GG, 2, [14].

13   Rahner, Karl, "Ignatius of Loyola Speaks to a Jesuit of Today," *Igantius of Loyola*, Rahner and P. Imhof, Rosaleen Ockenden, trans., (London/NY: Collins, 1979), p. 32. [*"Rede des Igantius von Loyola an einen Jesuiten von heute,"* Ignatius von Loyola, (Freiburg im Breisgau: Herder, 1978), p. 32.]

14   GG, 5, [17].

15   Karl Rahner, "On the Situation of Faith," ST, Vol. 20, Edward Quinn, trans., (London: Darton, Longman and Todd, 1981), pp. 14-15. [*"Zur Situation des Glaubens,"* B. 14, (Zurich: Benziger, 1980), p. 25.]

16   GG, 5-6, [18].

17   GG, 4, [16].

18   GG, 4, [16-17].

19   GG, 7, [19].

20   *I Remember*, p. 92.

21   GG, 7, [19].

22   GG, 8, [19].

23   GG, 8, [19-20].

24   Karl Rahner, "Justifying Faith in an Agnostic World," ST, Vol. 21, Hugh M. Riley, trans., (NY: Crossroad, 1988), p. 130. [*"Glaubensbegründung in einer agnostishen Welt,"* B. 15, (Zurich: Benziger, 1983), p. 133]. Rahner makes a similar point in another essay where he talks about gnoseological pluralism in terms of concupiscence; see "On the Relationship Between Natural Science and Theology," ST, Vol. 19, Edward Quinn, trans., (NY: Crossroad, 1987), p. 21. [*"Zum Verhältnis von Naturwissenschaft und Theologie,"* B. 14, pp. 69-70.]

25   Ibid., p. 132, [134].

26   Rahner, "On the Situation of Faith," p. 16. [*"Zur Situation des Glaubens,"* pp. 26-7.]

27   Ibid., p. 131, [133].

28   Ibid., pp. 132, 136, [135, 138]. Also see Karl Rahner, "The Church and Atheism," ST, Vol. 21, p. 137. [*"Kirche and Atheismus,"* B. 15, p. 139.]

29   Ibid., p. 133, [136].

30   GG, 9, [20].

31   GG, 9, [21].

32   GG, 10, [22].

33   GG, 10, [22].

34   GG, 12, [23].

35   Rahner, "The Church and Atheism," p. 142. [*"Kirche and Atheismus,"* p. 143.]

36   GG, 10-11, [22].

37   GG, 11, [22-3].

38   GG, 11, [23].

39   Rahner, "On the Relationship Between Natural Science and
      Theology," p. 21; see also p. 19.   *["Zum Verhältnis von
      Naturwissenschaft und Theologie,"* p. 69; see also p. 67.]

40   GG, 14, [26].

41   GG, 14, [26].

42   Kant, *Prolegomena*, 293.

43   GG, 15, [27].

44   GG, 15, [26-7].

45   GG, 16-17, [27-8].

46   GG, 17, [28].

47   GG, 18, [28-9].

48   GG, 18, [29].

49   GG, 18, [29].

50   GG, 19, [30].

51   GG, 19, [30].

52   GG, 20, [31].

53   GG, 20, [31].

54   GG, 20, [31].

55   Karl Rahner, "Natural Science and Reasonable Faith," ST, Vol. 21,
      pp. 42-3. [*"Naturwissenschaft und vernüftiger Glaube,"* B. 15, p. 50.]

56   GG, 20, [31].

57   GG, 20, [31].

58   GG, 20, [31].

285

59   GG, 20-21, [32].

60   GG, 21, [32].

61   GG, 21, [32].

62   GG, 21, [32].

63   GG, 21-2, [32-3].

64   GG, 21-2, [32-3].

65   GG, 21, [32].   Also see Karl Rahner, "The Human Question of Meaning in the Face of the Absolute Mystery of God," ST, Vol. 18, Edward Quinn, trans., (NY: Crossroad, 1983), pp. 101-102; ["Die menschliche Sinnfrage vor dem absoluten Geihemnis Gottes," B. 13, (Zurich: Benziger, 1978), pp. 124-26.] Here, human interpersonal love is used as an analog for the fullness of the human relationship to God: "At the point where one person encounters another in really personal love is there not an acceptance of what is not comprehended, an acceptance of what we have not ourselves perceived and consequently not mastered in the other person, the person who is loved? Is not personal love a trusting surrender without reassurance to the other person, precisely insofar as the latter is and remains free and incalculable. . . . Only in the act of resigned and self-forsaking surrender of the subject to the incomprehensibility of God as such (which then ceases to be a limitation and become the very content of our relationship to God) does the most fundamental nature of love really dawn upon us, of which interpersonal love is merely a creaturely reflection."   A similar point is also made in Karl Rahner, "The Inexhaustible Transcendence of God and our Concern for the Future," ST, Vol. 20, pp. 175-6; ["Die unverbrauchbare Transzendenz Gottes und unsere Sorge um die Zukunft," B. 14., p. 408.]

66   Kant, Critique of Pure Reason, B295.

67   Rahner, "Natural Science and Reasonable Faith," p. 23; ["Naturwissenschaft und vernüftiger Glaube," p. 31].   Also see Rahner, "The Human Question of Meaning in the Face of the Absolute Mystery of God," p. 95; ["Die menschliche Sinnfrage vor dem absoluten Gehemnis Gottes," p. 118.] In the context of a the modern ideal of knowledge, talk of God's incomprehensibility is tantamount to a death sentence on the question of meaning.   Compare Rahner's

analysis of knowledge to that modern ideal "according to which knowledge gains its true nature and reaches its goal only when it sees through and thus dominates what is known, when it breaks down into what for us is unquestionable and obvious, when it seeks to work only with clear ideas and seeks to reflect to the very last detail the conditions of its own possibility, when as autonomous it seeks itself to decide the limits of what concerns it and what does not, when it seeks to be silent about those things in which it is impossible to speak clearly, when it is interested only in the functional connections of the details of its world of experience."

68   GG, 22, [33].

69   Rahner, *I Remember*, p. 57; [*Erinnerungen*, pp. 60-1]. Also see Rahner, "The Human Question of Meaning", p. 97; [*"Die meanschliche Sinnfrage"* p. 120]. Rahner's conception of rationality does not accommodate mystery but is based in mystery: "Reason must be understood . . . as the capacity of excessus, as going out into the inaccessible. If reason is not understood from the very outset as the capacity of incomprehensibility, of unfathomable mystery, as perception of the ineffable, then all subsequent talk of the incomprehensibility of God comes too late, falls on deaf ears, and can be understood only as an intimation of what happens to remain of objectivity, of what has not yet been processed by all-consuming reason but will sooner or perhaps later be so processed."

Chapter IX
1   GG, 24, [35].

2   GG, 24, [35].

3   GG, 25, [36].

4   GG, 25, [36].

5   GG, 25, [36].

6   GG, 25, [36].

7   GG, 25, [36].

8   Rahner, "Ignatius of Loyola Speaks," p. 20; [*"Rede des Ignatius von Loyola,"* p. 19.]

9   Ibid. p. 32, [31-2].

10   GG, 26, [37].

11   GG, 26, [37]; see also 34-5, [45].

12   GG, 27-8, [38-9].

13   GG, 29, [40].

14   GG, 30-1, [41-2].

15   GG, 29-30, 32; [40-1, 42-3].

16   GG, 32, [43].

17   GG, 32, [43].

18   GG, 33, [43].

19   GG, 33, [44].

20   GG, 33, [44].

21   GG, 33, [44].

22   GG, 33, [44].

23   GG, 33, [44].

24   GG, 34, [45].

25   GG, 34, [45].

26   GG, 34, [45].

27   GG, 35, [46].

28   GG, 35, [46].

29   GG, 36, [47].

30   GG, 36, [47].

31   GG, 36, [47].

32   GG, 36, [47].

33   GG, 38, [48-9].

34   GG, 38, [49].

35   GG, 39, [49-50].

36   GG, 39, [50].

37   GG, 39, [50].

38   GG, 40, [50].

39   GG, 40, [51]; emphasis added.

40   See pp. 79-85, 91-2, 99-102.

41   GG, 41, [52].

42   Rahner, *I Remember*, p. 101; [*Erinnerungen*, p. 114.]

43   Ibid., p. 104, [118]. "Ultimately, of course, one cannot anticipate death, not even by committing suicide, but to a certain extent, one can do something like anticipate death by practicing renunciation, by enduring loneliness, silence, and perhaps by forgetting oneself."

44   Karl Rahner, "Eternity from Time," ST, Vol. 19, pp. 171-2; [*"Ewigkeit aus Zeit,"* B. 14, p. 425.]

45   Ibid., p. 173, [427]. Pace Locke and Hume, of course, who claim to have undermined this claim in their analysis of substance.

46   Ibid., pp. 173-4, [427-8].

47   Ibid., pp. 174-5, [428-9].

48   Ibid., p. 175, [429].

49   Ibid., pp. 176-7, [430-2].

50   GG, 41, [52]. See also Karl Rahner, "Profane History and Salvation History," ST, Vol. 21, p. 14; ["Profangeschichte und Heilsgeschichte," B. 15, pp. 21-2.] In this essay, Rahner is equally emphatic about the irreducibility of the individual: "Quite candidly, and without any apology to the spirit of the times, it must first of all be said that there are in the world histories of freedom for which individuals as such are responsible, and these cannot be transferred or sloughed off. As far as the meaning of history is concerned, no one is dissolved in a collective mass, be it secular or ecclesiastical."

51   Rahner, "Ignatius of Loyola Speaks," p. 37; ["Rede des Ignatius von Loyola," p. 37.]

52   GG, 42, [52-3].

53   GG, 42, [52].

54   GG, 43, [53].

Chapter X

1   GG, 44, [54].

2   Rahner, "Ignatius of Loyola Speaks," p. 15; ["Rede des Ignatius von Loyola," p. 14.]

3   GG, 45-6, [55-6].

4   Heidegger, "On the Essence of Truth," Section 6, p. 134.

5   GG, 48-9, [58-9]. See also Rahner, "Ignatius of Loyola Speaks," p. 38; ["Rede des Ignatius von Loyola," p. 38.] Rahner's Ignatius gives this assessment of a hypothetical world where no one inquired after God: "If it were so, it would leave me unmoved. Men would have evolved backwards, as individuals or as the whole human race, into resourceful animals, and mankind's history of freedom, responsibility, guilt, and forgiveness would then be at an end—and only the manner of the end would have altered, for we Christians awwait an end in any case. Men who deserve the name of men would have found eternal life."

6   GG, 50, [60].

7   GG, 51-2, [61-2].

8   GG, 53, [62].

9   GG, 52, [62].

10   GG, 53, [63].

11   GG, 54, [63].

12   GG, 54, [63].

13   GG, 54, [63-4].

14   GG, 55, [64].

15   GG, 55-6, [64-5].

16   GG, 56-7, [65-6].

17   GG, 58, [67].

18   GG, 54, [63].

19   Heidegger, "On the Essence of Truth," pp. 134-5. Here "insistent existence" means holding fast to what is offered by beings as if they were open in and of themselves.

20   GG, 59, [68].

21   GG, 60, [69].

22   GG, 61, [70].

23   GG, 61-2, [70-1].

24   GG, 65-6, [74].

25   Karl Rahner, "Thomas Aquinas on the Incomprehensibility of God," [a lecture given at the University of Chicago, 8 November 1974], *The Journal of Religion*, 58(Supplement 1978), p. S108.

26   Ibid., pp. S108-9.

27   Ibid., p. S109.

28   Ibid., p. S113.

29   Ibid., p. S115.

30   Ibid., p. S116; see also p. S110.

31   Ibid., p. S117.

32   Ibid.

33   Ibid.

34   Ibid.

35   Ibid., pp. S118-9.

36   Ibid., pp. S119-20.

37   Ibid., p. S121.   See also Karl Rahner, "The Human Question of Meaning," p. 98; [*"Die menschliche Sinnfrage,"* p. 121.] In this essay, Rahner shows how, even if reason does not reflect on its unfulfilled transcendentality, it cannot avoid acting through it: "For when it grasps and understands any object, it has already transcended the latter into an infinity that is present as unexplored, precisely as such and not otherwise; it always seizes the individual object by being tacitly aware of the fact that the object always is and remains more than what is grasped of it. It locates the individual object with reference systems which themselves are not precisely fixed and determined and in which such an individual reality has a place without being absolutely and forever settled there."

38   Ibid., p. S121.

39   Ibid, p. S120; see also GG, 51, [61]. A similar point is made in Karl Rahner, "The Human Question of Meaning," p. 99; [*"Die menschliche*

Sinnfrage," p. 122.] See also Karl Rahner, "The Question of Meaning as a Question of God," ST, Vol. 21, p. 202; [*"Die Sinnfrage als Gottesfrage,"* B. 15, p. 200.]

40   Ibid., p. S120.

41   Ibid., p. S122.

42   Interviews with Leonhard Reinisch, 1982, and with Siegfried von Kortzfleisch, Hanover, 1981, KRD, Paul Imhof et al, eds., (NY: Crossroads, 1986), pp. 338, 293.

43   Rahner,"Thomas Aquinas on the Incomprehensibility," p. S121. See also Rahner, "The Question of Meaning as a Question of God," p. 198; [*"Die Sinnfrage also Gottesfrage,"* p. 197.]

44   Ibid., p. S125.

45   Interview with Patrick Granfield, 1965, Washington, D.C., KRD, p. 18. See also Rahner, "The Human Question of Meaning," p. 104; [*"Die menschliche Sinnfrage,"* p. 128.] Rahner argues that a mere affirmation of God does not alone constitute "surrender to the mystery": "Recourse to God as answer to the question of meaning of man in his wholeness is right and indispensable. But it becomes the creation of a human idol if it does not bring man forsaking himslef, self-surrendering and blessed only in that way, into the presence of the incomprehensibility of God."

46   Rahner,"Thomas Aquinas on the Incomprehensibility," p. S123.

47   Rahner, "Ignatius of Loyola Speaks," p. 17; [*"Rede des Ignatius von Loyola,"* p. 16.]

48   Rahner,"Thomas Aquinas on the Incomprehensibility," p. S123.

49   Ibid., p. S124.

50   Ibid., pp. S122, 124.

51   Rahner, "The Question of Meaning as the Question of God," pp. 197-8; [*"Die Sinnfrage als Gottesfrage,"* p. 196.]

52   Ibid., p. 199, [197].

53   Ibid., p. 204, [202]. The idea of a *docta ignorantia*, of course, is not original to Rahner; the Renaissance thinker, Nicholas of Cusa, elaborated this theme in his *De Docta Ignorantia*: "[T]he quiddity of things, which is the truth of beings, is unattainable in its purity; though it is sought by all philosophers, it is found by no one as it is. And the more deeply we are instructed in this ignorance, the closer we approach the truth." (*Nicholas of Cusa on Learned Ignorance*, Jasper Hopkins, trans., [Minneapolis: Banning Press, 2nd edition, 1985], Book I, C. III, para. 10, p. 53.) Rahner has more to say on this theme of "learned ignorance" in his essay "On the Relationship Between Natural Science and Theology," [*"Zum Verhältnis von Naturwissenschaft und Theologie,"* B. 14.]

54   GG, 69, [78].

55   GG, 70-1, [79].

56   GG, 69, [78].

57   GG, 63, [71-2].

58   GG, 63, [72].

59   GG, 63, [72].

60   GG, 71, [79].

61   GG, 72, [79-80].

62   GG, 72-3, [80].

63   GG, 72-3, [80-1].

64   GG, 73, [81].

65   GG, 73-4, [81-2].

66   GG, 75, [83].

67   GG, 74, [82].

68   GG, 77, [84].

69   GG, 77, [84].

70   GG, 77. [85].

71   GG, 77-8, [84-5].

72   GG, 78, [85].

73   GG, 80-1, [87-8].

74   GG, 80, [87-8].

75   GG, 81-2, [89].

76   GG, 84, [92].

77   GG, 85, [92].

78   GG, 83-4, [90-1].

79   GG, 87, [94].

80   GG, 88-9, [95-6]; see also 85, [93].

81   Karl Rahner, "On the Theology of Worship," ST, Vol. 19, pp. 142-3; ["Zur Theologies des Gottesdientes," B. 14, pp. 327-28.]

82   Ibid., p. 143, [229].

83   Ibid., p. 146, [232]; see also p. 149, [237]. For a fine overview of the Rahnerian view of worship, see Michael Skelley, "The Liturgy of the World and the Liturgy of the Church: Karl Rahner's Idea of Worship," Worship, 63(March 1989), pp. 112-132.

84   Ibid., p. 147, [234].

85   Karl Rahner, "Christianity's Absolute Claim," ST, Vol. 21, pp. 173-4; ["Uber den Absolutheitanspruch des Christentums," B. 15, p. 173.]

86   Ibid., p. 174, [173].

87   Ibid., p. 174, [174].

88   Ibid.

Conclusion

1   Paul D. Molnar, "Can We Know God Directly? Rahner's Solution from Experience," *Theological Studies*, 46(1985), p. 229. For a sustained critique of the effort to reconcile Thomist realism with transcendental philosophy, also see also Etienne Gilson, *Thomist Realism and the Critique of Knowledge*, Mark A. Wauck, trans., (San Francisco: Ignatius Press, 1986), Chapter 2; see especially pp. 82 ff.

2   Ibid., p. 234. Also see Dewart, "On Transcendental Thomism," 389-401 and "A Response to J. Donceel," 452-62. Fabro has similar complaints about transcendental Thomism, though from the rather different perspective of his participation-based Thomism; see Cornelio Fabro, *La svolta antropologica di Karl Rahner*, (Milano, Rusconi editore, 1974).

3   GW, 219-20, [228].

4   Donceel, "Transcendental Thomism," p. 78.

5   Dewart, "On Transcendental Thomism," p. 396.

6   Sheehan, p. 114.

7   Dennis Bradley, "Rahner's Spirit in the World: Aquinas or Hegel?" *The Thomist*, 41(April 1977), p. 184.

8   Peter Eicher, *Offenbarung: Prinzipneuzeitlicher Theologie*, (München: Kösel-Verlag, 1977), pp. 403-4. Also see Molnar, p. 238.

9   Hentz, p. 439.

10   Leo O'Donovan, "Karl Rahner: Foundations of Christian Faith," *Religious Studies Review*, 5(1979), pp. 198 ff; similarly in Klaus P. Fischer, *Der Mensch als Geheimnis. Die Anthropologie Karl Rahners*, (Freiburg: Herder, 1974), Preface. Cp. O'Donovan and Fischer with Larz Pearson, "Book Review of Foundations," *The Thomist*, 43(January 1979), 186-194; the latter sees Rahner as deeply influenced by Hegelian dialectic with all its attendant difficulties.

11   J. C. Roberston, "Karl Rahner: Foundations of Christian Faith," *Religious Studies Review*, 5(1979), p. 193; he defends Rahner against the objection about the neglect of historical particularity. For more on the theological version of this objection, see Eicher, p. 404. For more on the philosophical roots of the problem see Bradley, p. 169; also see Metz, *Faith in History and Society*, p. 65.

12   O'Donovan, p. 198.

13   Metz pp. 13 (n. 15) and 160ff.

14   Rahner, "Ignatius of Loyola Speaks to a Jesuit of Today," p. 37.

15   Clodovis Boff, Theology and Praxis: Epistemological Foundations, Robert Barr, trans., (Maryknoll, NY: Orbis Books, 1987).

16   HW, 107, [132].

17   GG, xiii.

18   Hans Urs von Balthasar, *Cordula oder der Ernstfall*, Einsiedeln: Johannes, 1966), pp. 91-2.

19   Karl Rahner in interview with Albert Raffelt, 1974, KRD, 124.

20   Karl Rahner, "The Concept of Existential Philosophy in Heidegger," p. 136. The Novalis quote is taken from an unidentified lecture of Heidegger which Rahner attended as a student at Freiburg. Novalis (1772-1801) was the pen name of the early German romanticist Freiderich Leopold Freiherr von Hardenberg.

Bibliography

Works by Rahner

Books

The Dynamic Element in the Church. New York: Herder and Herder, 1964. [*Das Dynamische in der Kirche.* Freiburg: Herder.]

Foundations of Christian Faith, William V. Dych, trans. New York: Seabury (Crossroad), 1978. [*Grunkurs des Glaubens: Einfürung in den Begriff des Christentums.* Freiburg im Breisgau: Herder, 1976.]

Hearers of the Word, Michael Richards, trans. New York: Herder and Herder, 1969. [*Hörer des Wortes.* München: Kösel-Verlag, 1963.]

Spirit in the World. William Dych, trans. New York: Herder and Herder, 1968. [*Geist in Welt,* München: Kösel-Verlag, 1957.]

Theological Investigations, [*Schriften zur Theologie*],

> Vol. XVIII, *God and Revelation,* Edward Quinn, trans. New York: Crossroad, 1983. [A translation of the first four sections of *Schriften,* B. XIII. Zurich: Benziger, 1978.]

> Vol. XIX, *Faith and Ministry,* Edward Quinn, trans. NY: Crossroad, 1987. [A translation of selected articles from *Schriften,* B. XIV. Zurich: Benziger, 1980.]

> Vol. XX, *Concern for the Church,* Edward Quinn, trans. London: Darton, Longman, and Todd, 1981. [A translation of selected articles from *Schriften,* B. XIV. Zurich: Benziger, 1980.]

> Vol. XXI, *Science and Christian Faith,* Hugh M. Riley, trans. New York: Crossroad, 1988. [A translation of the first three sections of *Schriften,* B. XV. Zurich: Benziger, 1983.]

w/P. Imhof. *Ignatius of Loyola*, Rosaleen Ockenden, trans. London/NY: Collins, 1979. [*Ignatius von Loyola*. Freiburg im Breisgau: Herder, 1978.]

Articles and Essays

"Aquinas: The Nature of Truth," Andrew Tallon, trans., *Continuum*, 21(1964). [No published version of the German original exists; this translation is based on a Portuguese transcript of a conference given by Rahner at Innsbruck: *"A Verdade em S.Tomás de Aquino."* Revista Portuguesa de Filosofia, 7 (1951), 353-370.]

"The Concept of Existential Philosophy in Heidegger," Andrew Tallon, trans. *Philosophy Today*, 13(1969). [A Rahner-approved translation of an article originally published under the name of Rahner's brother Hugo in *Recherches de Sciences Religieuses*, 30(1940), 152-71.]

"Thomas Aquinas on the Incomprehensibility of God." *The Journal of Religion*, 58(Supplement 1978), S107-25. [Based on a lecture given by Rahner at the University of Chicago on November 8, 1974.]

Interviews

Karl Rahner in Dialogue: Conversations and Interviews. Imhof, Paul, Hubert Biallwons, Harvery Egan, ed. NY: Crossroad, 1984. [This edition is based on the more complete, two volume German edition *Glaube In Winterlicher Zeit: Gespräch mit Karl Rahner aus den Letzten Lebensjahren.* Imhof, Paul and Humbert Biallovans, ed. Dusseldorf: Patmos, 1986.]

I Remember: An Autobiographical Interview with Meinhold Kraus. Harvey D. Egan, trans. NY: Crossroad, 1985. [*Erinnerungen: Im Gespräch mit Meinhold Krauss.* Freiburg im Breisgau: Herder, 1984.]

Bibliographies

Bleistein, R. and E. Klinger, eds. *Bibliographie Karl Rahners—1924-1969.* Freiburg, 1974.

Klinger, E. and K. Wittstadt, eds. *Glaube im Prozess.* Freiburg, 1984.

Neufeld, Karl and Roman Bleistein. *Rahner-Register: Ein Schlüssel zu Karl Rahners Schriften zur Theologie I-X und zu seinen Lexikon Artikeln.* Zurich: Benziger, 1974.

Pedley, C.D.   "An English Biographical Aid to Karl Rahner."   *Heythrop Journal*, 15(1984), 319-65.

Works About Rahner

Books

Bonsor, Jack Arthur. *Rahner, Heidegger, and Truth: Karl Rahner's Notion of Christian Truth, The Influence of Heidegger.*   Lanham, MD: University Press of America, 1987.

Carr, Anne E.   *The Theological Method of Karl Rahner.*   Missoula, MT: Scholars Press, 1977.

Fabro, Cornelio.   *La svolta antropologica di Karl Rahner.*   Milano: Rusconi editore, 1974.

Fischer, Klaus P.   *Der Mensch als Geheimnis. Die Anthropolgie Karl Rahners.* Freiburg: Herder, 1974.

Kress, Robert.   *A Rahner Handbook.*   Atlanta: John Knox Press, 1982.

Sheehan, Thomas.   *Karl Rahner: The Philosophical Foundations.*   Athens, OH: Ohio University Press, 1987.

Vorgrimler, Herbert. *Karl Rahner.* New York: Paulist, 1966.

_____.   *Understanding Karl Rahner: An Introduction to His Life and Thought.* New York: Crossroad, 1986.

_____. *Wagnis Theologie.* Freiburg, 1979.

Articles and Essays

Baker, Kenneth.   "Rahner: The Transcendental Method."   *Continuum*, II(1964), 51-59.

Bradley, D.   "Rahner's Spirit in the World: Aquinas or Hegel?"   *The Thomist*, 41(April 1977), 167-99.

Galvin, John P.   "Grace for a New Generation."   *Commonweal*, 25(January 1985), 40-42.

Hentz, Otto. "Foundations of Christian Faith." *Thought*, 53(1978), 433-41.

Hurd, Robert. "Heidegger and Aquinas: A Rahnerian Bridge." *Philosophy Today*, (Summer 1984), 105-137.

Molnar, Paul D. "Can We Know God Directly? Rahner's Solution from Experience." *Theological Studies*, 46(1985), 228-61.

O'Donovan, Leo. "A Final Harvest: Karl Rahner's Last Theological Writings." *Religious Studies Review*, 11(October 1985), 357-61.

_____. "A Journey into Time: The Legacy of Karl Rahner's Last Years." *Theological Studies*, 46(1985), 621-46.

_____. "Karl Rahner." *New Catholic Encyclopedia*, XIII(Supplement '78-'88). D.C.: CUA Press, 1989.

_____. "Karl Rahner. Foundations of Christian Faith." *Religious Studies Review*, 5(1979), 190-198.

_____. "Living into Mystery: Karl Rahner's Reflections at 75." *America*, 140(March 10, 1979), 179-180.

_____. "The Word of the Cross." *Chicago Studies*, 25(April 1986), 95-110.

Pearson, Larz. "Book Review of Foundations." *The Thomist*, 43(January 1979), 186-194.

Robertson, J.C. "Karl Rahner: Foundations of Christian Faith." *Religious Studies Review*, 5(19979), 190-198.

Skelley, Michael. "The Liturgy of the World and the Liturgy of the Church: Karl Rahner's Idea of Worship." *Worship*, 63(March 1989), 112-132.

Stevens, Clifford. "The Rahner Equation." *Listening*, 17(Autumn 1982), 239-43.

Tallon, Andrew. "Getting to the Heart of the Matter: Spirit." *Louvain Studies*, 11(Spring 1969), 277-82.

_____. "Karl Rahner—Philosopher (1904-1984)." *Philosophy Today*, 28(Summer 1984), 102-104.

301

Other Works

Books

Aristotle. *Metaphysics.* W.D. Ross, trans., contained in *Introduction to Aristotle*, Richard McKeon, ed. NY: Random House, 1947.

_____. *Nichomachean Ethics*, W.D. Ross, trans., contained in *Introduction to Aristotle*, Richard McKeon, ed. NY: Random House, 1947.

_____. *On the Soul*, Hippocrates G. Apostle, trans. Grinnell, Iowa: Peripatetic Press, 1981.

Augustine of Hippo. *Homilies on the Gospel of St. John*, Vol. I., H. Browne and J.H. Parker, trans. Oxford: Library of the Fathers, 1948.

Bernstein, Richard J. *Beyond Objectivism and Relativism: Science, hermeneutics, and praxis.* Philadelphia, PA: U. of Penn. Press, 1983.

Boff, Clodovis. *Theology and Praxis: Epistemological Foundations*, Robert R. Barr, trans. Maryknoll, NY: Orbis Books, 1987.

Brezik, Victor B. *One Hundred Years of Thomism: Aeterni Patris and Afterwards, A Symposium.* Houston: Center for Thomistic Studies, 1981.

Caputo, John. *Heidegger and Aquinas: An Essay on Overcoming Metaphysics.* New York: Fordham U. Press, 1982.

_____. *Radical Hermeneutics: Repetition, Deconstruction, and the Hermeneutic Project.* Bloomington, IN: Indiana U. Press, 1987.

Clement of Alexandria. *Stromata*, contained in *Greek and Roman Philosophy after Aristotle*, Jason L. Saunders, ed. NY: The Free Press, 1966.

de Guibert, Joseph. *The Jesuits: Their Spiritual Doctrine and Practice.*, W.J. Young, trans . St. Louis: Institute of Jesuit Sources, 1972.

Denzinger, Henry. *The Sources of Catholic Dogma*, Roy Defarrari, trans. London/St. Louis: B. Herder Book Co. 1957 [Based on H. Denzinger and J. Schönmetzer, ed. *Enchiridion Symbolorum, Definitiorum, et Declaratiorum*, 30th Edition.]

Derrida, Jacques. *Of Grammatology*, Gayatrix Charkravorty Spivak, trans. Baltimore: John Hopkins University Press, 1974.

Descartes, René. *The Philosophical Writings of Descartes*, two volumes, John Cottingham, trans. Cambridge, UK: Cambridge University Press, 1988.

Egan, Harvey. *Ignatius Loyola the Mystic*. Wilmington, DE: Michael Glazier, 1987.

_____. *The Spiritual Exercises and the Ignatian Mystical Horizon*. St. Louis: The Institute of Jesuit Sources, 1976.

Eicher, Peter. *Offenbarung: Prinzipneuzeitlicher Theologie*. München: Kösel-Verlag, 1977.

Festugière, A.J. *Contemplation et vie contemplative selon Platon*. Paris: Vrin, 1950.

Fleming, David L., ed. *Notes on the Spiritual Exercises of St. Ignatius of Loyola*. St. Louis: Review for Religious, 1983.

_____. *The Spiritual Exercises of St. Ignatius: A Literal Translation and a Contemporary Reading*, literal trans. by Elder Mullan. St. Louis: Institute of Jesuit Resources, 1978.

Galilei, Galileo. *Discoveries and Opinions of Galileo*, Stillman Drake, trans. NY: Anchor Books, 1957.

Gilson, Etienne. *Reason and Revelation in the Middle Ages*. NY: Charles Scribner's Sons, 1963.

_____. *Thomist Realism and the Critique of Knowledge*, Mark Wauck, trans. San Francisco: Ignatius Press, 1986.

Hegel, G.W.F. *Phenomenology of Spirit*, A.V. Miller, trans. Oxford: Oxford University Press, 1977.

Heidegger, Martin. *Being and Time*, J. MacQuarrie and E. Robinson, trans. NY: Harper and Row, 1962.

_____. *Basic Writings*, David Farrell Krell, ed. NY: Harper and Row, 1977.

_____. *An Introduction to Metaphysics*, Ralph Manheim, trans. NY: Doubleday (Anchor), 1961.

_____. *Kant and the Problem of Metaphysics*, James S.Churchill, trans. Bloomington, IN: Indiana University Press, 1962.

Husserl, Edmund. *Cartesian Meditations*, Dorion Cairns, trans. The Hague: Martinus Nijhoff, 1960.

Ignatius Loyola. *The Spiritual Exercises*, Elisabeth Meier Tetlow, trans. Lanham, MD: Univeristy Press of America, 1987.

John, Helen James. *The Thomist Spectrum*. New York: Fordham University Press, 1966.

Kant, Immanuel. *Critique of Pure Reason*, Norman Kemp Smith, trans. . NY: St. Martin's Press, 1965.

_____. *Prolegomena to Any Future Metaphysics*, James Ellington, trans. Indianapolis: Hackett, 1977.

Kierkegaard, Soren. *Concluding Unscientific Postscript*, D. Swenson and W. Lowrie, trans. Princeton: Princeton University Press, 1974.

Kristellar, Paul Oskar. *Marsilio Ficino and His Work after Five Hundred Years*. Leo S. Olschki Editore, 1987.

_____. *Renaissance Thought*. NY: Harper Torchbooks, 1961.

Laudan, Larry. Progress and its Problems. London: Routeledge and Kegan Paul, 1977.

MacIntyre, Alisdair. *Whose Justice? Which Rationality?* Notre Dame, IN: University of Notre Dame Press, 1988.

Maréchal, Joseph. *A Maréchal Reader*, Joseph Donceel, ed. and trans. New York: Herder and Herder, 1970. [Includes excerpts from *Le Point dé départ de la métaphysique*, Vol. I-V. Paris: F. Alcan, 1926.]

_____. *Studies in the Psychology of the Mystics*, Algar Thorold, trans. London: Burns, Oates, and Washbourne, 1927.

Metz, Johannes Baptist. *Faith in History and Society*, David Smith, trans. New York: Seabury, 1980.

McCool, Gerald. *Catholic Theology in the Nineteenth Century*. New York: Seabury, 1977.

Nicholas of Cusa. *On Learned Ignorance*, 2nd Edition, Jasper Hopkins, trans. Minneapolis: Banning Press, 1985.

Nietzsche, Friederich. Excerpts from *The Gay Science* and *Thus Spoke Zarathustra*, contained in *The Portable Nietzsche*, Walter Kaufmann, trans. NY: Viking Press, 1968.

Pico della Mirandola, Giovanni. *On the Dignity of Man and Other Works*, Paul J. Miller, ed. Indianapolis: Bobbs-Merrill, 1965.

Pieper, Josef. *The Silence of St. Thomas*, John Murray and Daniel O'Connor, trans. New York: Pantheon, 1957.

Plato. *The Republic*, Alan Bloom, trans. NY: Basic Books, 1968.

Porreco, Rocco, ed. *The Georgetown Symposium on Ethics*. Lanham, MD: University Press of America, 1984.

Richardson, William. *Heidegger: Through Phenomenology to Thought*. The Hague: Martinus Nijhoff, 1962.

Rousselot, Pierre. *The Intellectualism of St. Thomas*, James E. O'Malony, trans. New York: Sheed and Ward, 1935. [*L'Intellectualisme de saint Thomas*. Paris: Beauchesne, 1924.]

Tertullian. *Prescription Against the Heretics*, contained in *Greek and Roman Philosophy after Aristotle*, Jason L. Saunders, ed. NY: The Free Press, 1966.

Thomas Aquinas. *St. Thomas Aquinas: Faith, Reason, and Theology: Questions I-IV of His Commentary on the De Trinitate of Boethius*, Armand Mauer, ed. Toronto: Pontifical Institute of Medieval Studies, 1987.

_____. *Questions on the Soul,* James H. Robb, trans. Milwaukee: Marquette University Press, 1981.

_____. Excerpts from *Summa Theologiae*, contained in *Basic Writings of St. Thomas Aquinas*, Anton Pegis, ed. NY: Random House, 1944.

von Balthasar, Hans Urs. *The Moment of Christian Witness*, Richard Beckley, trans. New York: Paulist (Newman), 1969. [*Cordula oder der Ernstfall*. Einsiedeln: Johannes, 1966.]

Weisheipl, James. *Friar Thomas D'Aquino*. Washington, DC: Catholic University Press, 1983.

Wisser, Richard, ed. *Martin Heidegger im Gespräch*. Freiburg: Alber, 1970.

Articles and Essays
Bukowski, Thomas P. "Siger of Brabant vs. Thomas Aquinas on Theology." *The New Scholasticism*, LXI(Winter 1987), 25-32.

Deely, John. "The Situation of Heidegger in the Tradition of Christian Philosophy." *The Thomist*, 31(April 1967), 159-244.

Dewart, Leslie. "On Transcendental Thomism." *Continuum*, 6(1968), 389-401.

_____. "A Response to J. Donceel." *Continuum*, 7(1969), 453-462.

Donceel, Joseph. "A Thomistic Misapprehension?" *Thought*, 32(1957) 189-98.

_____. "On Transcendental Thomism." *Continuum*, 7(1969), 164-68.

_____. "Transcendental Thomism." *Monist*, 58(1974), 67-85.

Dudley, John. "La Contemplation Humaine Selon Aristote." *Revue Philosophique Louvain*, 80(August 1982), 387-413.

Hennessey, James. "Leo XIII's Thomistic Revival: A Political and Philosophical Event." *The Journal of Religion*, 58(1978 Supplement), 185-97.

Kraut, Richard. "The Peculiar Function of Human Beings." *The Canadian Journal of Philosophy*, 9(September 1979), 467-78.

McCool, Gerald. "Neo-Thomism and the Tradition of St. Thomas." *Thought*, 62(June 1987), 131-40.

_____. "Twentieth Century Scholasticism." *The Journal of Religion*, 58(1978 Supplement), 201-202.

Moline, Jon. "Contemplation and the Human Good." *Nous*, 47(March 1983), 37-53.

Peter, Carl. "A Shift to the Human Subject in Roman Catholic Theology." *Communio*, 6(Spring 1979), 56-72.

Tassi, Aldo. "Modernity as the Transformation of Truth into Meaning." *International Philosophical Quarterly*, XXIII(September 1982), pp. 185-93.

Wippel, John. "The Condemnations of 1270 and 1277 at Paris." *Journal of Medieval and Renaissance Studies*, 7(1977), 169-201.

Index

Absolute Being, (see "Being")

absurd, absurdity, 180, 207, 232

abyss: God as, 149, 213; of non-being, 188, 136, 141, 187; of existence, 149; of Being, 187; of mystery, 191

Aeterni Patris, 40ff.

affirmation: pre-conceptual a. of God's existence or Holy Mystery, 19, 107, 194, 208, 219, 225; implicit in judgment, 8, 70, 94-96, 102, 146, 167, 222; or. judgment, 51, 60, 92, 105ff., 199

agent intellect, 19, 61, 104-5, 223, 228

agnosticism, 153ff, 163, 167, 179, 196ff., 227, 231

ahistorical: conceptions of the human subject, 28, 169; conceptions of human reason, 28, 40, 44, 73; principles of rational justification, 28, 156, 171

always already, 116, 127, 176, 227 (*immer schon*), 238

analogical existence, 209 ff., 229

analogical speech, 98, 209, 217, 219

analogy, 210ff., 219

Angst, 133ff., 142

Ansichsein, 64

anthropology: 24, 38, 152; metaphysical, 46ff., 67ff., 75,

203; philosophical, 33, 75, 84ff., 216, 222, 235, 237; Rahner's, 2, 33, 46, 48, 70ff., 148, 173ff., 190-1, 227-230; theological,174-176, 182, 190

anticipatory aspect of knowledge, 85, 105, 109, 139

apologetics: contemplation and, 3, 9, 237ff.; nineteenth century Catholic, 37ff., 46, 68, 196; apologetic use of philosophy, 14-5

a priori: structures revealed in *a posteriori* experience, 104; knowledge, 104; laws of reason, 28, 163-64; principle of unification, 105; structure of mind, 26, 28, 105, 165

apriorism, 223

Aristotle: 18, 24, 56, 80, 134, 204; and contemplation, 3, 5-6, 99, 102

asceticism: 6, 8, 72, 85; and indifference in Ignatius, 123-124, 128; radicalized in Heidegger, 128, 141ff.; of a careful intellectual reflection in Rahner, 148ff., 158, 168

atheism, 44, 153-156, 172, 209, 239

Augustine (of Hippo), 17

Averroes, Averroism, 18-24

Bacon, Francis, 25

beatitude, natural, 99-100, 106

will, volition, 96, 106, 117, 123,
(see also "intellect")
wonder, 57, 99, 190, 204, 231
Woraufin, 62-3, 199, 211, (see also
"transcendence")
Word, listening for a word.spoken
by God in history, 1, 47, 52,
69ff., 100, 150, 174ff., 186,
191, 193, 196ff., 206, 208,
211, 213, 219, 227-229, 240

worldiness: as a contemplative
characteristic, 67, 185-6, 235;
in the *Spiritual Exercises* ,
118, 120, 122-3; in Heidegger,
136
worship, 22, 206, 215-6, 228, 230,
239
Wirklichsein, 64